CHANGE TO U.S. PRESIDENTIAL SYSTEM OF GOVERNMENT

GOOD FOR INDIA

KATTOJU SITARAMMA RAO

White Falcon Publishing

www.whitefalconpublishing.com

Dedicated to the Indian people who are looking for a better life for themselves and their families and the future for their children.

ACKNOWLEDGMENTS

Thanks to all my friends and my family for their support and encouragement

PREFACE

After obtaining independence on 15 August 1947, India has come a long way. Successive governments have played an important role in building the country, along with a great contribution by the people of India. In fact, more credit should be given to the people of India; in spite of the politicians letting them down economically, they have come up on their own for the first 44 years, though by the hard way. However, what the country has achieved in 20 years could have been achieved in 10 years, not being the fault of the people but due to the fault lines in the political system. India has plenty more to do to achieve a good life for the citizens, their children, and grandchildren. India has lost a lot of valuable time, and now the country has to move at a faster pace, and in some important areas, at a galloping speed.

A government is judged by how they look after the 'National Security' and how well they develop the 'Economy', especially in developing countries; how well they take social welfare measures to uplift the people from below the poverty line, not by pampering them or giving them freebies before the elections and forgetting them after the elections, but by meeting them halfway in their overall development, especially with education and healthcare that will get them a job and a job gives them a tremendous jump, away from the miseries of life and a vertical lift, socio-economically.

National security is of paramount importance as the country cannot progress with external threats; it may be a physical attack, an economic blockade, political interference, or a cyber-attack. The country has to be protected from all these four directions at all costs.

The armed forces should be provided all the manpower and weapons, including force multipliers and equipment they require to maintain their operational efficiency at all times.

Expecting the armed forces to protect our land borders, sea routes, and air without providing adequate resources is like sending the armed forces into war with one of their hands tied behind their back. For example, the Air force requires 42 fighter squadrons to take on two fronts, i.e., Pakistan and China at the same time, if the eventuality arise. Currently, they have only 31 squadrons; they have to make up the deficiency of 11 squadrons.With the recent purchase of 36 Rafael fighter aircraft of the fifth generation from Dassault Aviation Company in France,which will be delivered between 2019 and 2022, forming two squadrons with 18 aircraft each, the strength will go to 33 squadrons; the shortage will still be 09 squadrons. The manufacturing of Rafael fighter aircraft in India with a partnership between Dassault and Ambani's, as part of the 'Make in India' policy, will take some time. So far, only around 6 to 8 Teja fighter aircraft of the fourth generation, manufactured by HAL, have entered the Air force. The Air force is going to be short of fighter aircraft for some time to come. For offensive and defensive operations over land and sea, effective air power is essential; the present situation is very bad for 'National Security'. The politicians in power are to be blamed.

Even when we are sleeping at night and going about our work during the day, a large part of the army, part of the Air Force and a smaller part of the Navy guard our borders, air space, and sea lanes throughout the day and night [24x7]. India's political leadership should have a clear, far-reaching political and economic aim, must maintain the momentum of this aim, and should never neglect the Armed Forces; the Indo-Chinese 1962 debacle should never be repeated. Having a strong military is a deterrent against any hostility.

In the present day world, 'economy' plays an important part. Countries that pay attention to 'Foreign policy' based on economic consideration and internally carry out reforms and structural changes prosper, benefiting the maximum.

Since 1991, with the economic reforms and structural changes, under a very able Prime Minister, late P. V. Narasimha Rao, India slowly climbed to the status of a leader amongst the developing nations with the world's fastest moving economy and with a potential of becoming one of the economic leaders of the developed world, together with USA and China. Now, the developed countries, like the USA, UK [once India's masters], Japan, Germany, France, Italy, Canada, Australia, Russia, and even China are wanting to do more business with India, but are waiting and watching to see the reforms being unfolded that will ease taxation and remove the hindrance and in some cases hurdles in the clearing of projects.

We have carried out crucial reforms on the amendments to the 'Goods and Services Tax' and 'Insolvency and bankruptcy laws'. Our economy still needs constructive amendments to the 'Land Reforms', amendments to the 'Banking system' and reducing the number of Public Sector Banks [PSB] to 3/4, 'Labour reforms' and 'Administration reforms' for better development and growth, and to curb corruption, by starting with election reforms.

The pace of reforms has been slow. This is because of the low calibre of Members of Parliament at the central level and Members of the Legislative Assembly at the state level; most of them do not understand the importance of a sound economy, barring a few. The education standards of the majority of our politicians are low to almost non-existent, and above all, the negative mindset of the opposition.

For any nation to grow to a sound economy, savings and investments, exports, and two figures GDP growth are very essential. The government has taken action to boost investment but too little to boost the consumption that increases demand. The government has to put more money in the hands of the people; this can be done by reducing the taxes, but that will cause a loss in revenue. To make up for this loss, the government should reduce unnecessary expenditure on unproductive schemes, including some welfare schemes that are there to catch votes, trim the expenditure on running the government and unnecessary expenditure on politicians, including their security concerns. Security concerns should be on threat perception, not to boost their status.

To stimulate the economy, the government should spend more on development. To get the huge amount required for this purpose, the government should de-invest 'Public Sector Units' [PSU's] running at a loss.

Exports have hardly grown for the last five years. This is because India is a 'high-cost economy' that cannot compete with its Asian peers. The high cost is due to the high cost of land, labour, capital, electricity, railway freight, air freight, corporate, and income tax rates. For higher export growth, all these rates have to be lowered to the Asian level.

Inflation has to be controlled so that the steep prices of commodities for day to day living do not pinch the common citizen's pocket, but at the same time, concentrating only on inflation at the expense of growth is not the answer, focusing on growth should also be given importance to create more jobs. There has to be a balance between inflation and growth. The fiscal deficit can be increased from the present 3.5% to 4.5% to balance revenue and expenditure. The capital deficit has to be checked so that we have enough money to look into the crucial areas of development like infrastructure, education, skilled education, higher education, and health care that will accelerate growth. Our foreign exchange reserves have to be increased tremendously by reducing our taxation in line with other countries to make exports more competitive in the global market. Reducing corporate tax was a good move, but other areas need attention too. No country had ever grown fast without buoyant exports, apart from GDP, savings, and investment.

The government has to modernise agriculture for better output and higher income for our farmers.We should look at co-operative farming [on the Israeli model], with multi-produce that will help around 85% of farmers with small landholdings who are hit very badly, especially when there is a calamity. The farmers will earn the maximum if they can sell their produce directly to the whole sellers who, in turn, will sell to the retailers. This will remove the collecting agencies in between the farmers and the wholesalers. The collecting agencies in the rice bowl of Andhra Pradesh make around 300% commission.

Building industrial corridors/nodal points among a group of villages to move the surplus farm labours to industries will be a very bold move that will help jobs in the rural areas; all developed countries have gone through this process. At present, nearly 60% of the rural population depend on agriculture.

Farm loans on reasonable interest from organised banks should be encouraged. When there is less/no produce, the government should help the farmers by meeting them halfway to pay back their loans; subsidising the farm insurance premium is one way of doing it.

The government has to encourage manufacturing, including the manufacturing of defence equipment, to reduce import and create more jobs in both urban and rural areas. Encourage the private sector to grow faster by offering incentives to improve the availability of jobs, and also encourage both private and public sector participation in the building of infrastructure that creates more jobs, and encourage both private sector and public sector involvement in education, including research and development, and health care. Jobs will give everyone, including people below the poverty line and those on the marginal line, an opportunity to earn their livelihood.

So far, manufacturing in India concentrated only on the domestic market. As a result, when people have no money, consumption goes down, leading to demand going down. Therefore, manufacturing should concentrate on the domestic and foreign markets to lift up the demand.

Encourage domestic and foreign investment. India took a lot of time in allowing 'Foreign Direct Investments [FDI]' flowing into the country. Even developed countries encourage foreign investment.

A sound economy, apart from providing jobs, will increase the per capita income that will provide a better living standard to the Indian people.

And above everything, we should maintain cordial relationships with our neighbours and the developed/developing world by improving trade for mutual benefits; in fact, our 'Foreign Policy' should be based on economic considerations.

Domestic law and order should be tactfully controlled by maintaining 'Communal Harmony' by adhering to 'Human Rights'.Lastly, it is most important that we control our population, to two/three children per family. This is adhered to mostly by the rich and higher middle class in the urban population. The middle and poorer classes in the urban/rural areas need to understand the importance of family planning. Unfortunately, the politicians do not mention this aspect; they are only interested in the vote bank, more the population, more the votes. Some of them encourage illegal migration. All the development and growth is negated if the rate of growth of population and illegal migration is not checked.

Everybody knows that there is a lot to be done. Then, why is the country not moving ahead with the required concern and speed? This is because of lack of 'implementations' and old and outdated mindset of the political set-up and the lethargy of the bureaucracy; bureaucracy will only function effectively if a proper and clear roadmap is set and some pressure is put on them. Implementations are crucial, and course corrections at every stage a must as we move along. Even in our personal lives, we become better human beings when we sort out our personal problems and commitments by taking corrective steps at every stage of our life.

With the present mindset of the politicians and political power groups, as well as corruption at all levels, the current system in the Indian political environment is showing cracks, and we are facing a lot of hindrances and hurdles to make crucial reforms that will help the economy for better development and growth that will create jobs for everyone for a better life. Even a structural change in our institutions to strengthen them and make them more effective and transparent with timely delivery is being hindered. The essential reforms, starting with elections, land, labour, banking and administration, and structural changes in each sector and institution are badly required for future development and growth; time is running out, and if the politicians in power do not move fast enough, the country will lose out.

The main lacuna is that the Central Government makes all the major policies, including the ones that the states should do, and the State Governments have to implement them. Major policies and a major part of the finance with the centre and the implementations with the state, when there is partial or no delivery, each one blaming the other, this is why the end results are disappointing. At the outset, most of the policies are sound, though some of them do not address some of the regional requirements. The Centre has no tools to carry out the implementations; it has to be done at the State level. This is where we are all stuck, and this is the main concern of everyone. Further, with the Centre controlling a major part of the finance, the States have very little money; this needs a second look.

Because of the disparity between the centre and the state, the number of regional parties have grown. Today, we have so many parties that it is unmanageable; one can witness the chaos during the proceedings in the Lok Sabha and in the Rajya Sabha. More chaos is created when there are legal cases against the parliamentarians; the legislature should not get involved with legal cases against individual politicians. The Parliament is not the place for this; it should be left to the courts to deal with such cases. The legislatures are elected by the people for passing crucial bills that make sound and sustainable policies and to discuss crucial matters concerning the people.

To avoid the parliamentary procedures at the Centre and assembly procedures at the State from being hi-jacked, it is better to separate the executive from the legislature with some checks and balances, where the Executive Head at the Centre and the Executive Head at the State can function effectively. In addition, go for a complete federal system to allow the states more elbow room to implement what is good for the people of the State. This can only happen in a 'Presidential System of Government'.

Out of the 43 Presidential Systems of Government spread throughout the world, the USA seems to be the best, and India should look at it. The USA has a President, who is elected by the people through a process called the 'Electoral College' [which is itself directly elected] and is responsible to the 'constitutional council'. Though the people of the United States do not directly elect the President, they usually have a President of their choice through the directly elected members of the 'Electoral College'.

Once the President takes the oath, he does not belong to any political party; he is the head of the nation and the executive head, the commander-in-chief of the armed forces and the chief diplomat, leading the executive branch that is separate from the legislative branch. There is the separation of powers between the executive, the legislature, and the judiciary but follow the principles of checks and balances in place already.

The President can give 'Executive Orders' on some matters that concern the country that is implemented immediately, provided the orders are within the ambit of the Constitution and are legally correct. He does not have to go through the legislature that may take time to pass or not pass.

Governors in States are directly elected by the people and are responsible to the 'State constitutional council'. The Governor is the Head of the State and the Executive Head. The people of the state have a Governor of their choice, and the Governor is responsible to them.

This model has seen the test of time in the USA and will be workable in India.With this Federal structure, the governance at the centre and state will improve. Above everything, the states can have their own policies suiting their local requirements and aspirations, and control their finance the best way possible. This will ensure that the implementation of policies is carried out with acceptable results.

The US's Central Government looks after the foreign policy, national and homeland security, intelligence, commerce [keeping creation of jobs an utmost priority], energy, broad policies on education, health and human resources, justice, treasury, and veteran affairs. Emphasis is given on human rights and communal harmony; social issues like immigration, LGBTQ and gun control are addressed threadbare, and aspects of climate change and the environment are given importance.These aspects in the Indian perspective have been covered in part-2 of the book.

Now, how do we change the present system??? To change to the presidential system of government, the constitution of India needs an amendment. For this to happen, 2/3rd of the members in both the houses should agree to the amendment, and half the number of legislatures of states should ratify the amendment.

At present, the NDA with 343 seats in the Lok Sabha and no substantial support in the Raja Sabha, with a hostile, badly behaved, and unreasonable opposition, even introducing the issue in Parliament will be impossible. Further, the political parties will not be for the change as they will look into their own interest. The answer is to have discussions on this change through the national and regional electronic media and the print media to make people aware of the good in the change. It has to be a movement for a change peacefully. People together with the independent media can do a lot.The paid media that sways to a particular political party that does not want a change will scuttle the movement.

If most of the people are for the change and with their pressure, the government of the day may bring it up in Parliament for discussion. Most likely, no headway will be made, then the people should ask for a referendum democratically, similar to the referendum on 'Britain's-exit from EU'. It has to be a peaceful people's movement. In case the government does not call for a referendum, the people should take up the matter to the Supreme Court of India.

The best for our country is to change to the Presidential System of Government on the USA model and the President to be in power for not more than two terms. This change will slowly bring in the two-party systems at the centre; in all probability, the two parties will be the BJP, representing the Hindu majority and a few minorities, and the Congress, representing a small part of the Hindus and a large part of the minorities. Some of the regional parties and the communist will remain in their states of domination. Slowly, these parties will also wither away, with individual politicians joining one of the main parties. This transformation will be good for the country.

There is a school of thought that feels that instead of changing completely to the US presidential system, why not identify the portion of the Indian Parliamentary system that has shown negative results and replace it with the portion of the presidential system that has shown positive results. But some feel that any change in one aspect will have a side effect on another aspect. Either India sticks to the present constitution or changes totally to the US presidential system of government, as it cannot be a half-baked system.

A caveat, I am neither for the BJP, nor for the INC, nor for any of the Regional Parties, nor for the Communist Party, so, when I speak well of any party, it does not mean my leanings are towards that party. Likewise, if I speak about the drawbacks of any party, that does not mean that I am against that party.Every party has the good, the bad and the ugly; the shade may differ from one another. Some parties have done some good for the country, some have done something bad for the country, and some have taken some ugly actions, which the country is facing today, like the 'Himalayan blunder-1962', 'unjustified imposing of the emergency on the country-mid 1975', 'Massacre of Sikhs-1984', 'Demolition of the Babri Majid-1992', that led to the riots in Mumbai -1992/1993 and the burning of the train with 'Kar-Sevaks', returning from Ayodhya in 2002, that led to the 'Gujarat riots-2002'. My aim is to bring out the good, the bad, and the ugly as a lesson; good, advisable to follow; the bad, advisable to immediately carry out a correction; and the ugly, never to be repeated.

When one suggests a change to a different system, some political parties, especially the communists, dub the person as a foreign agent. To clarify, I am not an agent. I am a simple citizen, retired from the Indian army. Now, as an ordinary citizen and a veteran, I care for the well-being of my country. I am deeply disturbed with the way the Indian parliament functions and the calibre of the majority of the politicians who have got into the seats of power to help their own interests instead of serving the people.For them, the country and the people are secondary, even though the people have chosen them to bring a better future for everyone.

When one finds a number of things going wrong, there is one crucial change one must make so that 'Everything Falls in Place'. Therefore, I strongly advocate that India should change to the presidential system of government, preferably on the USA model.

K S Rao [author]

CONTENTS

Part I

INDIAN PARLIAMENTARY SYSTEM

The Parliamentary System of Government is a system of democratic governance of a state where the executive branch derives its democratic legitimacy from the legislature [Parliament] and is also held accountable to that legislature. The central principle is that there is a fusion of the executive and the legislature powers. The head of the state is a different person from the head of the government. This, in contrast to a presidential system in a democracy, is where the head of the state is also the head of the government, and most importantly, the executive branch does not derive its democratic legitimacy from the legislature.

Countries with parliamentary systems may be constitutional monarchies, where the head of a state can also be a monarch, while the head of the government is a member of the legislature, such as in the United Kingdom, Sweden, and Japan, or parliamentary republics, where usually a ceremonial president is the head of a state while the head of the government is from the legislature, such as in India. In a few parliamentary republics, such as Botswana, South Africa, and Suriname, as well as German states, the head of the government is also the head of the state but is elected by and is answerable to the legislature.

There are a total of 71 nations [including India] with a parliamentary system of government that are spread throughout the world. 5 nations in Africa, 13 nations in South and North America and the Caribbean, 16 nations [including India] in Asia, 32 nations in Europe, and 5 nations in the Pacific.

Some of the prominent nations are Canada, Iceland, Jamaica, Ireland, the United Kingdom,Norway, Finland, Sweden, Denmark, Serbia, Netherlands, Germany, Poland, Hungary, Belgium, Austria, Spain, Italy, Greece, South Africa, Israel, Iraq, Turkey, Pakistan, India, Myanmar, Malaysia, Singapore, Thailand, Cambodia, Japan, Australia, and New Zealand. Others are smaller nations.

There is some difference in these governments in terms of the connection between the legislature and the executive branch, and the appointment/ election of the head of the state, the election/ appointment/ approval of the Prime Minister, and the appointment/ approval of the council of ministers.

The parliamentary system in the developed nations, like Canada, the United Kingdom, Norway, Finland, Sweden, Denmark, Netherlands, Germany, Poland, Belgium, Austria, Spain, Italy, Israel, Singapore, Japan, Australia, and New Zealand are stable and running smoothly. The parliamentary systems in the developing nations, including India, are not really running smoothly.

Out of the developing nations, comparatively, India generally follows a parliamentary system as per the norms, but there are fault lines between the functioning of the Executive and the Legislature. As a result, the implementations of the service to the people and the nation, as per the promises the government had made in their manifesto, is only partially achieved. Thus, the governance is far below what is expected. The main reason is that the developing nations still follow the feudal system under the umbrella of democracy. The political parties are led by political families, and there is a lot of self-interest and corruption.As far as India is concerned, the intellectuals feel that if this is not checked, India will be ruled by 100 political families; this does not speak well of the Indian Parliamentary System. In one case, the functioning of the Head of State was questionable in 1975; the Head of State proclaimed an emergency that was not warranted. The emergency was the turning point in the democratic process in India.

India follows the Parliamentary System, based on the 'Westminster Model'. This model laid the foundation for the political system in free India. This system has two chambers of Parliament [or houses]: an elected lower house known as Lok Sabha, elected by the people and an upper house known as Rajya Sabha, which is elected by a different mechanism, candidates being elected by the members of the parties in the state assembles, the vacancies for the Rajya Sabha for each party is based on the number of their elected members in their assembly. As per the amendment to the constitution, a candidate residing in one state can represent the people of another state in the Rajya Sabha.

We have a ceremonial President, who is the head of the country, with no executive powers; he is elected indirectly by the people, in the sense that he is elected by the MPs in the Rajya Sabha and Lok Sabha. The President, in his role as head of the legislature, has full powers to summon and prorogue either house of Parliament or dissolve the lower house [Lok Sabha]. Parliament is the supreme legislative body of India.

We have a Prime Minister, who is the head of the government, with executive powers. The Prime Minister is also indirectly elected by the people, in the sense that he is elected by the party members as their leader of the party before or after the elections. If the party has the majority in Parliament, the President as the head of the state appoints him as the Prime Minister, like it is done in the United Kingdom, Canada, Australia, and New Zealand.The PM needs to survive a vote of confidence; otherwise, a new election must be called. The Prime Minister's term is for 5 years, and the number of terms is not restricted.

As the executive head, he presides over the Council of Ministers [cabinet],which is responsible for the legislature. The council of ministers are appointed by the Prime Minister.Their selection is based more on the political clout rather than on their qualification and experience in the portfolio they are to take over. The Prime Minister is chosen by the party he belongs to by the other elected parliamentarians of his party, and since the Prime Minister is indirectly elected by the people, in the true sense, the people may not get a Prime Minister, the executive head of their choice.

The legislature can typically be dissolved at any stage during its life by the head of the state on the advice of the PM alone, or the PM and cabinet, or by the cabinet.

The legislature has two chambers- the lower house and the upper house. The lower house [Lok Sabha] has 543 members, covering the whole country, and each member represents a constituency and is elected by the people of that constituency; their term is for 5 years. The upper house has 245 members, covering the whole country. However, the number of representatives from each state depends on the number of MP's elected from each state; their term is for 6 years [One third rotating after every two years].

Governors are the head of the states and are appointed by the President. The Chief Ministers are the executive heads of the states and are elected by the members of the political party that has got the maximum number of members of the legislature; usually, it is the leader of the party who becomes the Chief Minister; his tenure is for five years, i.e., till the next election. For the elections to take place, the Chief Minister dissolves the house and resigns.The Governor subsequently appoints him as a caretaker Chief Minister till a successor is elected.

The Chief Minister selects his cabinet ministers from the legislature only, usually with political compulsion. In case he wants someone from outside, he can use the Rajya Sabha route. The Chief Minister governs the state through the Commissioners of a group of districts, Municipal Commissioners in cities and towns, and Director General of Police and the state Attorney General.

Parliamentary governments produce serious debates as seen in the United Kingdom parliament, but in India, the greater part of the opposition creates a lot of noise, and there is so much shouting and ruckus to the extent of not allowing any debate; several precious hours are wasted, and no business is carried out for a number of days. The Members of Parliament collect their salaries and allowances without doing any work. Further, after a five-year tenure, they are given a pension for a lifetime, and there is a tremendous financial loss to the exchequer.

A recent World Bank study found that parliamentary systems are less associated with corruption. This is not true in India. Cash for even asking questions during the question hour in Parliament and cash for voting for membership to the Rajya Sabha [Upper House] has come to the notice of the public.

THE USA PRESIDENTIAL SYSTEM

A Presidential system is a system of government where a head of government is also head of state and leads an executive branch that is separate from the legislature branch. The central principle is that the legislature and executive branches of government are separate, and the President is constitutionally independent of the legislature and is the head of the executive branch.

There are 43 Republics that have a presidential system of government that are spread throughout the world; some of the prominent nations are the United States, Mexico, Argentina, Brazil, Cyprus, Iran, Indonesia, Philippines; others are smaller nations. And there are 16 Presidential systems with a Prime Minister; some of the prominent nations are Uzbekistan, Central African Republic, Yemen, and South Korea. There are Monarchical forms of the presidential system of government and Dictatorship, with one-party state or transitional governments.These systems have a number of problems and not worth considering.

The United States has a republican form of government with a full Presidential system. France and Sri Lanka have a semi-presidential system, where the President has powers over foreign affairs, and the Prime Minister has the powers over the day to day running of the country. The presidential system in the USA has been very successful, and the semi-presidential systems in France and Sri Lanka have been widely considered to be workable.

The United States of America has had a presidential system for the past 229 years; this form has seen the test of time in their political sphere. The system in the USA is most stable as compared to the presidential system of governments in other nations and is a workable model to follow.

The President is the head of the state, head of the executive and commander-in-chief of the armed forces. Once elected, he is not a member of any party. He has a set term of office of 4 years and cannot have more than two terms. The legislature also exists for a set term of office; the US have two legislative houses, the Senate with a set term of six years [1/3rd returning or seeking re-election every two years] and the Congress with a set term of two years and both cannot be dissolved ahead of schedule. The President is responsible to the legislature and cannot dismiss it. The legislature has the right, in extreme cases, to dismiss the President through impeachment. However, such dismissals in extreme cases are rare; in normal circumstances, using normal means, the legislature cannot dismiss the President.

He functions with a number of departmental chiefs such as secretaries of state that form his cabinet; the departmental chiefs must carry out the policies of the executive and legislature branches; they are not members of the legislature. Secretaries of state are usually selected by the President based on their qualifications and experience in the department they are going to lead and have to be confirmed by the Senate. This is the reason why the President has to be very careful while selecting the secretaries of the state. The President is directly responsible to the people of the United States, who have elected him to the chair of the President, through the 'Electoral College'. The President can give 'Executive Orders' that should conform to the constitution and are legally correct; otherwise, the 'Executive Orders' can be struck down by the courts, but any bills that have to be passed have to go through Congress and the Senate to be passed.

The President usually has special privileges in the enactment of the legislation, namely the possession of powers of veto over the legislation of bills, in some cases subject to the powers of the legislature by weighing majority to override a veto, e. g; in 1832, US President Andrew Jackson vetoed a bill that would re-charter the Second Bank of the United States. Thus, the legislature and the President are expected to serve as checks and balances in each other's powers.

The system ensures that the President need not bother about his/her seat to due opposition from the legislature with vested interests. The President will be able to take tough and long-lasting decisions, and there will be stability in the government; with this, the people will benefit.

The USA constitution limits the influence of swings in public opinion by placing the election of the Head of the executive [in their case, the President] in the hands of the 'Electoral College', rather than the subject of direct election and the terms of office of the President and the two chambers of the legislature are all set at different lengths, President for four years, Senate for six years [one third rotating after every two years] and the House of Representatives for two years. The members of the Supreme Court serve for life.

The USA's constitution is built on a greater compromise between the Virginia plan [representation of population] and the New Jersey plan [equal representation of all states], which resulted in the 'House of Representatives', with more members, being constructed based onthe population and the 'Senate', with 100 members, being composed of an equal number of representatives regardless of the population to balance the smaller states with less political power with the larger states with more political power. This is why six states today have one member in the 'House of representatives' [Lower House] but have two members in the 'Senate' [Upper House]. The members of the Senate are responsible to the whole state, unlike in the Indian Parliamentary System, where the members of the Rajya Sabha [Upper house] are responsible only to their constituencies.

The Governor of a state is the head of the state government and leads the executive branch separate from the legislature. The Governor is directly elected by the people of the state; therefore, the people of the state get a Governor of their choice. The tenure of the Governor is fixed for four years and a maximum of two tenures. He cannot be removed but can be impeached through the legislature.

The Governor administers his state through the elected Mayor of the town/city and the Police commissioner of the town/city appointed by him. The District Attorney, also appointed by him, is usually the senior-most in the District Attorney's Office.

In most states, the other leaders in the executive branch are also directly elected, including the lieutenant governor, the attorney general, the secretary of state, auditors, and commissioners.

All 50 states have a Legislative branch made up of elected representatives, who consider bills brought forth by the Governor or introduced by its members to create a legislature that becomes law for the state. The legislature also approves the state's Budget and initiates tax legislation and articles of impeachment.

Except for one state, Nebraska, all states have a bicameral legislature made up of two chambers: a smaller upper chamber called the Senate, and its members generally serve longer terms, usually 4 years. The larger lower chamber is most often called the 'House of Representatives', but some states call it Assembly or 'House of Delegates'. Its members usually serve shorter terms, two years.

The state's Judicial Branch is usually led by the State Supreme Court, which hears appeals from lower-level State Courts. Court structures and judicial appointments/elections are determined either by the legislature or the state constitution.

Local governments generally include two tiers: counties and municipalities.

COMPARISON BETWEEN BOTH THE SYSTEMS

There are differences in the federal structure in the Indian and United States system. On gaining independence on August 15, 1947, the Union of India was first formed, followed by the states, whereas in then North America, the colonies already existed before the Union was formed; the colonies were re-named as states and became the United States of America. Thereby, the states in the USA are self-governed and have a lot of independence, whereas, in India, the states are quasi-federal at best and depend on the Union government, mainly for finance and policies in most matters, resulting in a mismatch.

There is a disparity between demographical and representation in India's Westminster model. The House of Commons [Lower House] has 640 seats, with 66 million [10,300 per representative], compared to Lok Sabha [Lower House] with 545 seats against a population of 130 million [23,853 per representatives]. This is not only a lack of adequate representation, but also widens the gap between the people and their representative, leading to the inaccessibility of politicians to the common people. In the United States system, each member of the lower house represents a population of 15,000.

In the Indian Parliament System, the real executive power is vested in the Prime Minister and his cabinet composed of members of the legislature who are individually and collectively responsible for the legislature. The central principle is that there is a fusion of the legislature and executive branches of the government. It is faster and easier to pass legislation, as the executive branch is formed by the direct or indirect support of the legislature branch and includes members of the legislature. Thus, the executive, as the majority party or coalition of parties in the legislature that has a majority of votes, can pass legislation at will. In practice, this is not happening in the Indian Parliamentary System as this is due to the lower calibre of most of the members of Parliament and the opposition not allowing the Parliament to function.

Whereas, in the American Presidential System, the executive is chosen independently from the legislature and the real executive powers are vested with the President. If the executive and the majority of the legislature are from different political parties, then a stalemate can occur. Thus, the executive might not be able to implement its legislative proposals. However, Stalemate is taking place even in the Indian Parliamentary System.

The President can pass 'executive orders' for immediate execution but be within the ambit of the constitution and be legally correct. The Prime Minister cannot pass any 'executive orders', but his government can pass 'ordnances' for immediate action that is valid for only six months and must be rectified thereafter to be effective; otherwise, the ordnances become ineffective. Ordnances have found to be time-consuming.

In the Indian Parliamentary System, the executive powers are more evenly spread out among more people. The Prime Minister is seldom as important as a ruling president, and there tends to be a higher focus on voting for a party and its political ideas than voting for an actual person. This prevents one person from getting too much power. Whereas, in a Presidential System, the executive powers are with one person, but there are checks to ensure he does not become too powerful.

Unlike the American Presidential system, where the President has a set term of office of four years and can have a maximum of two tenures, and the legislature for a set term of office [Senate –six years with one third retiring every two years and the House of Representative – two years], and cannot be dissolved ahead of schedule, the fixed tenures allow elections twice in four years. Whereas the Indian Parliamentary System allows dissolving the Parliament and going for election at any time if the need arises; however, the lack of a definite election calendar can be abused. A ruling party could pre-pone the scheduled election date when it is felt that it is likely to retain power; the same is with the ruling party in the states. As a result, there are state elections six months in a year in some state or the other, and the governance in the state where elections are being held is badly affected due to politicians and the civil administration being in an election mode, and the code of conduct coming in that means no policy decisions can be taken during the election period. Though simultaneous election in India started from the first elections in 1950 due to the Central government falling prematurely several times and re-elections taking place.Similarly, State governments falling, followed by Governor's rule and re-elections taking place, this situation has arisen.

Further, in the American System, the President is more a less elected directly by the people and get a President of their choice, whereas, in the Indian System, the Prime Minister is indirectly elected by the people, and the people may not get a Prime Minister of their choice; the Executive Head is chosen by the legislature, and it depends on the members of the party and their personal ambitions. There is nobody to veto/check legislation passed by Parliament. This can result in the legislative branch gaining too much power.

Whereas, in the presidential form of government, the people elect the President through the 'Electoral College' [which itself is directly elected], allowing for a higher feeling of legitimacy. Though the people do not elect the President directly, the people would get a chief executive more a less of their choice. There is no scope of having two power centres, like in a parliamentary democracy, where it has one power centre under the Prime Minister and the other more powerful, under the President of the ruling party who has a lot of say in selecting the members of the cabinet council, on political support consideration. In a presidential system, separation of powers allows the President and Legislature to monitor and check each other.

In the presidential system, the President need not choose cabinet members commanding the support of the legislature; he has the flexibility to select from a much larger pool of potential candidates, with ability and competence and above everything who can deliver; there won't be any legislature or any coalition compulsions. Though, the appointment of cabinet members has to be agreed upon by the Senate. Thus, stability extends to the cabinet chosen under the system, compared to the parliamentary system where cabinets must be drawn within the legislative branch. In India, keeping in mind representation from religion, Caste, and socio-economic background, in many cases, cabinet posts are given to legislatures who are loyal to the Prime Minister/President of the political party. In the presidential system, cabinet reshuffles are unusual, whereas, in the parliament system in India, cabinet reshuffles are common, where Ministers are often moved between portfolios. Further, to satisfy various political groups, even the cabinet is expanded to accommodate their leaders. Maintaining a large cabinet is a drain on the exchequer.

In the higher judiciary in India, the judges appoint judges. This bypasses the elected representatives and leads to a lack of accountability. It was looked into, and a National Judiciary Committee proposed, which was struck down by the very same judges who took part in the agitation outside the court. Much like the inefficiency of the Parliament, this is also a thorn in transparency and efficiency in the delivery of the system. In the United States system, judges are appointed by the executive and confirmed by the Senate, represented by all the political parties.

The President usually has special privileges in the enactment of the legislation, namely the possession of powers to veto legislation bills. In some cases, subject to the powers of the legislature of weighing majority to override a veto, the legislature and the President are thus expected to balance each other's powers.

The President is the Commander-in-Chief of the armed forces, a constitutional title, and he is very effective. This can be seen by the support he gives to the servicemen and veterans, whereas the President of India is a ceremonial figurehead and non-affective.

The Presidential system ensures that the President need not bother about his/her seat due to opposition from legislatures with vested interests.The President will be able to take tough and long-lasting decisions, and there will be stability in the government. Small parties led by strong political individuals or families wither out, and there is no chance of coalition governments. As a result, two major parties emerge that suits the countries overall political situation; with this, the people benefit. Most important is that the Presidential System has fewer ideological parties than the Parliamentary System.

There is a feeling that in the presidential system, with the executive powers centred on one person, it may lead to Dictatorship; in the USA, this has never happened. Some countries in South America, Africa and the Middle East have a presidential form of government that has led to Dictatorship; this has normally been, in most cases, due to the President being from the armed forces, thus had influence/ backing from the forces and in most cases, used the armed forces to quell any rebellion. But the Presidential System that the USA follows is very democratic.

There is also a feeling that there can be political deadlocks since the presidency and the legislature are parallel structures, resulting in long periods of no-decision. This has taken place in exceptional cases, like 'Obama health Care', but it was resolved. In the Indian Parliamentary System, there was a deadlock initially passing the 'G S T bill', a crucial taxation bill, during the UPA era. However, it was resolved during the last NDA era by compensating the losses to the manufacturing states.

The USA constitution limits the influence of swings in public opinion by placing the election of the Head of the executive [in their case, the President] in the hands of the 'Electoral College', rather than the subject of direct election and the terms of office of the President and the two chambers of the legislature are all set at different lengths, President for four years, Senate for six years [one third rotating after every two years] and the House of Representatives for two years. The members of the Supreme Court serving for life.

India, like the USA, is also a large country with problems of communications and a population of varied backgrounds and education. Therefore, there is a swing in public opinion. The swing in public opinion affects the selection of MPs for the Lok Sabha and the final election of the leader of a political party from their elected MPs, who subsequently becomes the Prime Minister. The procedure followed in the Indian Parliamentary System does not limit the influence of swings in public opinion.

In the Indian Parliamentary System, the terms of office for the Prime Minister, the Executive Head and the lower house, Lok Sabha representatives are five years and for the upper house, and the terms of office of Rajya Sabha representatives is six years [One third rotating after every two years]. The Prime Minister's terms of office and the terms of office of the representatives of the Lok Sabha are the same. The swing in public opinion is not fully taken care of. It appears that the swing in public opinion was not kept in mind when the Indian constitution was drafted.

The USA constitution is built on a greater compromise between the Virginia plan [representation of population] and the New Jersey plan [equal representation of all states], which resulted in the 'House of Representatives', with more members being constructed based on the population and the 'Senate', with 100 members, being composed of an equal number of representatives regardless of the population to balance the smaller states with less political power with the larger states with more political power. This is why six states today have one member in the 'House of Representatives' [Lower House] but have two members in the 'Senate' [Upper House]. The members of the Senate are responsible to the whole state, unlike in the Indian Parliamentary System, where the members of the Rajya Sabha [Upper house] are responsible only to their constituencies.

In India, like the USA, the states are of different size in terms of population, and the political powers are in the hands of the larger states with the number of seats in the Lok Sabha based on the strength of the population, the number of seats in the Rajya Sabha is also based on the strength of the population, reviewed by the Election Commission, as necessary. As a result, the smaller states have less political power. The maximum strength of the Rajya Sabha is 250 [including 12 nominated by the President]. The Rajya Sabha seats per state are Uttar Pradesh – 31, Maharashtra – 19, Tamil Nadu – 18, Bihar and Bengal – 16 each, Karnataka – 12; Andhra Pradesh , Gujarat, and Madhya Pradesh – 11 each, Odisha and Rajasthan – 10 each, Kerala – 9; Telangana, Assam, and Punjab – 7 each, Jharkhand – 6, Haryana and Chhattisgarh – 5 each, Jammu & Kashmir – 4, Himachal and Delhi – 3 each; and Arunachal, Goa, Manipur, Meghalaya, Mizoram, Nagaland, Sikkim, Puducherry, and Tripura – 1 each.

Further, there are a number of power lobbies at the centre and states as it is in the USA, but the difference is that in the USA, the lobbies are open and transparent.

Within states, political party's nominate members, the assembly then elects its state MPs for the Rajya Sabha. Political Party composition in the state assemblies decides how many Rajya Sabha seats a party will get. For example, if the BJP has 55% of seats in the Maharashtra Assembly, BJP will get 55% of the 19 seats earmarked for Maharashtra in the Rajya Sabha, and the 55% will include the seats already occupied by the BJP and the vacated seats to be filled in, after every two years [one third rotating every two years]. This is not a constitutional requirement, but this is the practice followed and is acceptable to all political parties.

To give equal political powers to the smaller states, all states should have the same number of representatives in the Upper House regardless of the population. It appears that the disparity in the political power from one state to another was also not kept in mind when the Indian constitution was drafted.

The disparity in political power can be seen in the case of Utter Pradesh, which has 80 MPs in the Lok Sabha.As a result, out of 13 Prime Ministers, we have had 7 PMs from Utter Pradesh, namely, Pandit Jawaharlal Nehru, Lal Bahadur Shastri, Indira Gandhi, Rajiv Gandhi, Choudhary Charan Singh, V P Singh, and Chandra Shekar. The other six are from other states; they are Morarji Desai and Narender Modi from Gujarat, P V Narasimha Rao from Telangana, H D Deve Gowda from Karnataka, I K Gujral from Punjab and Atal Bihari Vajpayee from Madhya Pradesh.

The states in the United States are governed by a Governor, and he is the head of the state and chief executive head of the government. He is directly elected by the people of the state, and they get a governor of their choice. The tenure of the Governor is fixed for four years, with two tenures only. Like the President, he cannot be removed but can be impeached through the legislature. The Governor administers his state through several executive departments. Each office term is limited to two, four-year terms. The executive and the legislature are separate.

Whereas, in the Indian states, the Governor is nominated by the ruling central government, he is the ceremonial head of the state, and the real executive powers are with the chief minister of the state, who is indirectly elected, the people don't get a chief executive of their choice. In addition to 28 states, India has 8 Union Territories [UTs], out of which 3 UTs have a Lieutenant Governor, head of the UT, an elected Chief Minister, and an elected assembly and 5 UTs that are directly governed by the Centre, through a Lieutenant Governor, without an elected assembly.

State governments of the United States are institutional units in the United States exercising some of the functions of the government at a level below that of the federal government. In most states, the other leaders in the executive branch are also directly elected, including the lieutenant governor, the attorney general, the secretary of state, and auditors and commissioners.

In Florida, the Senate has 40 members [4-year-term with 20 senators up for election every two years], and the house has 120 members [2 years tenure]. Members of both houses are term-limited to serve a maximum of eight years. There are four types of local governments in Florida: counties [67 in number], municipalities, school districts and special districts. Other states are on the same line but differ from one another in their composition, selection, and functioning.

In India, the state governments administrate the state through the mayors of the municipalities, sheriffs, and police commissioners [in cities/towns], and Director General of police and state attorney general, and through the Divisional Commissioners with 4 to 5 districts under him, districts are headed by a District Collector; he administrates his district through the block officers and village Gram panchayats. The mayors [in cities/towns] are figureheads. Sheriffs [in cities/towns] have very little functions; he is more a less another figurehead.

With the separation between the executive and the legislature, the President of the United States, as the executive head, is in a better position to govern the country better than the Prime Minister of India, who has many political compulsions. As a result, the governance in the Presidential System of Government in the United States is far superior as compared to the Parliamentary System of Government in India.

Implementing the centre's policies and reforms has to be carried out at the state level. In the US system, the governors are in a better position to carry out the implementation, as the Governors of states are directly elected by the people and are responsible to the people of the state.

In India, implementation of centres policies and reforms suffers, as the people do not get a chance of electing a capable Chief Minister of their choice. The Chief Minister himself is not sure of holding his job due to political uncertainty.

Indian Political Events

4.1   Pre-Independence-1947

Most parts of the Indian subcontinent was under the Mughal Empire from 1526 to 1757 [for over two centuries] and later under the East India Company from 1757 to 1858. Subsequently, the whole of India was directly under the British colonial power from 1858 to midnight of 14/15 August 1947. Side by side, 565 Maharajah's, Raja's and Nawab's ruled over one-third of India. Except for the Maharaja of Patiala, who ran a 'Model State', the others spent most of the revenues of the state on themselves for exceptional good living and on young ladies in their harems, and hobbies like hunting and playing polo.

With the Mughals, we were under foreign rule, and India remained in the feudal system and did not gain much, except for the period under Emperor Akbar, who improved the administration and maintained Communal Harmony. His second wife was a Hindu; he even banned the consumption of Beef. Under the British Empire, the political and administrative unification of India happened, and India became one nation. Though India was still under foreign rule, the country gained substantially. For India, this was the best thing that had happened. The British laid the foundation for the legal, civil administrative and educational institutions, military, dams for harnessing water, electricity, connectivity in roads, railways, shipping, and telecommunication, on an all India grid; though the British did all the developments for their own requirements, they left the infrastructure behind when they left, and India benefitted. Above everything, what Britain gave the diverse people of India is the English language that bonded them with each other and gave them the opportunity to communicate with people from all over the world.

But, by the time the British left, 24% of the world's wealth that India possessed as known at that point of time before they came into power came down to 4%, and the industrial output from 27% came down to 2%; the worst-hit being the handloom weavers, their backs were broken, and they went into poverty. Indian handlooms were world-famous; the raw materials were shipped to England, spun and sold back to India at a very high cost. This is the darkest side of British rule.

The Indian National Congress [INC] was founded on 28th December 1885, by 65 educated individuals with the active help of Alan Octavian Hume, a retired British civil officer, and with the blessings of the Viceroy of British India, as an exclusive debating club, voicing the desire of India's small educated and westernised elite for a larger share in the administration. It was not a nationalist party but was considered the largest and most prominent Indian public organisation and functioned as a loyal constructive opposition. The British allowed it as they wanted to have a platform for civic and political dialogue of educated Indians with the British Raj. In 1906, the Muslims of India also formed the 'All India Muslim League' on the same basis.

In 1916, Mohandas Karamchand Gandhi, later known as 'The Mahatma' came back to India, fresh from his experience with non-violent action in South Africa, started by him and joined the Indian National Congress [INC].On 18 September 1941, he made it into a political party.Therefore, INC was a political party from 18 September 1941 but under the British Raj. Under the leadership of Mahatma Gandhi, the INC spear headed the peaceful movement struggle to gain independence from the British, the colonial rulers. Hereafter, the INC became the main focus in the fight for independence and had a defining influence on the Indian Independent Movement. Initially, Gandhiji never asked the British toleave India; he asked them"to give us our freedom", a positive, legitimate demand.When Gandhiji found that nothing had changed in the direction of obtaining freedom, he started a civil disobedience movement, called the 'Quit India Movement' on August 8, 1942, during World War II, it was also known as the 'India August movement [August Kranti], in Hindi, it was known as the 'Bharat Chhodo Andolan'. The movement was accompanied by mass protests across the country on non-violent lines in which, Mahatma Gandhi called for 'an orderly British withdrawal from India'. Thereafter, the 'Quit India Movement' accelerated the freedom struggle.

Subash Chandra Bose also accelerated the freedom movement from outside India by leading the 'Indian National Army [INA]' that he raised against the British in Burma [now Myanmar] and Malaya [now Malaysia]. With the Indian people against the British and the 'Indian National Army's' offensive posture during World War II, the British had decided to give Independence to India at a later date as they did not want the Brahmin community to dominate Indian politics, but it was the subsequent 'British Indian Naval Mutiny' that made them bring forward the date to 15 August 1947. The demand for freedom was met without bloodshed, and India became a free country at the midnight hour of 14th/15th August 1947, and the British left India. The credit for gaining independence should go to Mahatma Gandhi and Subhash Chandra Bose.

After gaining independence, the function of the erstwhile Indian National Congress [INC] ended. In fact, Gandhiji did not want the INC to continue since the goal of gaining independence was achieved. He wanted the INC to be dissolved and a new political party to be formed to run the country.

4.2   The Political Events -1947 to 2021

Independent India started off as a 20th century democracy in a social environment comparable to that prevailing in Europe in the 18th century. Out of the two types of parliamentary democracies, namely the Westminster system and the Consensus system, India opted for the Westminster system, which is found in the Commonwealth Nations influenced by the British political system. This system of government laid the foundation for the Indian Parliamentary System in free India; there was nothing wrong in doing so, and the country benefited. As a result, we have a democracy with representatives from all religions and communities, with various social-economic levels, including Other Backward Classes [OBCs], *Dalits* and the *Tribals;* it has been a great achievement indeed.

Sardar Vallabhbhai Patel, as Deputy Prime Minister and Home Minister, played an important part in bringing the princely states under the Indian Flag by granting concessions to the Maharajas and Princes in the form of a privy-purse in 1947, in return for their peaceful accession to the Indian Union. Except for the Nawab of Hyderabad and the Nawab of Junagarh, who wished to go to Pakistan, everyone agreed. The military was ordered to take over Hyderabad and Junagarh by force. The military action was justified as both Hyderabad and Junagarh, geographically, were well within the Indian Territory. For uniting India to its present form, Sardar V Patel is known as 'The Iron Man'.

Pandit Jawaharlal Nehru, as the first Prime Minister [August 15, 1947, to May 27, 1964], did not dissolve the INC, as per Gandhiji's wishes. He kept the same organisation with changes in the political structure and portfolios, and the INC became a main political party.Thus, the birth of INC as a political party in its present form took place on August 15, 1947, and, in reality,is about 73 years old and is the oldest political party in independent India.

Parliamentary democracies have worked very well in the political environments of Canada, the United Kingdom, Spain, Netherlands, Denmark, Sweden, Germany, Israel, Singapore, Japan, Australia, and New Zealand. France has a semi-presidential system with both the presidential and parliamentary system by combining a president with executive responsibility to Parliament; this system has also worked very well.

But in India, the parliament democracy has shown some cracks from the very beginning. Firstly, with only one political party in the fray and no opposition.Secondly, the whole country was in the hands of one family [three generations] for nearly 38 years [initially for around 28 years and later for around 10 years]. There is feudalism at the centre, the state, and down to the village level, right from the beginning that still exists to a great extent, even today. Normally, a parliament democracy thrives when the voters are educated. In India, even today, the bulk of the voters are not educated or not educated enough to understand the importance of electing a leader who can deliver.

Unfortunately, even today, feudalism is in the political parties at the national and regional level. At the national level, in the Indian National Congress [INC], it has to be a member from the Nehru-Indira Feroz Gandhi family who can be the Party President to head the party and another member who has to be the Prime Minister to run the country. Similarly, at the regional level, Samajwadi Party [SP], with Mulayam Singh's family in Utter Pradesh which is the largest state that can influence the political alignments in the country with 80 seats in the Lower House [Lok Sabha]; Rashtra Janata Dal [RJD], with Lalu Prasad's family in Bihar which is the second-largest state that can also influence the political alignment with 50 seats in the Lower House [Lok Sabha]; Shiromani Akali Dal [SAD], with Badal's family in Punjab; DMK, with Karunanidhi's family in Tamil Nadu; National Congress Party, with Sharad Pawer's family in Maharashtra, and Shiv Sena, with Thackeray's family also in Maharashtra; Janata Dal [S], with Deve Gowda's family in Karnataka and all these regional parties want to have a Chief Minister/Deputy Chief Minister to run their respective state, when they are in power. This does not speak very highly of the parliamentary democracy practised in India. With feudalism in Indian politics, the people cannot get the best person to govern the country/state.

Initially, the country, under Nehru did well with the 1st and 2nd - 5 years plans, when the basic Infra-structure came up, like construction of dams to harness the water, steel plants to help the industrial base, expansion of railways for better connectivity; importance was given to Agriculture, and more food was grown; importance was given to higher education by establishing Indian Institute of Technology. However, health was not given enough importance, and public transport in cities was neglected.

Unfortunately, the two strong leaders, Sardar Vallabhbhai Patel, had died of a heart attack, on 15 December 1950, at Bombay [Mumbai] and Netaji Subhas Chandra Bose was presumed dead in an air crash on 27 Aug 1945, at Taipei [Taiwan], the loss of two great stalwarts was a great loss to the country. There was no opposition to Nehru. He was the undisputed leader. He followed the Parliamentary Democracy of Britain but with the economic socialism of Karl Marx.

At the outset, INC represented the whole country. The one political party government, initially under Nehru, ran the country till he died on May 27, 1964, later from June 9, 1964, by Lal Bahadur Shastri for a very short time till he died on Jan 11, 1966, at Tashkent, followed from Jan 24, 1966, by Indira Gandhi, daughter of Nehru and wife of Feroz Gandhi, till Mar 24, 1977, when the Janata Party came into power. Thus, since independence for almost 30 years, there was one party ruling the country without any opposition party.During this period, the Nehru-Indira Feroz Gandhi dynasty ruled the country for around 28 years, and the remaining very short period under Lal Bahadur Shastri.After the fall of the Janata Party on 14 January 1980, Indira Gandhi once again became the Prime Minister till she was assassinated on 31 October 1984. Thereafter, her son Rajiv Gandhi became the Prime Minister [October 31, 1984, to May 22, 1990] till he lost the next election, due to the 'Bofors scandal'; the Nehru-Indira Feroz Gandhi dynasty had ruled for another 10 years. This brings it to nearly 38 years; the country was under one family. This period saw the military reverses the country suffered at the hands of the Chinese army during Nehru's period, the imposition of the emergency that crippled the parliamentary democratic system during the Indira Gandhi period and the Bofors scandal with Italian connections and other middlemen that took place while purchasing Military Hardware during Rajeev Gandhi's period.On the economic front, during the Nehru-Indira Feroz Gandhi Dynasty rule of 30 years, the average GDP was 3.5%; the 'License-permit raj' thrived with corruption at every level, resulting in debts and, at the end of this period, defaulted loan payments and the governments there after had to face a very bad economic situation, due to lack of economic reforms.

Under Jawaharlal Nehru, the state of the armed forces operational preparedness was neglected, and the Prime Minister did not take the military advice on national security. When General K S Thimayya, as Chief of the Army, advised him to take the threat from China more seriously, he brushed it aside.

The launching of the 'Forward Policy' without sufficient troops aimed at pushing Indian patrols and forward posts into Chinese held territory claimed by India had annoyed the Chinese. As retaliation, on October 20, 1962, the Chinese attacked our north-eastern border in Arunachal Pradesh [earlier known as North Eastern Frontier Agency] and simultaneously attacked our northern border at Chushul in Ladakh. To make matters worse, Nehru sent Lt Gen B M Kaul [groomed by Nehru to be the future Chief of the Army] to take over the newly formed IV Corps to take on the Chinese at the north-eastern border. Lt Gen B M Kaul could not command well, and the lower formations of the IV Corps suffered several casualties and were unable to stop the Chinese army, which came in waves. The Indian 7 Mountain Brigade at Thangdar Ridge, under Brigadier John Dalvi, were surrounded by the Chinese. Many were shot dead,and many were taken POW's, including Brigadier John Dalvi, and very few escaped. Subsequently, a Mountain Brigade at Se-la, under Brigadier Hushier Singh, were surrounded by the Chinese. The Commander gave orders to withdraw, and in the hasty move, some were killed, including Brigadier Hushier Singh; some were taken POW, and some managed to escape,and finally, a brigade at Bomdi-La, made a hasty withdrawal. Lt Gen B M Kaul was replaced by Lt Gen Sam H F J Manekshaw, popularly known as 'Sam Bahadur. Some formations from Nagaland [incharge of the rural insurgency area] and Ferozpur [guarding the Pakistani border] were milked out and inducted. They held onto the foothills, thus prevented the Chinese from moving down to the plains of Assam. It was a 'Himalayan Blunder'. 'Jane's Magazine' stated, "the finest army in the world was beaten by the Chinese." This debacle affected the morale of the Army. Lt Gen Sam Manekshaw later became the Chief of the Army Staff, in the rank of a General, and retired as a Field Marshall for his contribution to the subsequent action - 'Liberation of Bangladesh', in 1971.

However, a brigade formation under Brig Naveen Rawley held on to Wallong in NEFA but suffered several casualties and subsequently withdrew after blowing up their artillery guns to the mountain ranges in-depth and consolidated their positions. This was a well-planned organised withdrawal. Another brigade formation under Brigadier T N Raina held on to Chushul and prevented the Chinese from taking over Leh, the capital of Ladakh.Brigadier T N Raina later became the Chief of the Army Staff, in the rank of a General. Brigadier N Rawley later became the Vice Chief of the Army Staff, in the rank of Lt Gen.

The National Security was undermined, and the political leadership was to be blamed. To save Nehru, the defence minister, Krishna Menon, resigned. If Nehru had taken General K S Thimayya's advice and built up the army operationally to take on any threat from the north, the Chinese would have thought twice before embarking on their ambitious mission.If there was political opposition to Nehru's foreign policies, especially towards China, this debacle would not have taken place. Unfortunately, Sardar Vallabhbhai Patel died in 1950; before his death, he had advised Nehru to take the threat from China seriously and also recommended remedies, but Nehru took it lightly.

On the economic front, the government controlled everything. After Nehru's visit to USSR, he was impressed with how the communists in USSR had dealt with the economic progress; he made the Indian state to be involved in the building of heavy industries, as he felt that the Indian private sector would not be able to handle it, he left only the small industries to the private sector, thus, following some sort of a mixed economy with more leaning towards the public sector.

Nehru's vision had three pillars – self-reliance, some sort of a mixed economy, and non-alignment. Nehru's first and second Industrial Policy Resolution of 1948 and 1956 declared that India would strive to establish a 'socialistic pattern of society'. Government regulations were perpetuating inefficiency and promoting corruption; this curbed the private sector from growing. There was no viable private sector that helped in the economic growth that provided Jobs. Mostly, government Jobs were available, even that was limited. Again, if there was an opposition to Nehru's economic policies, the private sector, the backbone of any economy, would have thrived, and the availability of Jobs would have been improved.

But a strong opposition only comes when there are at least a minimum of two main national parties. Apart from the INC, the only other parties at that period were the Swatantra[Freedom] Party, a conservative political party, the two communist parties [CPI[M] and CPM] in Bengal and Kerala and the Bharatiya Jana Sangh in Madhya Pradesh, Maharashtra [mostly around Nagpur], and a portion of Rajasthan and Uttar Pradesh.

The party with the most liberal ideas was the Swatantra Party, founded by Chakravarti Rajagopalachari in 1959. The founder was the first and last Indian Governor General of India. The Party stood up for democratic freedom, personal liberty, social liberalism, pluralism, and individual initiative that were brilliantly articulated by Rajaji, Piloo Modi and Minocher Rustom Masani. The party was formed as a reaction to Jawaharlal Nehru's dominant Indian National Congress [increasingly socialist] and with a statist outlook and had a widespread response in Orissa, Bihar, Rajasthan, and Gujarat. The Party stood for a market-based economy with 'Licence-permit Raj' dismantled. It was located right of the political spectrum; it was not communal like the Bharatiya Jan Sangh.

Incidentally, the 'Licence-permit Raj' was dismantled in 1991, after nearly 44 years, and the economy was liberated by P V Narasimha Rao [a Congressman] when he became the 9th Prime Minister and found that the country was in bad debts and defaulted in paying back loans. After gaining independence from the British, it took India nearly 44 years to kickstart the economy. The country wasted a lot of time.

In the 1967 general elections, the Swatantra Party won 44 seats with a vote share of 8.7%, the same number of seats that the Indian National Congress won in the general election of 2004 and a little more, 55, in 2019. Swatantra Party could have been an alternative to the Congress, but unfortunately, the founder, C Rajagopalachari, died in 1972, and the party declined rapidly. On 4 August 1974, the party president, Piloo Modi, dissolved the party and merged with Charan Singh's Bharatiya Kranti Dal [BKD]; this was a great mistake. Subsequently, the remaining leaders, including Rajmata Gayatri Devi of the erstwhile Swatantra Party, were put in jail during the 'emergency', by Indira Gandhi. After the emergency, the party never got a chance of reappearing in the political arena. This was a great setback for the Indian political system.

After Nehru, Lal Bahadur Shastri took over as Prime Minister on June 9, 1964; he was Nehru's choice for the next PM, but unfortunately, he died on Jan 11, 1966. He was a decisive leader. He went on merits and decided to make Swaran Singh the foreign minister, though Indira Gandhi [Nehru's daughter and wife of Feroz Gandhi [no relation of Mahatma Gandhi]] was keen for this post. When Pakistan attacked India in September 1965, he gave a free hand to General JN Choudhary, the then Chief of the Army, to take on the Pakistani army. The Indian Army defeated the Pakistani army and regained its prestige. His motto, "Jai Jawan- Jai Kisan", built the image of the Jawans [soldiers] and Kisans [farmers] who were contributing the maximum to the nation. His death was a great loss to the nation and to the Indian National Congress [INC].

After Shastri's death, Indira Gandhi became the PM [the first lady PM]. However, she was an autocratic leader, she did some good for the people of the country, like nationalising the banks [though nationalising 70% of the banks was not a sound decision, today we are facing the problem of 'Non Performing Asset's [NPAs], and Devaluation of Rupee that adjusted the Rupee with foreign currency, abolishing the privy purse that was a drain on the economy, allowing abortion that helped out the women, strict action on dowry deaths, that was a black mark on the Indian society; stopping bonded labour that nearly amounted to slavery in another form, etc. Some were bad decisions, like causing a division in the Indian National Congress [INC] and promoting family dynasty, both were her bad contributions that are still haunting the country; her son, Sanjay Gandhi, was to be the next PM, without having any political and administrative experience; some ugly, like the imposition of the emergency, thus crippling the democratic system in India.

She took the political decision to liberate East Pakistan from the tyranny of the Pakistan army. The leader of the Awami League, Sheikh Mujibur Rahman, had won an absolute majority in the election for the Pakistan National Assembly in the beginning of 1971. Awami League captured every seat from East Pakistan on a 'six-point programme' of maximum provisional autonomy, which verged on secession. Though East Pakistan formed a majority of the country's total population, Pakistan's politics had been dominated since independence by a small group of well-connected politicians, bureaucrats, generals from the western wing and particularly from the Punjab province. Sheikh Mujibur Rahman was not given a chance to become the Prime Minister of Pakistan; instead, he was put in prison by General Yahaya Khan, who declared martial law and took over the country, as the Executive head [President], with the concurrence of Zulfiqar Ali Bhutto. Sheikh's second in command proclaimed the independence of Bangladesh and directed an underground resistance movement by the Mukti Bahini-the Awami League's guerrilla arm. There was an uprising in East Pakistan; to quell the uprising, on 25th March 1971, a corps under General Tikka Khan was sent in; the Pakistan army indulged in a number of atrocities, and about ten million refugees [30,000 per day] landed in India. The refugee problem was a drain on the economy of India, amounting to ₹2,75,00,000 per day, despite international aid. Apart from the refugee problem, there was a possibility of a country from outside interfering with their internal problems and even sending in manpower into then East Pakistan, maybe China or Myanmar; this would not have been in the interest of India.

The Indian armed forces, under the leadership of General Sam H FJ Manekshaw, crushed the Pakistan army and liberated the people of East Pakistan. Initially, the Indian Air Force wiped out the Pakistani Air Force in East Pakistan. The Indian Navy dominated the Bay of Bengal and blocked the sea routes to East Pakistan; the Indian Army came from the Northern, Eastern and Western direction and surrounded Dacca, capital of East Pakistan.After closing the last open flank by dropping a parachute battalion group, Dacca fell, and the Pakistani corps surrendered; it was a well-coordinated effort by all three forces. East Pakistan became Bangladesh, an independent nation, with Sheikh Mujibur Rahman as the Prime Minister. Indian armed forces took around 93,300 Pakistani POWs.

Though the liberation of Bangladesh was a feather in Indira Gandhi's cap, while negotiating with Zulfiqar Ali Bhutto, the president of Pakistan, during the Shimla Agreement of June 1972, she agreed to send back 93,300 Pakistani POWs but failed to bring back around 54 Indian POWs who were languishing in Pakistani civilian Jails. The Pakistan army established POW camps, with effect from 15th December 1971; the war started on 3rd December 1971, with the pre-emptive airstrike on Indian forward airfields late in the evening; the Indian POWs were taken from 4th December 1971 onwards, when their army started their advance- to 14th December 1971 were put into Pakistani civilians Jails with other criminals and were given prison clothing; they did not follow the "Geneva Convention" that says that all POWs will be put into separate camps and be treated as per the convention.

2nd Lieutenant AGJ Switten [later retd as Colonel] was taken POW on the early morning of 4th December 1971, at Kakian Wala in Chamb Sector and was put into Rawalpindi civilian jail. On 7th December 1971, the Indian Army HQ declared the young officer as 'missing believed killed'. The Pakistan army did not make efforts to declare him as a POW and shift him to the POW camp when it was established on 15th December 1971. In February 1973, a Swiss lady of the 'Red Cross', part of the 'Amnesty International', on her visit to Rawalpindi jail, took a photograph of Switten and on his request, sent his photograph addressed to his father- Mr Switten, Light House, Alleppey, India. Mr Switten received the photograph in July 1973 and wrote to the Indian army HQ and MOD. As there was no headway, he spoke to the local MLA, who brought up the case in the Kerala assembly and later requested a local MP to take up the case in the parliament. RAW was put into action, and as per their inputs, there was nobody by the name of 2nd lieutenant Switten in Rawalpindi civilian jail. The Pakistani's had changed Switten's name to Wasim Khan Akram to hide his identity as they faltered in not shifting him to a POW camp.

Switten's father mobilised many people from his native place, Alleppey and had demonstrations in front of the Pakistani embassy, showing Switten's photograph. This caught the notice of one of the leading national newspapers, and they sent a journalist to get feedback from the Swiss lady, who confirmed meeting the young officer, taking the photograph and sending a copy to his father on his request.

MEA requested the US Ambassador to interfere. Finally, Pakistan bowed to international pressure and, to save their face, admitted that they did have a person in Rawalpindi jail having a name Wasim Khan Akram or such name arrested for murder in general area Kakian Wala. If the Indians think that he is one of their army officers, Indians can have him back. Sometime in September 1973, after nearly two years, 2nd Lieutenant AGJ Switten crossed the Wagha border and returned to India. Likewise, there were more POWs who were not transferred to POW camps were languishing in Pakistani civilian Jails.The best time to get back 44 Indian prisoners of war was when the Pakistanis wanted their 93, 300 prisoners of war back, to which India agreed, but did not press to return 44 Indians during the process of the Shimla agreement. In such a sensitive human issue, the Prime Minister failed.

Further, though India had the upper hand, she failed to get the Line of Control [LOC] drawn beyond point NJ 9842, in the northern direction in Siachen. To date, India is still guarding the area beyond point NJ 9842, in Siachen, at a huge monetary cost and losing several lives. This is when one feels that India needs a Defence Minister with a military background who could advise the PM on issues of military concern.

During her leadership, there was no inner-party democracy; there was dissent in the INC. In 1969, caused by her own desire to establish supremacy in the party and in the country, she split the INC and formed her own party, the Congress [Requisitioned], later changed to Congress [I], 'I' stood for Indira. In the same year, Chaudhary Charan Singh, an experienced politician and leader of the Jat farmer community, left the INC and formed his own party, 'Bharatiya Kranti Dal'. Stalwarts like K Kamraj and Morarji Desai, both experienced politicians and good administrators, also left the INC and formed their own party, Congress [Organisational].

The worst that followed was the proclamation of the internal emergency on June 26, 1975, which was not justified. People lost confidence in the democracy in India, and the world saw us as a nation going towards a 'Dictatorship Government'. The emergency showed the defects of according to primacy to personal factors in decision making and showed how things can go wrong when instruments of governance are subordinated to the interests of those in power. This was the first time we saw a major crack in the functioning of the President of India. The then President, Fakhrudin Ali Ahmed, sanctioned the imposition of emergency in the dead of night, based on the proposal put up by the Prime Minister, on a flimsy ground that there will be a law and order problem in the whole country due to the Allahabad High Court verdict against Indira Gandhi for using the state machinery for her election campaign. Actually, the ground reality was that she would have to step down as Prime Minister and stay away from politics for six years, if she had done so, then, most likely, she would not have come back to power after six years of gap. The President did not apply his mind, neither did he ask the Prime Minister if she had got the nod from her council of ministers, nor did he take any legal advice. The President acted like a rubber stamp. As a result of the emergency, anyone who was a threat to Indira Gandhi, or her party was put in prison. The opposition was crushed, and there was no 'Freedom of Speech'. The media was muzzled.

In February 1977, during the emergency, Babu Jagjivan Ram, an experienced politician and respected leader of the scheduled Caste, resigned from the Union Cabinet and with Congress poised on a nationwide parliamentary poll, he looked forward to forging alliances with opposition parties for the forthcoming elections and announced forming a new party, 'Congress for Democracy'. This move was more due to Indira Gandhi giving more seats to members of the Youth Congress to make her son Sanjay Gandhi, the then head of the Youth Congress, stronger with more political support to fight the forthcoming elections by milking out seats from Jagjivan Ram's strong political bastion that would have resulted in Jagjivan Ram's political support within the Congress becoming weak.

On the economic front, based on Nehru's Industrial Policy Resolutions of 1948 and 1956, Indira Gandhi was for more state-directed Industrial development policy in 1973, thereby initiated the 'licence-permit raj' and nationalised a number of companies, including foreign companies, and imposed restriction on the growth of firms with a view of curbing the 'concentration of economic power' among the industrialists. One of the first to be targeted was J R D Tata, she nationalised 'Air India' without even consulting him, and now Air India is in a mess and has been put up for sale, and no one wants to buy it. She neglected the economic growth of the country by neglecting the private sector; as a result, the required Jobs were not created. Only populism welfare measures were undertaken, keeping the vote bank in mind. Though she followed her father's socialistic approach, most of the Congress governed states did not improve the quality of education, skill development, health care and benefits for the social-economic backward people; even the public transport system was not developed; except for Mumbai. The 'Licence-permit Raj' encouraged corruption at the political and bureaucratic level. This was the start of corruption in India, apart from the tampering of land records. Even the Average GDP growth from 1950 to the 1980s of 3.5% did not make the leaders realize that economic reforms had to be carried out. Decades of central planning, licence-permit raj, and government handling of the economy badly, and high levels of corruption had crushed the confidence of the Indian youth in their ability to compete globally.

As a result of the emergency, under the overall leadership of Jay Prakash Narain, a national alternative party was formed, with the birth of the Janata [Peoples] Party. The party was coming together of the Jan Sangh, Bharatiya Lok Dal, the Socialist Party and the old Congress that included the powerful breakaway leaders like Morarji Desai, Babu Jagjivan Ram and Chaudhary Charan Singh. To have another main national party, it took India nearly 29 1/2 years. The Janata Party swept the election and formed the first non-Congress government. However, it lasted for only three years because of un-ethnical political movements, within and from outside.

Morarji Desai became the Prime Minister [24 March 1977 to 28 July 1979] with Chaudhary Charan Singh's support. Initially, Charan Singh wanted to become the Prime Minister but did not have enough support; his support base was mainly from his own party, the Bharatiya Lok Dal. Babu Jagjivan Ram had more support than Charan Singh; his support base was from the socialists and Young Turks, a larger number. The old Congress and the Jan Sangh wanted Morarji Desai to become the Prime Minister, but he did not have enough support. Charan Singh did not want Jagjivan Ram [a Dalit] to become the PM, so he supported Morarji Desai to become the Prime Minister; Jagjivan Ram was made the deputy Prime Minister.

Charan Singh's ambition was always to become the PM. The Congress knew of this, and there were back-channel talks between him and the Congress, with an understanding that he withdrew his support to Morarji Desai and Morarji's government fell after hardly two years and four months. Charan Singh, with outside support from Congress [I], formed the government on 28 July 1979. As the Prime Minister, his economic policies were not balanced, he emphasised only on Agriculture, and as a result, he brought down the overall economy by ten years. In a very short time, on 14 Jan 1980, Indira Gandhi cleverly withdrew her outside support, and Charan Singh's government fell, and the country went in for another election, a tremendous expenditure to the exchequer, economics was sacrificed at the altar of politics. In the end, the people of the country lost out.

Morarji Desai was an experienced politician and a good administrator but not flexible; his first important appointment was as an assistant collector of a district during the British Raj. He was a Finance Minister in Jawaharlal Nehru's government from Mar 13, 1958, to Aug 28, 1963, and in Indira Gandhi's Government from Mar 13, 1967, to 1970. As the Prime Minister, he tried to take the first step towards creating a political consensus in favour of economic liberalisation by appointing a high powered committee chaired by a highly respected economic journalist, Vadilal Dagdi, but before the 'Dagdi Committee' could submit their report, Desai's government fell.

However, he undertook a number of welfare measures for the betterment of the people; if he could have continued for his full tenure, then the amount spent on the ill-timed election could have been ploughed into the welfare measures that would have benefitted the people below the poverty line. If Indira Gandhi had not taken advantage of the situation by supporting Charan Singh that made him the Prime Minister, Morarji Desai would not have to step down, and his government would have completed its 5 years tenure. Maybe, the economy would have done better with more Jobs for the people. After the fall of the Janata government, the party disintegrated into small regional parties, with regional interest; the only party that resembled a party with national interest was the Bharatiya [Indian] Janata [Peoples] Party [BJP], under the leadership of Atal Bihari Vajpayee and Lal Krishna Advani, both experienced politicians. The fall of the Janata Party resulted in the emergence of the BJP that subsequently grew to become the second national party, which was good for India.

Indira Gandhi came back to power on 14 Jan 1980. Then, with her son Sanjay Gandhi, who was becoming powerful and with rumours that he was likely to be the next PM, began the family political dynasty. Bansi Lal, the union defence minister, in his rallies in Haryana, his home state, would introduce Sanjay Gandhi as their next Prime minister.In the army headquarters [operational room], for the briefing on the operational preparedness, the Defence Minister had brought Sanjay Gandhi along with him, maybe to educate Sanjay on military matters. The army brass politely told the Defence Minister that the briefings/discussions in the operation room are of a sensitive nature, and only authorised people are allowed to participate, and Sanjay should be asked to leave. To this, the Defence Minister took Sanjay to a corner and told him, "Ye army ka mamla hai, ap bahar jaingaye tho acha hai", meaning – this is an army matter, it is better if you go out. Sanjay left the room. Grooming of Sanjay Gandhi was done not only by Indira Gandhi but more by some of her loyalist who were doing all this, hoping to get a berth in her cabinet or appointment as a governor, when she became the Prime Minister.

However, Sanjay died in an air crash on 24 June 1980, and his elder brother Rajiv Gandhi stepped into his shoes as the heir apparent. In a parliamentary democracy, one does not hear the word 'heir apparent', but in the Indian parliamentary democracy, surprisingly, one hears it even today.

To everyone's surprise, Rajiv fired T Anjaiah, Chief Minister of Andhra Pradesh at the airport in the presence of a large group of people. He was then only a Congress member; he had no authority to admonish a Chief Minister. T Anjaiah was the third Congress Chief Minister to be sacked by the Congress central command. The sacking of Chief Ministers, one after another, cost the Congress a debacle in the January 1983 state election that resulted in the Congress losing power in Andhra Pradesh and Telugu Desam Party [TDP], a regional power, under N T Rama Rao coming to power.

Later, as the Prime Minister, Rajiv also sacked the Foreign Secretary, A P Venkataeshwaran, during the fag end of a press conference, at Delhi, by declaring – quote, "From tomorrow, you will see another foreign minister" unquote, and got up, and left. Late Venkataeshwaran was an outstanding officer of the Indian Foreign Services and well respected by his colleagues. As the gentleman that he was, neither did he represent his case nor make any statements to the press.

With dynastic politics, with no future at the national politics, Sharad Power, with his supporters, left the Congress and formed the Congress [Secular]. Later finding himself isolated, he rejoined the Congress. Political leaders with grass root support from states stayed away from the Congress and formed small parties with regional interest.

Unfortunately, Indira Gandhi was assassinated on 31 Oct 1984, and Rajiv Gandhi became the PM. He was the youngest PM and the third from his family. There was no selection based on 'first among equals', for the post of the executive head, he was not even a minister; leave alone the senior-most one. Since he was Indira Gandhi's son, he was the 'heir apparent', next to Indira Gandhi; he was the second most important and powerful person in the ruling party, without any political or administrative experience. Pranab Mukerjee was the senior-most with bags of political and administrative experience and would have been accepted by everyone, but he was sidelined. In the 1985 elections, Rajiv Gandhi won by 400 seats, the highest so far; it was due to a sympathy wave. Though in 1978, the Election Commission had declared the Congress [I] as the real Congress, it was only in 1986, the symbol 'I' was dropped during Rajiv's time.

Rajiv Gandhi lost the next elections in 1989 because of the Bofors scandal. With the Nehru-Indira-Rajiv era for 38 years, between August 15, 1947, to December 02, 1989, with economic socialism, India slowly drifted to an economic, fiscal crisis and defaulted in the Balance of Payments that resulted in a brink of bankruptcy in 1990. India had to mortgage gold to avoid default. It was sad for the people of the country to see gold being emptied from their treasury.

During Rajiv Gandhi's time, VP Singh fell out with Rajiv and formed his own party, 'Janata Dal' [JD]; later, N H Baghuna left the Congress. By then, most of the Congress stalwarts aspiring to become Prime Ministers one day left and the remaining stayed put and were happy with a cabinet berth followed by governorship and maybe a step into Rashtrapati Bhavan.

From December 1989 to June 21, 1991, we had another coalition government [National Front], initially with VP Singh, from the Janata Dal, as Prime Minister, with support from the allies and with outside support from the Bharat Janata Party [B J P] and the Left Front, headed by Communist Party of India [Marxist], till November 7, 1990. And later Chandra Shekar, popularly known as the Young Turk, as Prime minister, when V P Singh could not get a 'vote of confidence', Chandra Shekar withdrew his support to V P Singh's government and with support of 64 MPs and outside support from the Congress, under Rajiv Gandhi, formed the Government, from November 7, 1990, to March 9, 1991. Thereafter, he remained as a caretaker Prime Minister till June 21, 1991.

The fall of V P Singh was mainly due to two reasons- firstly, the implementation of the decade-old recommendation of the 'Mandal Commission', that gave 27% reservation of all central government Jobs to 'Other backward classes[OBCs]. This was in addition to the 22% reservations [meant for only 15 years] for Harijans [former untouchables] and Adivasis [most oppressed and exploited], officially called scheduled Caste and scheduled tribes. This resulted in the reservation going to 49%; this created upheaval amongst other communities that created a social divide in the society, and as a result, a number of riots took place around the country.

Secondly, L K Advani, leading the rath yatra or pilgrimage to Ayodhya, was arrested at Samastipur, on the border of Bihar by Laloo Prasad Yadav, a close supporter of V P Singh, and as a result, the Ayodhya Movement was not making any headway into Uttar Pradesh, and the construction of the temple at Ayodhya was being delayed, the BJP withdrew their support.

V P Singh, instead of resigning, went to prove his majority in the house with a hope of getting support from OBCs [supporters of the Congress and BJP] by sidestepping to his party due to the initiative he had taken on the 'Mandal Commission'. This did not take place. On November 10, 1990, he lost the 'vote of confidence', and his government fell.

Like Charan Singh, a decade earlier, Chandra Shekar fulfilled his life's ambition of becoming the Prime Minister, with the support from the Congress, under Rajiv Gandhi; he formed his government on November 10, 1990. In a short time of 120 days, on March 9, 1991, Rajiv Gandhi withdrew his support, and the government fell, and we had to go for another election in a short time, tremendous expenditure to the exchequer. In the end, the people of the country lost out once again. It was very bad for the country as two governments fell in succession within around one year and three months [December 1989 to March 9, 1991].

V P Singh was politically experienced and was a good Finance Minister from Dec 31, 1984, to Jan 23, 1987, under Rajiv Gandhi's government. As an FM, he introduced the Modvat, set a stage for VAT, the first step towards GST. At the start of his Prime Ministership, he brought Montek Singh Ahluwalia from the Finance Ministry into the Prime Minister's Office [PMO] to write a paper on the economic reforms. The paper was leaked out from the PMO and was known as the 'M' document; most probably, the 'M' abbreviated 'Montek'. Ajit Singh, who was the industrial Minister under V P Singh, had prepared the Industrial policy reforms, so did the commerce ministry on trade policy reforms. So, the start of the economic reforms was already on the cards.With the Prime Minister, a former Finance Minister who was well aware of the economic situation and Montek Singh Ahluwalia, an eminent economist and civil servant, the country at that period would have benefitted a lot economically, but this was not to be.

V P Singh, instead of concentrating on the economic agenda, concentrated on the social issues and did not tactfully deal with the Ayodhya issue. Earlier, Congress avoided taking up the recommendations in the 'Mandal Commission' to avoid social upheaval, but the government had to face it one day as there was a disparity in job opportunities between the socio-economically better off people and the people who were not. Though one appreciates the spirit of the intention, the formula worked out was wrong; maybe the reservation of 27% was too much; the reservation should have been at a reasonable level and only for families with 2 to 3 children.

Chandra Shekar was an effective Prime Minister, this is what scared Rajiv Gandhi, who thought that Chandra Shekar [an old Congressman] would overshadow him and get Congress' men/women to sidestep and support him, and as a result, he would become weak politically. This was the main reason Rajiv Gandhi withdrew support from Chandra Shekar.

In a short tenure of 120 days, from a nation that faced defaulting on 'Balance of Payment' and required Dollars to pay for oil and food, Chandra Shekar somehow managed to turn the tide in our favour by emphasising on economic corrections combined with a slight change in foreign policy towards the US.

Chandra Shekar government managed to get the International Monetary Fund [IMF] to sanction $1.8 billion support to India. The US was the largest shareholder on the IMF board and had veto powers to sanction loans. The government got the US on their side by permitting their C-141 Star lifter transport aircraft flying from the Philippines to the Gulf to overfly India and stop and refuel at Chennai, Agra, and Mumbai, in January/February 1991, for the planned attack on Iraq. On January 21, 1991, the USS Ford, a guided-missile frigate, also docked at the Mumbai harbour, also enroute to the Gulf from the Pacific; this was a big pro-American military decision.

Though there were objections to Chandra Shaker's government becoming friendlier with the US, Chandra Shekar paid no heed and went ahead and succeeded in getting the IMF loan. This demonstrated Chandra Shekar's ability to keep India's economic interest at the top by taking the right foreign policy decisions and, at the same time, not heeding to domestic politics that did not keep India's economic interest in mind. He took a political risk, but it worked.

Yashwant Sinha was the Finance Minister from 10 November 1990 to 20 June 1991, and his contribution is also commendable. He made the Budget for 1991-92 that covered the economic reforms, based on the inputs already available in the PMO and his thoughts and perception from his experience as an eminent former civil servant in the Finance Ministry that covered not only the ministry of finance but also the commerce and industry ministries. The most important issues covered under the Finance Ministry were the fiscal deficit, taxation reforms, foreign exchange reforms, public sector reforms, and Devaluation of the currency.

When the FM was to announce the Budget for 1991-92, the Congress felt a little jittery that part of the blame would go to them if there was political fallout because they were supporting the government in power.The Congress representatives went to the President of India, R Venkataraman, as they did not want the government to give out a regular Budget. The President, a former Finance Minister, who was aware of the benefit of the economic reforms in getting the IMF loan, explained to them the benefits, but Congress did not listen. Instead, Congress told Chandra Shekar that there should not be a regular Budget, only an interim one. Since Congress was supporting Chandra Shekar's government, they had the upper hand. Unfortunately, for the people of India, economics was sacrificed at the altar of politics.

Yashwant Sinha gave out the interim Budget for 1991-92. Ajit Singh had already announced the reforms in industrial policy, and the balance was almost ready to be announced, but Congress withdrew its support, and the government fell. Yashwant Singh had already moved on to the fiscal deficit reforms and was moving forward on the taxation reforms that was largely about bringing down the tax rates and cleaning up the procedure. Only a political decision on Devaluation of the Rupee was to be taken by the Prime Minister. Before the next government took over, a lot of water had flown under the bridge. At this stage, the people of the country did not lose out on the reforms due to the fall of the government because the next government went ahead with the economic reforms in full gear.

In addition to the benefits of the interim Budget and the IMF loan, Chandra Shekar, as the Prime Minister, authorised the mortgaging of gold to avoid default on its foreign exchange payment. 20 metric tonnes of confiscated gold, worth $200 million, held in its vaults, was made available by the Reserve Bank of India [RBI] to the State Bank of India for sale, with a repurchase option, to the Union Bank of Switzerland. This was the first time India was selling gold to avoid default in payment, and it was made in May 1991.

Later, P V Narasimha Rao, as the subsequent Prime Minister, authorised a second mortgaging of gold in July 1991, which involved the movement of 46.91 tonnes, valued at $405 million to the Bank of England in London.

Both the Bank of England and the Bank of Switzerland demanded the actual shipment of gold to their vaults, with no paper settlement. Gold bars of acceptable quality had to be airlifted and sent out. Though the final shipments began in July, after P V Narasimha Rao's government took over, the procedure of paperwork was done from March to June 1991. The entire operation was carried out in secrecy by the RBI governor, Venkataramanan and the deputy governor, C Rangarajan.

At this time, there was a complete political vacuum, the Congress coterie, with interest in the share of ministerial berths, both at the cabinet and lower level, thrust the Congress crown on an unwilling Sonia Gandhi, making her feel that she was the only one to help the Congress come back to power as if there were no other Congress' men/women to lead the Congress; most of the members of the coterie are the same who were with Indira Gandhi, Sanjay Gandhi, and Rajiv Gandhi. So, the leadership of the Congress was with Sonia Gandhi as it is today.

At this time, the country faced a crippling economic crunch, proliferating social conflicts, Pakistan backed secessionism and terrorism in Kashmir and Punjab and an international environment in which there was foreign interference in the internal affairs of the sovereign nations.

On 5th and 7th July 1991, India transferred 67 tons of gold to England and Switzerland to avoid defaulting on its foreign currency payment. When the country was almost bankrupt, in the July 1991 Budget, the finance minister had earmarked ₹100 crores for the Rajiv Gandhi Foundation, a private foundation; some members of the coterie around Sonia Gandhi cribbed that the amount was too small, though they knew that the taxpayers' money cannot be used for this purpose.

A coalition government [United Democratic Front], under Pamulparthi Venkata Narasimha Rao as the Prime Minister, was formed on 21 June 1991, the first coalition government to last for a full tenure till 16 May 1996. This was due to P V Narasimha Rao's vision, leadership, statesmanship, political skill, and administrative experience. P V had taken over the country during a period that was economically bad for India, there was a sharp increase in fiscal deficit and unsustainable Balance of Payments that were attributed due to a series of unsound policy measures taken by the governments during the period between 1985 to 1989 under Rajiv Gandhi and later, in 1990, under V P Singh. In addition, the effects were due to social conflicts within the country, secessionism and terrorism in Kashmir and Punjab backed by Pakistan and globally, the collapse of the Soviet Union that affected India in exports and import of Military Hardware.

P V Narasimha Rao had the wisdom and courage needed to implement radically new policies, both on the economic and foreign policy front. He was praised for enabling the economic reforms that transformed the country in 1991. He restored political stability by shared political management, pushed economic reforms, and steered foreign policy during the post cold-war. Politicians from across all the parties looked up to him.

In 1991, he de-licensed industry and opened the economy that saved India from bankruptcy. P V wanted I G Patel, a famous economist, to be the finance minister but I G Patel declined as he wanted to live a simple retired life, so the second choice was Manmohan Singh [a bureaucrat and an economist of repute], the choice, though, of the second one was very good. With P V as the Prime Minister who gave the overall directions and with his astute political management without which the reform Budget could not have moved ahead and Manmohan Singh as the finance minister who worked out the nutty gritty on the Prime Minister's direction, the economic trajectory was paved that we are following today.

This coalition worked because it was led by a major national party with 190 MPs, with support from allies; P V himself had viable support of 89 MPs, mostly from the southern states. The earlier coalitions did not work as they were led by Morarji Desai, who had the support of only 40 MPs but formed the government with the support of other leaders of the Janata Party. When Charan Singh, one of the leaders who supported him, pulled out, the government fell. Subsequently, Charan Singh, with weak support, formed a coalition government with outside support from Congress. This coalition also did not work as Congress pulled out, and the government fell. Yet, another coalition government led by V P Singh, a leader who did not have viable support, but took outside support from the BJP, also did not work as the BJP pulled out and the government fell. Subsequently, Chandra Shekar, with weak support, formed the government with outside support from Congress. This coalition also did not work as Congress pulled out, and the government fell. Some years later, another coalition government led by H D Deve Gowda, a leader who had the support of only 16 MPs, but had the outside support of the Congress, also fell due to internal squabbles and fighting. Yet again, another coalition government led by I K Gujral, a leader who individually also did not have viable support but had the outside support of the Congress also fell; this coalition also did not work as the Congress pulled out. The governments fell because each Prime Minister individually did not have viable support and had outside support from a major national party that pulled the rug to topple the government when it suited them.

P V Narasimha Rao was the second Congress Prime Minister outside the Nehru/Indira- Feroz Gandhi's dynasty; the first one was Lal Bahadur Shastri. P V became the Prime Minister because Sonia Gandhi was not ready to get into politics, and Rahul and Priyanka were too young. During his tenure, he requested the Election Commission to give the INC symbol to Congress.

The economic reforms finally succeeded because of P V Narasimha Rao's decision to go ahead with the economic reforms in full gear and with his political management and finer tuning. His actions were appreciated not only by the people of India, but also by the people abroad, and the leading papers in the USA had stated that P V was a very decisive Indian political leader.Through his sources, he found out the names of political leaders who were against the reforms. Once the names were established, he sent his trusted bureaucrats to explain the benefit of the reforms to them. Thus, there was clarity and transparency, and as a result, he won overthe majority of the political leaders.

Further, when Manmohan Singh advised him to devalue the Rupee at that point of time, he gave the political clearance, but when the Devaluation of the Rupee was announced, and there was a political uproar, he had asked Manmohan Singh to stop the second Devaluation. Manmohan Singh telephoned RBI Deputy Governor, C Rangarajan, to hold back the second Devaluation but was told that it was already announced 30 minutes ago. However, the Devaluations worked; it was a blessing in disguise.

On July 24, 1991, the Finance Minister's Budget contained several important economic policy decisions and defined a new framework for India's macro-economic policies. One day before the Budget, on July 23, 1991, the Minister of State for Industry, P J Kurien introduced the industrial bill that gave the historic dismantling of the infamous 'licence-permit raj'. During this period, the Finance Minister introduced the 'service tax'.

Prior to the historic Budget given by Manmohan Singh on 24 July 1991, most parts of the blueprint for economic reforms were already made by Yashwant Sinha and was available to him. Even the Budget speech made for the interim Budget for 1991-92 speech, written by the chief economic adviser, Deepak Nayar for Yashwant Sinha, was available to Manmohan Singh. Manmohan Singh himself was a bureaucrat in the ministry of finance, deputy chairman of the planning commission, RBI governor and later the economic adviser to Chandra Shekar. With all the inputs Manmohan Singh received and his vast experience and knowledge, he came out with a historic reforms Budget.Part of the credit for the historic Budget should also go to Yashwant Sinha, who himself was a bureaucrat in the ministry of finance and later a Finance Minister under Chandra Shekar government. But the overall credit should go to P V for his foresight, political stewardship and skill and some credit to Chandra Shekar for his efforts to revive the economy.

The first devaluation of the Rupee by 7% on July 1, 1991, and the second by 11% on July 3, 1991, was the right thing to do under the circumstances India was in, and it helped the reforms tremendously. The devaluation led to the Finance Ministry demanding abolishing cash compensatory support for exports. The devaluation was an intermediate step towards moving to a convertible and flexible exchange rate within two years. The Budget gave a clear signal to move to a more market-driven economy which unlocked India's growth potential, averaged about 7.7% growth in a span of 13 years, as compared to the 1980s when the average growth was 5.5%.This has been the major change.

In September 1991, the government issued an ordinance removing restrictions on capacity expansion, mergers, acquisitions, amalgamation, and takeovers that had all been closely controlled till then by the Monopolies and Restrictive Trade Practices Act, 1969.

On the International Affairs front, P V Narasimha Rao's foreign policy reached out to India's neighbours, adjusted to post cold-war situation after the fall of the USSR, new US and China friendship, and the post colonial-world-order, looking east policy and ASEAN, his visit to South Korea, building bridges with Malaysia and Singapore, reaching out to west Asia, his visit to Israel and recognising Israel, good relationship with Saudi Arabia, Iran, Egypt, and Iraq, extended cordial relations with Europe, changed India's foreign policy and India was no more isolated.

On the national security front, P V had pushed for nuclear tests and planned it in the winter of 1995. He did not go ahead because of the likely sanctions from the USA that would have affected the progress of the economy, which was his first priority but had briefed and advised Atal Bihari Vajpayee to go ahead with the nuclear tests at the first opportunity.

In the next election, BJP came to power with Atal Bihari Vajpayee as the Prime Minister, but he lost the floor test, and his government fell after 13 days [from 16 May 1996 to 1 June 96].

Another blow to the INC took place in 1996, with 'G K Moopanar leaving the Congress and formed his own party, 'Tamil Maanila Congress', thus weakening the INC further in Tamil Nadu.

In 1996, BJP, with 161 MPs and support from its allies, formed the government but lost during the 'floor test'.The government lasted for 132 days. The Janata dal [JD], with 143 MPs and with the support of 15 coalition partners, and outside support from the Congress [with 141 MPs], formed another coalition government [United Front], from 1 June 1996 to 19 March 1998. Initially, with H D Deve Gowda, from the Janata Dal, as the Prime Minister and later from April 21, 1997, with Inderjit Kumar Gujral as the PM. It is interesting to note that within the Janata Dal, Deve Gowda had only 16 MPs of his own and, with support from the coalition partners, became the PM. He had to step down because of the inner coalition squabbles.

Later, Congress withdrew their support to United Front, and the government fell, and we had to go in for another election within a short period [1 year and 9 ½ months], another huge cost to the exchequer.

The people of the country, for the third time, lost out. The first time was when the Janata Party coalition government that lasted for 3 years with Morarji Desai and later Charan Singh [the Congress pulled the rug], the second time was when another coalition government, initially with V P Singh [the BJP pulled the rug] and later, with Chandra Shekar [the Congress pulled the rug] that lasted for 19 months or 1 year and

7 months, third time, still another coalition government, initially with Deve Gowda [infighting and squabbles within the coalition] and later with I K Gujral [the Congress pulled the rug] that lasted for 21 months or 1 year and 9 months. In all these three cases, economics was sacrificed at the altar of politics. Ultimately, the people lost out.

On the economic front, Deve Gowda sticking to the tax slab of 10, 20 and 30 was a sound decision.Though the Finance Minister, P Chidambaram, was for a higher slab. If he had continued for his full tenure, maybe he would have taken more sound economic decisions that would have benefited the people.

Another blow to the INC came in 1999, with Sharad Pawar leaving the INC for the second time on the grounds of Sonia Gandhi's foreign origin and formed the Congress [S], the name of the party was subsequently changed to the National Congress Party [NCP]. Sharad Pawar is an important leader in Maharashtra and had an ambition to become the Prime Minister. His formation of a separate party affected the INC hold of Maharashtra State.

Thereafter, from 19 March 1998 to 22 May 2004 [initially 13 months and followed by 5 years], the NDA with BJP and its allies ran the government; it was the second non-Congress government with Atal Bihari Vajpayee as the PM that completed its full tenure. He was a good choice, like Narasimha Rao. He was intelligent, an experienced parliamentarian, a capable leader, and a statesman. He realised that the country cannot run with RSS interference, and tactfully, he kept them at bay and ran the coalition very effectively.

The government under him with Yashwant Sinha as the finance minister continued with the economic policies of P V Narasimha Rao's government and, economically, had brought up the middle class, the backbone of any society. Yashwant Sinha was aware of the policies, as he himself had earlier initiated the economic policies as Finance Minister under Chandra Shekar's government. Later, Jaswant Singh became the finance minister. In 2003, Jaswant Singh set up a committee under Kelkar, the former Finance Chief Secretary, to look into the economy of the country. The report was known as the 'Kelkar Committee Report.'During this time, 9 states set up 'Empowered Committee of FMs', the panel worked on VAT rollout. VAT was effective from April 2005 in most states except TN and UP. The centre allowed compensation for 3 years. In the last year of their tenure, the growth rate was 8.1%.Therefore, when they left, the economy was very sound, due to which the UPA benefitted.

On the Kashmir Policy, Vajpayee achieved bringing some healing touch to the people of Kashmir that brought in harmony between Kashmir and the Centre.

On the International Affairs front, Vajpayee followed P V's foreign policy towards the US, towards the Middle East, especially Israel; look east policy towards Japan, South Korea, Vietnam, and ASEAN countries.

On national security, Vajpayee went ahead with the nuclear tests to the displeasure of the USA; sanctions were imposed on India but did not have much impact. Indians managed to go ahead with their lives without the availability of some goods and services and monetary funds. The economy was on a good trajectory and with good relations with Iran, and so getting oil was not a problem.

The BJP was in power with support from the Trinamool Congress, with Mamata Banerjee as the railway minister [she had left the Congress in 1997 and formed her own TMC party], DMK and Telegu Desam Party [TDP]. They lost in 2004 due to the train burning incident at Godhra, that triggered the Gujarat riots in 2002. During the Gujarat Riots, about 1200 people were killed, about 700 Muslims and about 500 Hindus. As per the well-known police officer of repute, SPS Gill, who had taken over immediately as the security adviser, Modi should not be blamed for not controlling the riots, as he had taken over as CM two weeks before the riots and when he found that the police could not control the riots, he had called in the Army, within 24 hrs. **Special Investigation Team** [SIT] has also cleared Modi of any allegations. Prior to 2002, Muslim and Hindu riots had taken place in Ahmadabad a number of times under the Congress government; the worst was in 1967. Compared to the

Gujarat riots in 2002, the riots in 1984, after the assassination of Indira Gandhi, were the worst, killing of nearly 3000 people from the Sikh community took place in Delhi. It was genocide under the Congress government, and the army was called in after four days.

In the next elections, INC came to power and ruled for ten years, from May 22, 2004, to May 26, 2014, with Manmohan Singh, as the PM. His bringing in the Indo-American Nuclear Treaty was appreciated. The bifurcation of united Andhra Pradesh ,which resulted in the creation of Telangana, was a disaster for the Congress government. Various scams, like 2G, coal, railway and CWG, had a negative impact on Manmohan Singh's leadership and governance.The Congress lost out in the elections in 2014. Apart from the rampant corruption at the top, the economy was not in a sound state at the end of UPA -2 tenure, and above everything, there was nobody in the INC who could be better than or as good as Modi in delivery. So, the people voted for Modi, and as a result, the NDA, with BJP, the main national party, and its allies, TDP, SAD, LJP and Shiv Sena, came to power.

Modi won the 2014 election in the hope of a better life for aspiring Indians. They felt he was a man who had three successful terms as CM of Gujarat, and with his experience, he would be able to pull up the economy of the country at the National level where everyone will benefit in getting Jobs.

In the general elections in May 2019, the opposition parties threw up a number of Caste combinations and regional alliances, and their only aim was to stop Modi from getting back to power. The regional powers in the opposition, without any power at the national level, also wanted to stop the BJP from making further inroads into their regions of interest. The opposition parties had no alternative plans to sort out the main issues, the agrarian distress, unemployment, and the inefficient credit market.

Modi, as the PM, from May 26, 2014, to May 2019, had put the country's economy and foreign relationship on the right track. The welfare schemes, like Swatch Bharat [Clean India], the opening of bank accounts, providing cooking gas, cheap housing, mudra loans to start a small or medium business have benefitted the poor. The precision attack on militants launching pads on a wide front, deep inside POK by the army commandos in September 2018 and the deep air-strikes on Balakot by the Indian Air Force, in February 2019, destroying the main militants training camp, gave confidence to the people that the NDA government, under Modi could handle Pakistan.

With his performance in his first tenure, Modi won the 2019 election with a majority in the parliament. Now, he has to bring up the economy that will generate Jobs, and it is Jobs that the majority of the younger workforce want.

The recent general elections in May 2019 have shown that political parties cannot win seats based on Caste and Caste alliances and dynastic rule. The younger generation wants a Prime Minister who is strong, who can take the economy forward, protect the country from outside attacks and take more welfare measures that genuinely help more people below the poverty line.

In the state elections, in Karnataka, in 2016, the BJP was short of the half mark, the Congress was much below half mark and the Janata Dal [S], with the least seats. Since BJP could not muster the required seats, Congress cleverly supported the JD[S] and allowed them to have the Chief Minister and run a coalition government, and the JD[S] jumped into an unholy alliance. A very weak government was formed that had a lot of disagreements and confrontations. Ultimately, some of the Congress MLAs resigned to join the BJP, the Congress became weaker, and the coalition government of the JD[S] and Congress fell, and BJP came to power and formed the government. The people of the state did not have a stable government for nearly 1½ years.

In the state elections, in December 2018, the Congress had won with a majority in Chhattisgarh, a win in Rajasthan and won by a close margin in Madhya Pradesh, on the farmers not earning enough, though the BJP had built the infrastructure, like roads and marketplaces and provided direct transfer fertilisers, the farmers could not see the actual money in their hands, which would take some time. Lack of Jobs for the youth was also an issue that went against the BJP. The Jobs will grow when the economy picks up, and for the economy to grow, it takes time, as long as the government lays down the fundamentals, which the government has done.

However, in the subsequent general elections in May 2019, BJP had done well in all these states; this means that the people of these three states feel that NDA under Modi is the best bet at the national level, though they voted for the Congress at the state level.

In 2020, there was spilt in the Congress in Madhya Pradesh [MP], and the Deputy Chief Minister, Jyotiraditya Scindia, broke away from Kamal Nath's government and joined the BJP with his supporters, thus making the Congress weaker. Since the BJP had more of their MLAs in the assembly, BJP formed the government with Shivraj Chauhan as the Chief Minister. The people of the state lost out as they did not have a stable government for nearly two years.

The present political situation

May 2019 election has been a remarkable change from the earlier elections, in which Narendra D Modi's win is a watershed moment in the contemporary history of India. In 2014 and in 2019, the BJP, under the leadership of Modi and the general secretary, Amit Shah, with his organizational skill, have consolidated the Hindu vote to make the BJP a political force by emphasizing the Hindu identity.

BJP came to power because they consolidated around 67% of the Hindu support and brought confidence among the community. Whereas the Congress, which ruled from 15 August 1947 for around 54 years, neglected the Hindus and depended more on the Muslims for their support. A senior and a prominent MP from the Congress said in the 2018 state elections in MP that if 95% of the Muslims don't vote for the Congress, the Congress will be doomed in the elections.

The Hindus form nearly 80% of the total population of India; the Muslims form about 17%; Christians about 2%, Sikhs about 0.5%, Buddhists about 0.3%, Jains about 0.2% and Parsis about 0.1%.

Over the years, Congress won elections more due to Muslim support. However, they did not improve their livelihood, and as a result, Muslims went to the Samajwadi Party [SP], Bahujan Samajwadi Party [BSP], Rashtra Janta Dal [RJD], Telangana Desam Party [TDP], Communist Parties in Kerala, and Aam Admi Party [AAP] in Delhi. The Congress kept going down to only 54 seats in parliament. Congress now has realized that Hindu support matters a lot to gain power at the national level.

Prior to becoming an independent country, on 15 August 1947, the Hindus were ruled by the British [Christians] for nearly 200 years and before this period, under the Mughals [Muslims] for nearly 400 years. Naturally, the Hindus would not like to go back to those days. They would like to hold the maximum political power and steer the future of the people of the country for a safer and better life; this is understandable.

In Europe, the countries are small in size and have one religion, namely Christianity; there are no clashes for political power. As a result, there is stability and harmony in their countries that is very important for progress.

USA and India are similar in nature, large in size, with people of many different religions, Caste, creed, and colour. The whites [Christians] in the USA and the Hindus in India, being the largest in size of the total population in their respective country, wish to have the maximum political power; both the countries are moving towards Nationalism. In the USA, it is known as white supremacy, and in India, it is known as the Hindu majority.

With migration and the threat of ISIS, Germany, France, Turkey, the UK, Japan, and Australia are also moving towards Nationalism, giving maximum political space to the majority of the population.

If the majority of the population does not have a reasonable political space and the minorities have political power, there is bound to be political disharmony. If the majority has the maximum political space, allowing legitimate space to the minority, there is political harmony.

There is nothing wrong with nationalism, provided the majority, having the maximum political power, allow the minority to have their respective legitimate political space and governs effectively, taking into account the concerns of the minority and maintains sustainable social relations, then the country moves with no problems, and the minority also cooperate with the majority in moving the country in the correct direction for the betterment of all the people. Thus, stability and harmony are maintained.

Modi fought a presidential type of election and he was accepted by the people of the country as a strong leader who can take on Pakistan and take the economy forward; ten years are required to actually see tangible results. Further, with giving ₹1500 per family to build a toilet, no initial charges/deposit for gas connections, the opening of bank accounts with only ₹50 deposit, giving ₹1.5 lakhs per family for building a house, Mundra loans to start off a business for the poor, and above everything, direct deposit payments, the people, at the grass route level benefited, irrespective of their religion and those who did not get the benefits were confident that they would get it the next list.

The people realized that he is a leader who has a genuine concern for the people. In comparison, the people saw that the opposition leader for the PM's post had nothing to offer.

The mandate in 2019 has challenged Caste-based identity for the first time in 30 years since the Mandal Commission report to give job reservations to the OBCs that came into effect in 1990; it spurned backwards class politics, changed the power balance, and threw out the backward, class-based leaders like Mulayam Singh, Mayavati, Lalu Prasad, Nitish Kumar and Uma Bharati.

In UP and Bihar, the Modi wave also washed away Caste-based alliances.

In the new India, 50% of the population is under 25, and they are now aspiring for the fullfilment of their dreams through a larger identity.

SP and BSP rely on Caste mobilization and the BJP on Hindu consolidation. Elections 2019 has diluted Caste loyalties, but it has enforced religious identity. In his first speech, Modi gave a new dimension to Caste identity, and he said that there are two Castes; one is the poor and the other who want to alleviate poverty.

Modi realized that the only issue in the election was himself and the opposition concentrated on him, and he converted it into a presidential-style campaign. He steered the narrative towards nationalism and away from the performance of his government and altered India's political matrix by demolishing the dependence on Caste and dynasty. The incredible mandate is because many believe in him. Since he is from a very humble family, the people of India identify with him. He says that he may make mistakes, but he works selflessly for the nation. He has earned credibility because many of his schemes like free India from open defecation, affordable rural housing, free gas connections or medical insurance have been delivered, by and large. And those who did not get them hope to get them in the next list, so there is hope. Further, the schemes were for everyone irrespective of religion, Caste, creed, colour, or region. Many of the schemes he began during his first five years are clearly long-term projects, which now will materialize fully in the second five-year term.

On the other hand, his opponents had no credibility and no narrative in the eyes of the voters. Congress ran a disorganized campaign, and the allegation of corruption in the Rafale deal and the attempt to paint Modi as a 'Chor' backfired on Congress with a vengeance.

The BJP's victory is not a mandate for the Hindu Indians only but for all the Indians. Modi would do well if he reins in the extremist elements within the party. The electorate has united behind him, and the electorate expects him to protect the unity of the Indian people.

Further, the decisive majority has given Modi the mandate to reshape the agenda and future of India. But with great power, comes great expectation, and he needs to meet them with speed, strength, and senility.

The only drawback in this election is that there are 43% of the newly-elected Lok Sabha MPs across the parties have criminal charges against them, a 265 increase compared to 2014. The cases are related to rape, murder, and attempt to murder or crime against women as per the Association of Democratic Reforms [ADR], an NGO.

On the financial status, 475 [88%] of the 539 winners are crorepatis.

EC has asked TMC, NCP and CPI, why they shouldn't lose national party status. The criteria set by the poll panel, a national party needs to get at least 6% vote share each from a minimum 4 states or get 2% of the total seats in Lok Sabha from at least 3 states, or it should be recognized as a state party in at least 4 states.

The voting base is at the lower level that is 20% at the lowest level of the population and 20% at the marginal level, irrespective of Religion, Caste, creed, and colour, i.e., around 40% of the population. The Political parties cannot distribute freebies to win votes and give welfare promises that are not fully implemented anymore. The people want Jobs and higher wages so that their basic living standard is improved. The political parties should keep this in mind.

At present, the Bharatiya Janata Party [BJP], with support from the majority of Hindus and lesser percentage of the Muslims, and few minorities and the Indian National Congress [INC], with support from a lesser part of the Hindus and a larger part of the Muslims and other minorities are the two national parties that will remain to be so, this is good for India. The Aam Admi Party [AAP] is a young party with national aspirations; its bases are only in Delhi and partly in Haryana and Punjab.

In the recent Delhi state elections, AAP won 67 out of 70 seats and formed the government; this was due to giving free 200 units of electricity a month and free 20,000 litres of drinking water to every household and giving free transportation to all women and the senior citizens, in the metro and government buses and improving the infrastructure in schools, and developing the Mohalla Clinics, the people of Delhi voted for them. Except for improving the infrastructure in schools, developing Mohalla Clinics and free transportation to senior citizens, the rest are freebies that will be a drain on the taxpayers' money. However, the people of Delhi did not vote for them in the general elections of May 2019; BJP bagged 6 out of 7 seats. It appears that the people of Delhi want AAP at the State level and the BJP under Modi at the National level. Most likely, AAP will remain as a regional party.

The regional party in the opposition tend to obstruct anything the central government wants to do. The communists have lost power in West Bengal and are holding onto the power in Kerala; BJP is trying to make an entry into Kerala. Other regional parties, like the Samajwadi Party [SP], Bahujan Samajwadi Party [BSP] in Uttar Pradesh have also shrunk. Rashtriya Janata Dal [RJD] in Bihar has also shrunk. The Trinamool Congress [TMC] is feeling shaky as BJP has made inroads into West Bengal. The Telegu Desam Party [TDP] has been written off, with Jagan Reddy's Congress forming a majority state government. DMK seems to have the upper hand in Tamil Nadu; in the recent general elections, they bagged 26 seats in the Lok Sabha. AIDMK is losing their foothold in Tamil Nadu, and after the death of their dynamic leader, Jayalalitha, there is nobody to take her place. The forthcoming state elections will show their relevance. At present, they are leaning towards the NDA. The National Congress Party [NCP] and Biju Janata Dal [BJD] are in the opposition but play a constructive role. AAP came to power with an intention of sorting out corruption and a party that will work for the peoples 'day to day' requirements, but they have become like any other regional party. However, they will have relevance in Delhi only.

Now, the Congress [INC] hopes to make a comeback in the next general elections, i.e., in 2024. This will be possible if they have democratic elections within the party and elect a leader capable of holding the post of Prime Minister. The present form of selecting a leader for the top executive post will not take them very far, and the people want to see a new capable face who can deliver. However, it is unlikely that the Congress will do this; even if the present leadership of the Congress has a leader from outside the Nehru-Indira-Feroz Gandhi dynasty, the dynasty will still have control over the leader. With this configuration, it will be very tough for Congress [INC] to make a comeback in the next election in 2024; unless they sort out their in-house problems and put up a suitable candidate against Modi.

Out of 29 states and 9 Union Territories, the Congress [INC] control only 5 states and 1 Union Territory. This means that Congress [INC] has lost the support of 23 states and 7 Union Territories; this is not a happy situation. Even at the state level, Congress [INC] has to have party elections and select a suitable leader for the chief minister's post, the executive head of the state. Otherwise, they will lose more states and UTs. This will affect their position at the national level.

Future prediction in 2024 elections, with the likely negative results for the Congress [INC], the party will crumble, and there will be a revolt among the members and the party. This will force party elections and elect a suitable leader of the Congress Party on merits and not on dynastic considerations. The Nehru-Indira-Feroz-Gandhi dynasty will prefer to stay out and enjoy whatever privileges that they are left with. This is when the Congress [INC] will become a viable national party. So, all is not doomsday for them. Further, the people want two national parties; they would not like the Congress [INC] to wither away.

Some people from the Rashtriya Swayamsevak Sangh [RSS], Vishwa Hindu Parshad [VHP], Bajrang Dal and Hindu Sabha are still trying to force the Hindu way of life [Hindutva] on the minorities [Muslims, Christians, Dalits and Tribals]. This will affect the outcome of the polls in the 2024 elections. Forcing the Hindu way of life may result in Muslims, Christians, Dalits and Tribals not voting for the BJP.

Muslims in India are Indians and follow Indian and Islamic culture; Christians in India are Indians and follow Indian and Christian culture. Dalits are at the receiving end socio-economically; a number of them follow Buddhism, and more want to convert to Buddhism. The advantage is that they can have their own identity as there is no Caste system in Buddhism, apart from following a rich religion. Some Dalits follow Christianity, and they have benefited a lot in terms of education, and education gets them Jobs. Tribals are not Hindus; they have their own identity and follow their own religion and culture like other tribes across the world. A lesser percentage of Tribals having converted to Christianity have benefitted like the Dalits. This can be seen in the Eastern part of India.

If the BJP, under the leadership of Modi and the BJP president, can keep the communal forces out, they will be able to win over the confidence of all the Indians and govern better with no hindrance.

The advice from the RSS can be considered like any advice, but Modi should take his own decision in the interest of all Indians. Modi has to soften the 'Hindutva' brigade; development and growth cannot go hand in hand with 'Hindutva'. The RSS is a sensible organisation and does make course corrections. They will soon realise that it would be better to remain strictly as a social and cultural organisation, bringing out the good in 'Hinduism' but not force 'Hindutva' on everyone. When around 80% of the population follows Hinduism and the Hindu culture, why force the remaining 20% to follow the Hindu culture. In case the RSS is keen on politics, they should form their own party with Vishwa Hindu Parishad [VHP], Bajrang Dal and the Hindu Sabha, the communal forces and fight the elections without riding on the back of the BJP.

Since the BJP represents the maximum Hindus, it has to be the party that should have the maximum political space but allowing political space for the remaining non-Hindus. With maximum political space, it should steer the course to benefit Hindus and non-Hindus, then only BJP will justify its political space. Otherwise, the Hindus with the Congress and the non-Hindus [minorities] will fight tooth and nail for political space.

Except for the BJP and the Communists, the Congress and most regional parties have a dynastic rule. These parties will partially be affected as most of their other leaders who have been marginalised, or side-lined may leave their party and may organise their own parties; some may defect and join the BJP or the Congress for the 2024 election.

THE FAULT LINES

From August 15, 1947, to mid-June 1975 [nearly 28 years] and later from March 1979 to May 1990, [nearly 10 years], for a total of 38 years, India had one political party, the Indian National Congress [INC] ruling the country, with the post of the 'Prime Minister' [Executive Head of the Nation], occupied by members of one family [Father, daughter and daughter's son], except for 1 year and six months when Lal Bahadur Shastri of the INC was the Prime Minister. Having three Prime Ministers from one family is a remarkable achievement for one family, but it is a mismatch with the requirement of any democracy. Because of the family domination and support from the coterie [inner circle], they never allowed any other political party to come up. There was no opposition party, nor did they allow inner-party democracy within their party. This political situation is bad for any democracy. As a result, India went through a humiliating defeat in the 1962 Indo-Chinese war that demoralised the army, went through the worst days of the 'emergency' when the members of the opposition were unlawfully put behind bars, and there was no 'Freedom of Speech'; the private sector that was choked with the 'licence-permit raj' that led to politicians/bureaucrats indulging in massive corruption and the people looking forward only to government Jobs that were limited. Both on national security and on economics, there was a disaster. This shows cracks in the Indian Parliamentary System.

The emergency imposed on July 25, 1975, by Fakhrudin Ali Ahmed, the then President of India [the Head of the State], on the advice of the Prime Minister on the grounds of lawlessness and anarchy in the country was contrived to serve one individual, who felt threatened by the opinion of the law enforcing agency. The Prime Minister reacted in her self-interest. Before the opposition in splinter groups could react, the key figures were all arrested and put into prisons spread throughout the country, and the press was muzzled.

There were checks in the parliamentary government system. The president could have asked the PM to consult her cabinet and get back to him, and in the meantime, consult the judiciary, and he would have got a balanced picture of the situation. Further, if he had read the newspapers, heard the news on the TV, he could have been aware of what was going on in the country. All these inputs would have enabled him to turn down the proposal for the emergency. Instead, the President did not follow the democratic procedures; he did not apply his mind and acted like a rubber stamp. This was the first time there was a major crack in the Indian Parliamentary System at the highest level, and the people of India suffered.

Normally, we have a president who is accepted by the majority of the parties; by consensus, there are no proper elections. So, India had Fakhrudin Ali Ahmed as President, who imposed the emergency in June 1975 that was undemocratic and later, Pratibha Patil, as President, who had travelled around the world with her family members at the cost of the exchequer. The people of India did not get a president who was their choice. Though the system has a provision that the politicians from all the parties representing the people elect the president, but in practice, the personal requirement of the leader of the ruling party and his/her survivability dictates the choice. Normally, the leader of the ruling party wants a president who can be in their favour as and when required. This is bad for any democracy.

Swatantra Party – founded by Chakravarti Rajagopalachari, the first and last Indian Governor General, in 1959, was the only party that could have been an alternative to the Congress. The Party stood for liberal ideas in our political discourse, democratic freedom, personal liberty, social liberalism, and individual initiative. During the emergency, the members of the erstwhile 'Swatantra Party', including Rajmata Gayatri

Devi, the Maharani of Jaipur, and a prominent personality, were put into prison undemocratically. Even the coming back of the 'Swatantra Party' was crushed. There was no chance of another main political party coming up. So, the country had to accept one main political party till 1977, when the Janata [Peoples] Party came to power.

After Rajiv Gandhi's assassination, only on two occasions, the Prime Ministers were from a non-Nehru-Gandhi family, P V Narasimha Rao [from Congress], who headed the United Democratic Front and Manmohan Singh [from Congress], who headed the United Party Alliance. The former became Prime Minister, with the support of 89 MPs, mostly from the southern states, as Sonia Gandhi was not keen on taking up the top post as she was getting over her husband's untimely death and her children, Priyanka and Rahul were too young. In 2004, though Sonia Gandhi had the maximum support from the INC, but due to the objection by Subramaniam Swamy that she was of Italian origin and born in Italy and cannot become the Prime Minister of India as per the Indian laws, she withdrew and nominated Manmohan Singh for the top executive post. Since Sonia Gandhi was of Italian origin and was born in Italy, as per the Indian laws, India has to follow the Italian law that says that anyone not of Italian origin and not born in Italy cannot hold the top appointment.

In previous cases, there were no inner-party elections to select a PM from a number of aspirants. The most likely to become Prime Ministers on merit were R Venkataraman, P V Narasimha Rao and Pranab Mukherjee. R Venkataraman became the President; later, P V Narasimha Rao became the Prime Minister when no member of the dynasty was in a position to take up the top post and later, Pranab Mukherjee became the President. The choice of P V Narasimha Rao was a good one, and the people gained a lot. But he was an exception.

After P V Narasimha Rao, the ground realities changed, now Congress just holds the symbol of INC on paper for election and legal purposes, but the functioning and culture is the same as Indira Gandhi's time, i.e., of Congress [I] time. There is no inner democracy, and elections from the grass route level to the top are not there. There is no buzz word like 'first among equals'. It is a dynastic rule. Even the regional parties like DMK of Tamil Nadu, Janata Party [S] of Karnataka, YSR Congress of Andhra Pradesh , National Congress Party [NCP] and Shiv Sena of Maharashtra, Rashtriya Janata Dale [RJD] of Bihar, Samajwadi Party [S P] of Uttar Pradesh, Shiromani Akali Dal [SAD] of Punjab, National Congress [NC] and Peoples Democratic Party [PDP] of J&K are also following dynastic rule. In due course of time, India will be having 100 families running the country, and the destiny of 1.30 billion people will depend on them. This will be the ultimate blow to the Indian Parliamentary System of government.

Coalition governments coming to power with small parties coming together has been a failure. Janata Party government lasted 3 years, V P/Chandra Shekar's government lasted for about 1 year and 7 months and H D Devi Gowda/ I K Gujral's Government for around 1 year and 9 months. On March 24, 1977, when the Janata Party came to power after the emergency was lifted, one thought that India would, at last, have a second main national political party. But the Janata government fell within three years. This was due to inter-party rivalry and the outside support cleverly given by the Congress to Charan Singh that was subsequently withdrawn. Further, the political parties in the coalition came together on issue to issue based on a minimum programme; this might mean different things to different people or even to the same people at different times. Therefore, the coalition was not together with a sound binding force.

From 1989 to 1991, the growth rate was still low, and any economic reforms that the then Prime Minister Chandra Shekar's government was trying to take off were muzzled, even when India needed a World Bank loan to buy food and oil; the loan was not sanctioned due to defaulting in due payments to the World Bank. India had to send gold reserves to the banks in the UK/Switzerland. The economy was overshadowed by politics.

Both the two national parties, the Congress [on three occasions] and the BJP [on one occasion], gave outside support to a coalition leader to form the government. When they thought that things were not going as they wanted, and the time had come to go for another election to get back to power, they withdrew their support, and the governments fell without completing their full tenure. A cunning strategy that was good for them but not good for the people of the country, as the country had to go for pre-mature elections that sucked out a huge amount of money from the exchequer. This huge amount could have been used to elevate the socio-economic backward people. The same situation prevailed in the states, with state governments falling and president rule being imposed.

In 1950, India had its first elections, with central and state elections simultaneously held at the same time. Because of the falling of central and state governments at various time, India now has elections one or the other six months in a year, thus, affecting the governance, as most of the politicians and civil administration are on election modes and due to the 'code of conduct' being imposed one month prior to the day of voting when no policy decision can be taken. Now, the present government is trying to go back to simultaneous elections that will cost less and allow the politicians and the civil administration to pay more attention to governance.

When the coalition governments later came to power, like – P V Narasimha Rao's government [United Democratic Front [UDF]], and later, Atal Bihari Vajpayee's government [National Democratic Alliance [NDA]], followed by Man Mohan Singh's governments, [United Party Alliance [U P A-1 & 2]], with support from a few regional parties, they survived the 5 years tenure. These coalition governments were successful as the PM was from the party, with the maximum MPs, within the coalition that formed the government, with support from allies. Though the stalwarts from the regional parties created problems if they did not get their way, like in the Indo-American Nuclear Deal, when the CPI [M] in UPA-1 withdrew their support, and the government nearly fell, till they got support from Samajwadi Party [SP] and Rashtriya Janata

Dal [RJD]; the support from SP and RJD came when the government agreed to go slow on the CBI cases against their leaders. This is not the way a good parliamentary system should function.

When the average GDP growth from 1950 to the 1980s was 3.5%, why did the change in the economy for the betterment of the country not take place earlier? The main reason was that economics was sacrificed at the altar of politics. V P Singh had started the ball rolling for economic reforms, with Montek Singh Ahluwalia preparing the first paper on the reforms. But the BJP pulled out their support because the Ayodhya Movement was not progressing as per their schedule. However, Chandra Shekar, with Congress's support, formed the government and moved ahead on the economic reforms with Yashwant Sinha as Finance Minister. Yashwant made the complete blueprint for economic reforms, but Congress did not allow the regular Budget to be announced. Rajeev thought that Chandra Shekar may overshadow him, so he withdrew the support to Chandra Shekar's Government, and the government fell.

Re-elections prior to 1991 within a short time resulted in a huge financial loss to the country. No political leader had the capability or the political will to manage the politicians to give importance to the economy and build it up with reforms. The main jolt came when the country had defaulted on non-payment of debts and was forced to transfer its gold reserves to make up the shortfall. The major political parties, the Congress and the BJP, were not bothered about the economic burden on the country till P V Narasimha Rao turned the tide, and that was after nearly 44 years of gaining independence. The Indian Parliamentary System of government had no way to ensure that the country's economy was in good hands and the economic interest was not sacrificed at the altar of politics.

In the overall outcome, the people had no control over selecting the executive head. This political environment only benefitted most politicians, their family, and friends, who wanted power and money. This can be seen in the number of rich politicians and their rich cronies.

Prior to BJP coming into power and becoming a main political party, their first PM, Atal Bihari Vajpayee, was cleared by the RSS to become the PM, and the present PM, Narinder Damodar Modi, was also cleared twice by the RSS, in both cases, there were no inner elections within the political party to select a PM from all the aspirants. Though, one has to accept that the two PMs cleared by the RSS have been a good choice, and the people did not lose out. However, RSS is an educational and cultural organisation, and they cannot get into the election process of electing the party's leadership. This amounts to unconstitutional interference; however, they can suggest like anybody else. The present coalition government [NDA], under Narinder Damodar Modi, with a thumping majority in the Lok Sabha in 2014 and 2019, pulled through the full first 5 years tenure and should pull through the next five years; so did the coalition government [NDA] earlier, under PM Atal Bihari Vajpayee, complete the full 5 years tenure.

In the Lok Sabha, we have MPs directly elected by the people. Once they are elected, the people are not in touch with them as 90% of the MPs stay away from the people who have elected them and do everything in their personal interest. They seem to be in contact with the people only during the election. The promises they have made to the people disappear into the wind. Some of these Lok Sabha members have a close relative or close political friend to look after their constitution they control by remote, which is not what the people expect from their MPs.

Further, one cannot stomach to hear that most of the poor people have voted because they were lured by money or gifts and, in some cases, liquor. This will not happen if everyone has a job and the per capita income increases. Therefore, the whole economy should move in this direction; for this to happen, the present parliamentary system has to change.

When one witnesses the parliamentary proceedings, one can see the chaos. There is no proper debate and discussion, only personal charges, and counter-charges. Even when one is making a point, the opposition instigated by their leaders muzzles him or her by shouting together.

In the Rajya Sabha, the vacancies are given to each state on the basis of their population. Further, the vacancies are distributed to the state political parties based on the strength of their MLAs in the State Assembly. MPs to the Rajya Sabha are elected by the state legislatures in a particular political party and nominated to the Raj Sabha. In recent times, some MLAs have been taking money for their vote.

The constitution framers had laid down the qualifications for a Rajya Sabha member as the person who should ordinarily be a resident of the state where he or she seeks election. Even in the Presidential system of government in the USA, the American constitution laid down the qualification for a Senate [Upper House] member as the person should be an inhabitant of the state where he or she seeks election for 15 years. The person residing in the same state will be in a better position to put up their state's requirements as he is familiar with the state's ethos, comprising culture, language, and alike. The same goes for the members of the House of Representatives [Lower House].

As per the present qualifications as a result of an amendment, a Rajya Sabha member need not be a resident of the same state he or she is representing. Since there is no residential qualification, there are a number of Rajya Sabha members representing a state to which they are not residents for a reasonable specific period; just an address would do; this defeats the very purpose of people having a representative who will look into their state's interest.

Take the case of Tamil Nadu and Karnataka; the two states have a long drawn battle over the division of water from the Cauvery River. In this situation, if a politician, a resident of Tamil Nadu, becomes a Rajya Sabha member representing Karnataka, will the member represent Karnataka's interest in this case or have his loyalties to Tamil Nadu, where he has his political roots or vice-a-versa?

Take another case, the Shiv Sena, a political party in Maharashtra, is against the people from Uttar Pradesh and Bihar migrating to Mumbai for Jobs because they are biting into the Jobs that should be available to the people of Maharashtra. In this situation, if a politician from Maharashtra State becomes a Rajya Sabha member, representing Uttar Pradesh, will the member represent the interest of Uttar Pradesh in this case or have his loyalties to Maharashtra, where he has his political base or vice-a-versa?

Take another general case, some actors/actresses/sportsperson mostly living in Maharashtra [Mumbai] get into politics and are nominated to the Rajya Sabha but represent another state other than Mumbai and don't even attend parliament regularly, nor do they tour their state and keep in contact with the people. What interest can they take in the state they represent? And do the people of the state benefit? This also goes for some of the prominent lawyers from Delhi and Mumbai. Many actors and actresses feel that if Ronald Reagan could become the president of the USA, why can't they? In his earlier days, Ronald Reagan acted in 50 movies. When he was President of the actors' guild, he became interested in politics and left acting, and eventually opted for public life. Initially, he joined the Democratic Party and after a few years, left the party and joined the Republican Party and remained a Republican. He went through the mill of public life starting from the lowest rug and climbed to become the Governor of California twice before becoming the president of the USA for two terms. His biggest accomplishments were making the USA economically strong and ending the cold war between the USA and Russia; he is remembered as one of the best Presidents. Actor/sportsman Arnold Schwarzenegger was also the Governor of California twice [2003-2011]; his biggest accomplishment was 'cap on greenhouse emission on the whole of the United States'. A number of lawyers in the United States, the UK, France, Canada, Germany etc., have become MPs/Senators/Congressmen and Presidents/PMs, but they practised law for some time and then plunged themselves into public life at an earlier stage and then climbed the ladder from the lower rung; they were never parachuted down into becoming members of the 'House of Representatives' or the 'Senate' or governors of States. They also were all elected by the people at every stage.

The political parties get the actors/actresses and sportsmen into the Rajya Sabha since they have a fan following that can be used as a vote bank. Since a number of politicians have court cases against them, including criminal cases, they get lawyers into the Rajya Sabha to help them in their cases, this amounts to dual interests. governance has been sacrificed at the altar of personal requirements.

Rajya Sabha is a place where the bills passed by the Lok Sabha and bills directly introduced in the Rajya Sabha, other than money bills, are discussed and passed or returned to the Lok Sabha with constructive comments or with suggesting constructive amendments or additions for consideration. When a bill has gone through a select committee and discussed threadbare in the Lok Sabha and then put up to the Rajya Sabha, there is no question of sending the bill to a special select committee at this stage; the GST bill was one example. Precious time was wasted that affected the growth rate, affecting more job creation, which was the need of the hour. It was a loss for the people. The main reason is that many members in the Rajya Sabha are not elected and do not keep the interest of the people of the state in mind. Further, normally voting by voice is adopted instead of the ballot. The same takes place in the Lok Sabha.

In the Presidential System in the USA, proper voting by ballot takes place, and the yeas and nays are recorded in a journal that is from time to time published and is available to the public; for this purpose, $1/5^{th}$ of the house has to OK it. Thus, the people come to know how an individual member has voted and thus conclude his or her views on various bills. This enables the people to gauge a member's credibility and vote for him in the next election accordingly. In the Indian system, we have no procedure like this. This is one of the major lacunas in the Indian system.

Regional Caste and community are the bases on which political parties are used to adopt dynastic succession as a method of leadership transition. Land links up all the landowners and farmers who have a number of workers under them; thus, they have a powerful political base. Religious teachers, in whom people have a lot of faith, factory owners in rural areas with a number of workers under them [like sugarcane crushing factories] also have a powerful political base.

There are a number of power groups at all levels; most of these are with money/muscle power. Initially, viable vote banks are created by the Sarpanch of a village, who has the control of the land in their area of jurisdiction and are powerful. They tell the people who to vote for. Then step in the politicians, who can influence the lower socio-economic backward people, promising them a better life. They start off at the village level, then at the Zilla Parshad [block] level and later at the district level and finally at the state level.

Initially, they become MLAs, get into like-minded groups, and make a lot of money. With more money, they climb up to a prominent place in the state/centre politics and remove/threaten anyone who comes in their way with their money and muscle power. Some of them stay in politics for decades. The leadership of all the Indian political parties in the present political system depends on the vote bank; they are not bothered about the credibility of the candidate. After becoming an MLA, their next step is to become an MP. Some of the MLAs and MPs from politically influential families are parachuted directly, and they are the ones that hold the real political power.

For a candidate to be selected, there are no discussions on some of the important issues, such as National and internal security, Economy [Reforms/structural changes, infrastructure building, alternative energy, etc.], creation of more Jobs, education and health, law and order, Climate Change and environment, human rights, and Communal Harmony. These factors affect a common citizen.

The political speeches are normally a personal attack on opponents, falsely stating that their religion is being attacked, people of their community are not being looked after and suggesting the best way forward is to vote for their leader who will look after their interest.

They distribute a copy of their party's manifesto that seems very attractive, but one does not know how they would tackle the new manifesto. They do not mention what they had achieved in the last five years; the truth is that if they did so, they would most probably be hooted off the stage.

Some of the states are too huge, like Uttar Pradesh and Maharashtra; it is unmanageable to administer them. Further, the opinion swing differs from one part of the state to the other part. Likewise, political power also differs from one part to the other part. Mayawati, as CM of UP, had very rightly put up a proposal that the state should be divided into four states, Western UP, Central UP, Eastern UP and Bulandshahr [bringing the part of Bulandshahr in UP and Madhya Pradesh together]. UP is more problematic, and the political situation in UP affects the whole country, therefore, dividing UP should have been the first priority.

Manmohan Singh's UPA-2 government did not pay any heed to Mayawati. Instead, the UPA-2 government paid more attention to Andhra Pradesh and bifurcated the state to Andhra Pradesh and Telangana for electoral gains that backfired; in fact, Andhra Pradesh if it had to be bifurcated, it should have been bifurcated into Andhra, Rayalaseema and Telangana. There will be problems brewing later as Andhra is well off economically, and the Rayalaseema region of Andhra is backward economically.

Maharashtra is also a large state and is very difficult to administer. Further, the opinion swing and the political power differ from one part to the other. Vidarbha and Marathwada regions have water problem, and the farmers are always in distress. Most part of the Budget goes to the western region, where the actual development takes place. The politicians from the western region, especially from the sugarcane belt, dominate politics in Maharashtra. The state should also be divided into Western Maharashtra, Vidarbha and Marathwada.

The Governors in states are like the representatives of the ruling party, and in one glaring example that took place in Bihar State in 2005, when the assembly was in suspended animation, the governor, Buta Singh, recommended the assembly be dissolved without giving Nitish Kumar led JD [U]-BJP alliance, which had the largest tally, an opportunity to prove its majority on the floor of the house and recommended 'Presidents rule' in the state because Rajiv Gandhi did not want JD [U]-BJP alliance to form the government. The President, Dr A P J Abdul Kalam, was on an official visit to Russia, and he was woken up in the middle of the night by the Indian Ambassador to sign the proclamation. As a result, Bihar state saw another election the same year. Later, Abdul Kalam, in his book, 'My Journey', regrets signing the proclamation because of this mistake on his part, he once thought of resigning. During Indira Gandhi's period, in a number of non-Congress states, 'President Rule' was imposed, and a number of Chief Ministers were changed to break the stronghold of powerful regional bosses. This was the start of political instability in the states, and many regional parties mushroomed all over India. In a presidential system, the change of the executive or head of a state will not take place as the Head of the State [Governor] will be elected by the people of the state, and it is only the people who can throw him or her out.

In the Indian Parliamentary System of government, the Members of Parliament from the opposing parties at the Centre cause hindrance to the executive, and as a result, there is some issue or the other, in most cases, not pertaining to the parliamentary proceedings that stall the parliament and most of the time no business is done. The same goes for the Members of the Legislature at the state level. A time has come when the legislature and executive should be separated with some reasonable checks and balances, like the Presidential system of government in the USA.

The Indian political conditions have produced a greater percentage of a breed of legislatures who are not worthy of legislating. They have come into politics to better themselves with executive powers and money. The conditions have produced governments, which focus more on politics and less on governance [policy and implementation] and produced political parties that shift their alliances to suit their leader's interest, and the interest is not for the country but for the leader to stay in power;

if the leader is in power, then the political party is in power, and if the political party is in power, then, the members of the party are in power at their level.

The systems of governance require the formulation of the policies that are sound and sustainable and thereafter working out the modalities to achieve the aims and maintain the momentum of the aim of the policies, so that the people get what is due to them for a better life for themselves, their children, and grandchildren. The legislatures are elected to govern; they are not elected to look after themselves and their families. In the presidential system of government, the president can pass executive orders on matters that require immediate action, so that execution can be done without any delay in the interest of the people.

India, as of September 2016, has 1761 registered political parties, including 7 at the National level and 48 at the state level, both recognised by the 'Election Commission', and 1706 unrecognised by the 'Election Commission'. More political parties mean more 'opinion swings' and more unequal distribution of 'political powers'. At the centre, the political powers in the circus of Indian political conditions are the ruling Bharatiya Janata Party [BJP] with support from Janata Dal [United] [JD [U]], Shiv Sena, Shiromani Akali Dal [SAD], All India Anna Dravida Munnetra Kazhagam [AIADMK] and Lok Janshakti Party [LJP], Asom Gana Parshad [AGP]; and in the opposition the Indian National Congress [INC], Trinamool Congress [TMC], the Communist Parties [CPI [M] and CPI]], Dravida Munnetra Kazhagam [DMK], Samajwadi Party [SP], Bahujan Samaj Party [BSP], Rashtriya Janata Party [RJD], Telangana Rashtra Samithi [TRS], Telegu Desam Party [TDP]and Rashtriya Lok Dal [RLD]. There are too many parties; the presidential system will slowly bring in a two-party system that will be good for the country.

As per the present system, for a political party to become a national party, for the Lok Sabha, the party has to have 6% of votes share in 4 states and 4 Lok Sabha seats. For the Union territories, Delhi and Pondicherry state, 2% of votes share and 11 seats in at least 3 states.

For the state assemblies, 3% votes share with 3 seats and 25% in the Lok Sabha. Because of these criteria that have no proper base, we have landed up with so many political parties that are unmanageable. This can only change if we change to the presidential system that will slowly bring in a two-party system. For a national party to be viable, it should have representation spread throughout the country.

TMC has their base in West Bengal, CPI [M] and CPI in West Bengal and Kerala, BJD in Orissa, TDP in Andhra, TRS in Telangana, DMK and AIADM K in Tamil Nadu, Janata Dal [S] in Karnataka, NCP in Maharashtra, Shiv Sena in Maharashtra, JD [U] in Bihar, SP in UP with very small splinter group in Bihar and Maharashtra, BSP in UP with very small splinter group in Maharashtra, Karnataka, MP and Rajasthan, LJP in Bihar and UP, SAD in Punjab, NC and PDP in J&K and small parties in other very small states, like Goa and the Eastern Sector. These parties cannot come into the category of a national party, like the BJP and INC, as they have regional interests only. The BJP and the INC have national interests.

In the formulation of bills, the legislature suffers; most bills are drafted by the bureaucracy on the direction of the minister concerned; all the inputs from specialists and inputs from in house discussions are taken into consideration. The draft is gone through by the minister, and if need be, the minister consults the Prime Minister. Then the final bill goes through the Central Cabinet Committee, and after approval, the bill is put in front of parliament for scrutiny; there is discussion and debate, amendments are made if required and then it is passed. It is pertinent to note that there is hardly any discussion or debate that takes place in parliament, in some cases, less than 10 minutes. In the passing of most bills, there is voice voting. There should be proper ballot voting for all bills and should be recorded; otherwise, the performance of an individual MP is not known.

Chief Ministers of states are quite insecure about remaining in their position and more often are fighting for their own survivability. Chief Ministers are changed at the drop of a hat: the clear example was in the old state of Andhra Pradesh when three Chief Ministers were changed one after the other by the Congress high command. Apart from being vulnerable to the opposition parties, they are more vulnerable to their own cadres. In a situation like this, how can they govern properly? This is not a happy situation. This is not good for any democracy. In the long run, the people lose out.

In one case, when the Chief Minister of Bihar, Lalu Prasad Yadav, was jailed for the 'Fodder Scam' in which he was directly involved. As the president of his party, the Rashtriya Janata Party, made his wife, Rabdi Devi, the Chief Minister; she was a housewife with no political or administrative experience. He ran the state from the prison and later got out of prison through his wife, and the people of Bihar had to accept it. This was a mockery of our democratic system.

In another case, when the Chief Minister of Bihar, Nitish Kumar, realized that the then Chief Minister of Gujarat, N D Modi was a strong contender for the Prime Minister and would come in the way of his ambition of becoming the Prime Minister, he refused to support the candidate to the Prime Minister's post if N D Modi's name were proposed, and as a result, the BJP withdrew their support to his government. Nitish Kumar took the support of his rival, Lalu Prasad Yadav, and his government survived. Later, he fought the next elections with the support of Lalu Prasad Yadav and won. Eventually, N D Modi became not only the Prime Minister but a Prime Minister who is admired by the majority of the people of India and abroad. Seeing Modi's rise, Nitish Kumar resigned and formed the government with BJP support. It can be seen that personal ambition overrides good governance. This is not good for democracy.

In a state coalition government, each party that supports wants a pound of flesh. As a result, the Chief Minister cannot have ministers of his choice in his cabinet to run the state; he is handicapped.

Even at the state level, there are powerful families who can control the state. The examples are J&K, Punjab, HP, UP, Bihar, Assam, Orissa, Maharashtra, Andhra, Telangana, Karnataka, and TN [only DMK].

To overcome the above, it is advisable, like in the USA, to have the Governor of the state elected by the people and is responsible to them. This will ensure that the candidate has qualifications and administrative experience.

After being elected to Governor's office, since their ability to govern will depend on the ability to govern at all the levels below, the governors will ensure that capable people are elected or posted at the lower levels from the state level down to the village level. This will also eliminate corrupt officials at all levels.

First - in July 1997, the former Chief Minister of Bihar, Lalu Prasad Yadav, was found guilty in the 'fodder scam' by the Supreme Court and was put into jail; he retained the appointment of the president of the Rashtra Janta Party [RJD] and nominated his wife, Rabdi Devi as the Chief Minister, by-passing some of the capable members of the party; Rabdi Devi was just a housewife and had no qualifications/experience in politics nor administration to run a difficult state like Bihar. However, he managed to run the state by remote control from the jail, and the party just accepted it. This was the height of feudalistic and dynastic politics. The people of Bihar suffered. Can this happen in any good democracy?

Second- well before the state of Bihar's assembly elections, the present Chief Minister, Nitish Kumar, did not want to support Modi, the Prime Minister candidate for the 2014 general elections, as he believed he would lose the Muslim support; he dumped the BJP that supported his government, and he did well with their contribution in running the state, as he wanted to distance himself from the BJP, to get the Muslim support.

In 2015, Nitish Kumar joined up with Lalu Prasad Yadav of the RJD and won the elections. Lalu Prasad Yadav benefitted as his inexperienced son became the Deputy Chief Minister, another inexperienced son became a state cabinet minister, and his inexperienced eldest daughter became a Rajya Sabha member.

Nitish Kumar was short-sighted and very wrong in his judgement. Modi became the Prime Minister with a thumping majority, and the other corruption charges against Lalu Prasad Yadav were coming up in the public domain; this was affecting the image of his government. Nitish Kumar did an about-turn and withdrew support of his party to RJD. The government collapsed, and he then tied up again with BJP and formed the present government. With governments changing frequently, the whole governance of the state is affected.

Third – in 2018, state elections in Karnataka, BJP got the maximum seats, but short of half the mark, the Congress got the second-largest seats, and the Janata Dal [S] got the least seats. The people voted for the BJP. However, Congress tied up with the JD [S] and formed the government by offering the Chief Minister's post to the JD [S]. In a coalition, the CM should be from the party with the maximum seats in the coalition to have more stability, in this case, the Congress. This did not happen, and the coalition fell. Finally, the BJP formed the government with MLAs shifting their support to the BJP indirectly by resigning and then fighting for elections. In the meantime, the governance of the state was affected.

Fourth – in 2010, state elections in Maharashtra, the BJP again got the maximum seats [105], but short of half the mark, the people voted for the BJP. However, the Shiv Sena [56] withdrew its pre-alliance with the BJP and formed the coalition government with the support of NCP [54] and Congress [44], all three parties with different ideologies. The BJP was willing to give the DY CM's post and 50% of the cabinet posts, but Shiv Sena wanted the CM's post.

By forming the coalition with the NCP and Congress, the Shiv Sena got the CM's post and only 14 cabinet seats, less than the number BJP offered. Maharashtra has a Chief Minister without any political and administrative experience and a deputy Chief Minister, his son, who also has no political and administrative experience; it is all in the family. Will the people of Maharashtra gain from this coalition? Time will tell; it may follow what happened in Karnataka- BJP with Shiv Sena support.

Fifth – in Madhya Pradesh state elections, September 2018, the Congress was short of half the mark, and the BJP was behind them; with the support of BSP, SP and independents, the Congress formed the government, with Kamal Nath as the CM.

Within one and a half year, there was a split in the Congress and Jyotiraditya Scindia, the Deputy CM, resigned with his supporters and joined the BJP, and the government fell. Since BJP had more MLAs in the assembly, they formed the government.

In India, the Mayors and Sheriffs are glorified figureheads without much power and with minimum resources. The commissioner of the municipality and the commissioner of police are in the hands of the local politicians. We should have a Mayor who is directly elected by the people that makes his position legitimate and effective; it is then that he will be able to cater to all the civic needs of the people. A Sherriff of repute is appointed on merits to maintain law and order to give protection to the people, and similarly, an attorney general of repute is appointed on merits to look after the judiciary. These are the three pillars that bring a better life to the people of any city/town.

At the District level, a District Collector is from the Indian Administrative Services [IAS], and similarly, at the Divisional level [consisting of 4 to 5 districts], a Divisional Commissioner, who is also from the IAS cadre to provide sound administration to the people. But this does not take place; they are at the beck and call of the politicians of that area. This will not happen when the elected Governors are head of the state and the executive head of the state. Everyone from top to down will have to deliver.

The President of the Zilla Parshad [Block] that has a number of Gram panchayats [villages] under it has the real power and financial resources, and he is elected by the people, and the people have their choice. Similarly, the Sarpanch is the head of the Gram panchayat [village] and has the real power and financial resources, is elected by the Gram-panchayat, and the people have their choice. When there is real power and financial resources, there is bound to be corruption at these levels, especially at the Zilla Prashad [Block] level. Due to corruption, development suffers.

In 1990, during Chandra Shekar's government, the country had reached a point where we required dollars for basic imports, like oil and food, and his government was in the process of carrying out economic reforms to conform to the requirement of the IMF to get a substantial loan, even under these extreme circumstances, Rajiv Gandhi had withdrawn the Congress support, and the government fell. This is the height of political opportunism.

Congress was a movement to gain independence for the country, later w.e.f. August 15, 1947, Congress became a political party to run the country. Now the Congress has become a family enterprise; so have most of the regional parties.

During UPA -1 & 2, Sonia Gandhi had delegated the powers of the PM to Manmohan Singh but held on to the authority; thus, there were two centres of power. When the 2G, CWC, Coal and Railway scams took place in UPA-1, Manmohan Singh did not take any action against the defaulters in the Coal ministry that was directly under him as well as against the defaulters in Telecom, Sports and Railway ministries that were also under his watch, as he felt that Sonia Gandhi, as the Congress president, should have taken necessary action against the people from Congress involved and as the UPA president should have taken the necessary action against the politicians from the allies involved. At the same time, one can presume that Sonia Gandhi must have felt that the PM as the executive head should have taken the necessary action against all the defaulters, regardless of their affiliation to any party. This confusion would not have taken place if there was only one centre of power. This situation is bad for any democracy.

The creation of the National Advisory Council [NAC], a high profile advisory body, with Sonia Gandhi as the chairperson during UPA-1 & 2 was not correct; it created a dual system of formulating bills, thus, adding to the dual control. It was dubbed as the shadow cabinet. Most of the NAC members were social activists who have done an in-depth study of the problems, especially problems related to social issues, like education, health care, food for the poor, availability of clean drinking water, electricity and roads, upper-Caste domination, Communal Harmony, etc. The biggest problem with activists is that they will point out the problems and give solutions without having all the inputs, especially the availability of funds and since the availability of funds is always low, they do not give the priorities with time and space for implementation; everything revolves around the availability of funds.

Further, activists are very critical and don't give a balanced view. The problems with suggested remedies should come to the parliament through the MPs. The problems with suggested solutions should be left to the ministries to solve, with in house discussions and inputs from specialists. The solutions may take the process of formulating a bill. This is the way to go about problems, not by creating an unconstitutional organisation.

Further, a joint secretary in the PMO met Sonia Gandhi regularly and briefed her on the key policy issues of the day and showed her important files, she had asked for, for her perusal, files that were cleared or to be cleared by the PM. Sonia Gandhi was acting like a shadow PM. The fault is not wholly with Sonia Gandhi because firstly, it is the fault of the joint secretary who allowed this to happen and knowing very well that he had signed the official secret act where it is spelt out clearly that the official files can only be shown and dealt with by the concerned people. Secondly, the fault is also with the PM, who allowed this to happen under his watch.

After independence, there was another incident when the first post-Independence Congress Party President, Acharya Kripalani, demanded that he be taken into confidence on the policies of the government headed by the then PM Jawaharlal Nehru. Nehru rejected this demand, taking the view that while the party president could be briefed on the broad policy issues, it would not be possible for ministers sworn to secrecy and holding constitutional office to share the contents of government files with the party president. Nehru invited Kripalani to join the government as a minister w/o portfolio and secure his entitlement, drawing a sharp distinction between party and government.

The fault lines show that there is political uncertainty at the Centre and state level all the time. The overall governance suffers, and implementation, especially at the state levels, suffers, and the implementation at the state level is of paramount importance. The fault lines will be removed if the Nation changes to a system of government where the chief executives are at the centre and state level are elected by the people, and they have someone of their choice.

WHY THE CHANGE?

Though India is following the Parliamentary System of Government for the last 73 years, when one goes through the political events that have taken place, one sees a number of faults that have occurred over the years from the very beginning after obtaining its independence from the British colonial power, and if these faults are not mended, India may not be able to provide good living conditions to its people.

India, like the USA, is a large country with problems of communications and a population of varied backgrounds and education. Therefore, there is a swing in public opinion. The USA constitution limits the influence of swings in public opinion by placing the election of the Head of the executive [in their case, the President] in the hands of the 'Electoral College', rather than the subject of direct election and the terms of office of the President and the two chambers of the legislature are all set at different lengths, President for four years, Senate for six years [one third rotating after every two years] and the House of Representatives for two years. The members of the Supreme Court serve for life. The tenures are fixed, and as a result, elections are held twice in the President's tenure of four years.

In India, the terms of office for the Prime Minister, the Executive Head, and the representatives in the lower house [Lok Sabha] are for five years and for the upper house [Rajya Sabha], the terms of office of representatives is six years [One third rotating after every two years]. The Prime Minister's terms of office and the terms of office of the representatives of the Lok Sabha are the same.

Normally, in the first six months of the ruling government, the Prime Minister, the executive head, puts forward his government's thrust-line, and the people who voted for his party sees whether the government is going as per their manifesto, for which the party was voted for. In the next two and a half years, the ruling government achieves at least fifty per cent of their manifesto and lays the foundation for another twenty per cent. Keeping one year for preparation for the election; a total of four years tenure is required for the Prime Minister and not five years. Same with the house of representatives in the lower house [Lok Sabha], they are effective for only two years; their tenure should be for two years, not five years. This will enable two sets of the house of representatives within the tenure of the executive head. The tenure for the elders in the upper house [Rajya Sabha] can remain for six years as 1/3rd are rotated after every two years. To avoid elections taking place throughout the year, the tenures should be fixed. This way, the swing in public opinion is taken care of, and the parliament's time is fully utilised.

In the present Indian system, the swing in public opinion is not fully taken care of. It appears that the swing in public opinion was not kept in mind when the Indian constitution was drafted. This can be set right if India changes to the US system.

In India, like the USA, the states are of different size in terms of population, and the political powers are in the hands of the larger states with the number of seats in the Lok Sabha based on the strength of the population, the number of seats in the Rajya Sabha is also based on the strength of the population, reviewed by the Election Commission, as necessary. As a result, the smaller states have less political power. The maximum strength of the Rajya Sabha is 250 [including 12 nominated by the President]. The Rajya Sabha seats per state are: Uttar Pradesh – 31, Maharashtra – 19, Tamil Nadu – 18, Bihar and Bengal – 16 each, Karnataka – 12, Andhra, Gujarat, and Madhya Pradesh – 11 each, Odisha and Rajasthan – 10 each, Kerala – 9, Telangana, Assam, and Punjab – 7 each, Jharkhand – 6, Haryana and Chhattisgarh – 5 each, Jammu & Kashmir – 4, Himachal and Delhi – 3 each and Arunachal, Goa, Manipur,

Meghalaya, Mizoram, Nagaland, Sikkim, Puducherry, and Tripura – 1 each.

Within states, political parties nominate members, the assembly then elects its state MPs for the Rajya Sabha. Political Party composition in the state assemblies decides how many Rajya Sabha seats a party will get. For example, if the BJP has 55% seats in the Maharashtra Assembly, BJP will get 55% of the 19 seats earmarked for Maharashtra in the Rajya Sabha, and the 55% will include the seats already occupied by the BJP and the vacated seats to be filled in, after every two years [one third rotating every two years]. This is not a constitutional requirement, but this is the practice followed and is acceptable to all political parties.

The disparity in the political power can be seen in the case of Utter Pradesh, which has 80 MPs in the Lok Sabha. As a result, out of 13 Prime Ministers, we have had 7 PMs from Utter Pradesh, namely -Pandit Jawaharlal Nehru, Lal Bahadur Shastri, Indira Gandhi, Rajiv Gandhi, Chacha Charan Singh, V P Singh, and Chandra Shekar. The other six are from other states, namely - Morarji Desai and Narender Modi from Gujarat, P V Narasimha Rao from Telangana, H D Deve Gowda from Karnataka, I K Gujral from Punjab and Atal Bihari Vajpayee from Madhya Pradesh.

The USA constitution is built on a greater compromise between the Virginia plan [representation of population] and the New Jersey plan [equal representation of all states], which resulted in the 'House of Representatives' being constructed on the basis of population and the 'Senate' being composed of an equal number of representatives regardless of population. This is why six states have one member in the 'House of representatives'[Lower House] today but have two members in the 'Senate' [Upper House]. The members of the Senate are responsible to the whole state, unlike in the Indian Parliamentary System, where the members of the Rajya Sabha [Upper house] are responsible only to their constituencies.

To give equal political powers to the smaller states, all states should have the same number of representatives in the Upper House regardless of the population. It appears that the disparity in the political power from one state to another was also not kept in mind when the Indian constitution was drafted. This can be set right if India changes to the US system.

In the Indian System, the members of the political parties select their leader, and the President of India asks the leader of the political party that has got the maximum Members of Parliament elected to form the government and within a specified period to face a 'vote of confidence'. The people of India do not have an executive head of their choice.

Having a Prime Minister, the executive head of the nation has worked very well in the parliamentary systems followed by other countries, especially in the advanced countries, but in the Indian Parliamentary System, when one goes through the events, since 15 August 1947 to date, one sees a number of faults. The faults can be mended, but with dynastic politics from the topmost to the lowest level and with the mindset of the present-day politicians, it cannot be done; in fact, as the nation moves ahead, more faults will take place that will affect the people of the country. It is most undemocratic to have few families deciding on the destiny of 1.3 billion people. The people of the country have to decide the form of change they wish to have.

Further, there is a disparity between demographics and representation in our Parliamentary system based on the Westminster model. The House of Commons has 640 seats for the UK's 64 odd million people [1 seat for 1, 00,000 people], compared to the Lok Sabha with 545 seats for 1.3 billion people [1 seat for 23, 85,321 people]. In the US Presidential system, their lower house has 1 seat for 15,000 people. In India, it is not only a lack of adequate representation, but widens the gap between the people and their representative – leading to the inaccessibility of politicians to the common people.

There is more emphasis on the amendments to the Constitution, especially the first amendments, which are in direct contrast to one another. This difference in political attitude towards fundamental rights eventually leads to the basic structure doctrine [Keshavananda

Bharati Vs State of Kerala]. A good reference is 'Sixteen Stormy Days' by Tripurdaman Singh.

 The sheer size of the Indian constitution makes it counterproductive in many ways. This also reflects in over-legislation in other areas such as labour laws and so on... [Ambedkar's views on this are interesting].

The answer will be to go for a complete change to another system, and the US Presidential system of government suits India because the USA and India have similar conditions, the people of both countries are democratically orientated and want an effective government, both have a number of religious groups, like Hindus, Christians, Muslims, Jains, Buddhists, Sikhs and Parsis; except, Christians are the dominating group in the USA, and others are in the minority, and likewise Hindus are the dominating group in India and others are in the minority; both countries have a pluralistic and diversified society, and both have people who want to do well in their lives economically and socially. In addition, both countries have seen internal conflicts; the US has gone through a civil war that has unified the country more strongly, and India has fought for their independence from the British colonial power that has unified the country more strongly. The only difference is that the American civil war brought a lot of bloodshed; however, in the Indian fighting for independence, there was less bloodshed, but a lot of people were put in prison that shattered their lives.

There is a school of thought that feels that instead of a total change to the Presidential System of Government in the USA, why not identify the areas where India has gone wrong in their Parliamentary System of Government and Modify only the portion that requires change. But there is another school of thought that feels that any change made in piece meal may have side effects that will unbalance the whole system, so the answer is to either change completely to the Presidential System or stay put in the present Parliamentary System. With the present mindset of the present-day politicians, it is advisable to change completely to the Presidential System on the lines of the USA model.

Normally, in a parliamentary system of government, there is a fusion between the executive and the legislature because the Executive Head, the Prime Minister, and the cabinet members are from the legislature and the legislative business moves faster. But, in the Indian Parliamentary System of government, the business moves very slowly, and most of the time, there is a deadlock due to the power groups in the legislature not being on the same page as the executive and the ruling party allies, putting up unreasonable demands like the TDS asked for a special status for Andhra, and the opposition that is bent on stalling the proceedings since they are out of power. When UPA was in power from 2004 to 2014, NDA did not allow the parliament to function due to the scams, and the UPA initially did not take any action on the defaulters, and now, when the NDA is in power, UPA is doing the same without any cause, more as retaliation. This is like if one falls into the well, the other chooses to follow, but what happens to the parliamentary proceeding and the loss of money to the taxpayers on a daily basis; it is a huge loss of money and valuable time that can never come back. There is an urgent necessity to have a clear separation between the executive and the legislature and the executive head selecting cabinet ministers with qualification and experience, not on political compulsion, to allow the executive head to function more effectively. This can only be done in a US Presidential system of government.

India should get rid of the President, who is a ceremonial head; a lot of taxpayer's money is spent on maintaining the 'Rashtrapathi Bhawan', including maintaining the staff and security personnel. Instead, have a President who is the head of the country and the head of the executive; the 'Rashtrapathi Bhawan' can be converted to a residence cum office for the President and his personal staff on the lines of the White House that houses the office and residence of the US President. If the Executive Head has to govern a large country like India, which is soon to become a world power, he cannot govern with a handful of staff in a small office. He needs a larger, effective organisation, an organisation that can look after the 'National Security' from outside aggression and homeland threat, move the economy to a higher level, maintain a good relationship with other nations more on economic considerations and follow up the 'MOUs' signed between India and other nations that have economic and strategic implications, follow up the decisions taken in all the world forums, follow every policy and implement the execution at the national level and coordinate with the states, monitor Communal Harmony and immediately take pre-emptive action to counter unpleasant incidents.

In India, the swing in public opinion from one state to another affects the functioning of the central government, and likewise, the swing in public opinion from one portion of the state to another portion affects the functioning of the State Government, especially in large states like Uttar Pradesh and Maharashtra. To limit the influence of swings in public opinion, like it is done in the US presidential system, the election of the executive head of the central government should be placed in the hands of the 'Electoral College'. The terms of the office of president and the two chambers of the legislature are to be set at different lengths, with fixed schedules, executive head for four years with a maximum of two terms, keep the Lower House of Representatives for two years. And the Upper House of representatives for six years [one third rotating after every two years] as it is done at present in the Indian Parliamentary System and the members of the Supreme Court to serve for life. Having different lengths of service will balance the swings in public opinion. Having elections twice in a cycle of four years and on fixed schedules will allow the politicians, the bureaucracy, and the civil administration to be on election modes only twice in a cycle of four years. This will help in their availability for governance more and save a lot of money.

In India, like the USA, the states are of different size in terms of population. The political powers in India are in the hands of the larger states with more representatives in the Rajya Sabha as the number of representatives from each state depends on the population, and the smaller states have less political power as they have fewer representatives in the Rajya Sabha. Instead of using the upper house [Rajya Sabha] like a dumping place to cater for loyalists, vote catchers like actresses/sportspeople, lawyers to protect politicians, etc. To give equal political powers to the smaller states, all states should have the same number of representatives in the Upper House, regardless of the number of representatives from each state in the lower house.

The main lacuna in the Indian Parliamentary System is the swing in the public opinion and various political powers from one region to the other that affects the smooth functioning of the central government, the functioning of the state governments and the relations between the centre and the state. Efforts have to be made to counter the swing in public opinion and bring political powers in all states on the same level playing field; this can be done if India changes to the US Presidential system.

In the Indian Parliamentary System, the government has promoted dynastic politics at every level, from the top to the lowest. The very thought of only 100 families ruling India in the future and controlling the destiny of 1.30 million people, as predicted by the political pundits, is frightening. Growing powerful political families have to be checked. To avoid dynastic politics with one family occupying the top political posts at the central and state level, India should change to the US presidential system.

India has far too many political parties and too many leaders aspiring to occupy the top executive post. Coalition governments, with a regional party with maximum MPs heading the government, have been failures because of political manoeuvring. In the US presidential system of government, there is no scope of having too many political parties, too many aspirants and also no chance of having coalition governments. In fact, there is more scope of moving into a two-party system.

In the Indian political system, the executive head has to select members of his cabinet only from the legislative representatives. In contrast, in the US presidential system, the executive head has the flexibility of selecting the best for his cabinet and not due to political compulsion. The latter is desirable.

A nation has to be protected from external aggression, and homeland Security is of paramount importance. The executive head in the US presidential system is in a better position to deal with any situation that is detrimental to national and inland security, as he is the Commander-in-Chief of the armed forces and has the flexibility to deal with any situation.

For people to live a good life for themselves, their children, and grandchildren, they should have Jobs with good pay, and for this to be achieved, the economy has to be sound. The Executive Head in the US presidential system is in a better position to improve the economy.

In the presidential system, the representatives from various constituencies within a state for the lower house and representatives from each state for the upper house have to be inhabitants of the state for at least 15 years so that they are conversant with the people and the problems of their area of responsibility. In the Indian Parliamentary System, it is not there. Anyone can show a local address and can represent a constituency, even if it is far from his permanent place of residence.

In the Indian Parliamentary System, the leader of the political parties are elected by the members of the political party, and the governor asks the leader of the political party that has the maximum elected MLAs to form the state government, and he becomes the executive head of the state [the Chief Minister]. The people of the state do not have a choice in selecting the Executive Head of the state. Whereas in the US presidential system, the people elect the executive head of the state [Governor]. The latter is desirable for better governance at the state level because most implementations have to be done at the state level. The present governor's house can be used as office cum residence of the governor [executive head] and his staff.

To avoid politics over economic considerations, India should never again be in an awkward situation where we have to send our gold reserves to the banks abroad.

A proper record of voting pattern for bills in the Lok Sabha and Rajya Sabha should be maintained to know what the leaders stand for and how much they have contributed to enable the people to know their capabilities for the next elections is a requirement. A periodic journal should be issued, and the public should be allowed to see it. This is not being adhered to. In the US System, the public can go through the journals.

The fault lines in the present parliamentary system will carry on for a long time if not checked. There has to be a separation of powers between the executive and the legislature, with proper checks and balances. The functioning of the present parliament with the calibre of MPs is undesirable.

The parliamentary system in present Indian conditions has produced at least 80% of legislative who have barely any qualifications or qualities in the field. They have sought elections only to wield executive powers and stay in power to achieve their self-goals; good governance is secondary. 'The welfare and well-being is for themselves and their family which comes first and the welfare and well-being of their country, and fellow men and women come second'.

Political parties shift alliances to cater for their leader's interest. There is no difference between one political party and another as all of them embrace socialism, secularism, and mixed economy, and in foreign policy, non-alignment; the shift does not affect their functioning.

To change to a more effective form of government for the citizens to have a better life, a course correction to change to the presidential system of government is required, with preferably two national parties in the fray.

In all respects, the change to the US Presidential System of Government will improve the governance, and the people will benefit and, in the long run, will do well for India.

HOW TO BRING ABOUT THE CHANGE

The fault lines cannot be cleared in the present functioning of the parliamentary system because it is too deep. Even if some people, who care for their country, try to get into the system to clean it up, they will not be able to do it; in fact, before they realise it, they will get sucked into the present system and even cut a sorry figure.

The people of the country have to think out of the box; they should organise a movement to force the change to the presidential system of government on the model of the USA. Presently a lot of politicians will not even think of this change, as they are well rooted in the present parliamentary system. The only person who seems to understand and can forcefully talk about a change is the present Prime Minister, N D Modi, but it cannot be a one-man show. In a way, he is fighting for the elections, and after being elected, he is running the country in a quasi-presidential system. Two politicians who can influence a change are Rajeev Chandrashekhar and Baijayant Panda. Rajeev Chandrashekhar has been advocating changes for better governance and has written a number of articles on various aspects in this regard. Baijayant Panda has also been advocating changes for better governance and has done an in-depth study in various areas, and has written a number of articles. Both these politicians are the right people to lead the movement. However, they both have to leave their political affiliations so that they can act forcefully without any influence from any political party or any so-called 'high command'. Incidentally, the term 'High Command' is used in the military chain of command, but in Indian politics, the term is often loosely used to show how powerful the leader of a party is.

Shashi Tharoor, with his knowledge and exposure at the international level and having stayed in the US for a long time and interacted with many key personalities across the society, can contribute a lot for the change; he can also be considered, provided he learns to speak in simple English language. Unfortunately, Kuldeep Nayar is no more. He was a political thinker, and his contribution to political journalism/books have been very useful. If he had been alive, he would have given constructive suggestions and may have also led the movement.

The people of the country, especially the younger generation, should talk about it because their future and their children's future are affected, organise discussions through social and print media, conduct seminars/panel discussions/lectures/talk shows/distribution of leaflets to make the people aware of the benefits.

Fault lines should not be hammered as if everything is wrong with the system but discussed objectively; the discussion should be on various faults and see how to overcome the faults if there is a need to change to the US Presidential System of Government – in most cases, the tilt will be towards this change. Now, how do we change the present system??? To change to the presidential system of government, the constitution of India needs an amendment. For this to happen, 2/3rd of the members in both the houses should agree to the amendment, and half the number of legislative of states should ratify the amendment. This is not possible, as the ruling party has a 2/3rd majority in the lower house, but in the upper house, the party is below half the mark.

At present, the NDA with 353 seats in the Lok Sabha and with 111 members in the Raja Sabha, with a hostile, unreasonable opposition, even introducing the issue in parliament will be impossible. Further, the political parties will not be for the change as they will look into their own interest. The answer is to have discussions on this change; through the national and regional electronic media and the print media to make people aware of the good in the change.

If most of the people are for the change and with their pressure, the government of the day may bring it up in parliament for discussion. If no headway is made, the people should ask for a referendum in a democratic way, similar to the referendum on 'British-exit from EU'. It has to be a peaceful people's movement. In case the government does not act on the referendum for change, the people should take the matter up to the Supreme Court of India.

The best for our country is to change to the Presidential System of Government on the USA model. This change will slowly bring in the two-party systems at the centre; in all probability, BJP and Congress, will be good for the country. Some of the regional parties and the communist will remain in their states of domination; slowly, these parties will also wither away, with individual politicians joining one of the main parties.

The present generation will probably not see the change; our children and grandchildren may see it. And they will be grateful to us for bringing about this 'change'.

....

Part II

The government of a country is judged by how well it has handled the economy and how well it has handled the 'National Security and homeland Security', apart from handling 'Communal Harmony' and 'Human Rights', 'Climate Change' and 'Environment Protection'.

With the economy moving forward, the GDP Growth hovered at around 7% till the last quarter of 2018-2019. After going through the drawbacks of demonetization and the time taken to decide on different slabs in the GST that brought temporary hardship to the people, it was reasonably a good achievement, under the unacceptable political situation, especially with an unreasonable opposition.

However, in the first quarter of 2019-2020, the GDP growth was 5%, and in the second quarter of 2019-2020, the GDP growth was 4.5%; the dip in the GDP growth was expected as the structural changes take time to be effective. In the first, second and third quarter of 2020 -2021, the GDP growth has seen a downward swing because there was less economic activities due to the effect of the coronavirus. By the time the present NDA government finishes its second five years tenure and the country heads towards the next elections in 2024, the economy is bound to go to a GDP growth of around 7% as sound economic fundamentals are in place.

In the handling of the 'National Security', at the beginning of his first five years tenure, with Pakistan, Prime Minister Modi tried to reach out to the political leadership of Pakistan during the tenure of former Prime Minister, Nawaz Shariff, but due to Pakistan's military leadership overshadowing the political leadership and dictating the relationship with India, both the Prime Ministers could not take the relationship foreword. A good opportunity was lost.

On July 27, 2015, militants sponsored by the Pakistan army attacked an Indian army base at Gurdaspur, followed by an attack, on January 02, 2016, on the Indian Air Force fighter base, at Pathankot. However, when they carried out an attack on the Indian army rear administrative base at Uri, in J&K, on September 18, 2016, the Indian Government gave a befitting reply by giving direction to the army to retaliate. On September 29, 2016, the Indian army successfully conducted a precision strike, deep inside Pakistan Occupied Kashmir [POK], on a wide frontage of 150 kilometres, on 6 to 8 targets. The targets selected were the launch-pads where the militants concentrated for infiltrating into the Kashmir Valley to attack our installations. This action shook up Pakistan's military leadership.

On February 14, 2019, the militants again attacked a convoy carrying Central Reserve Police Force [CRPF] men returning from leave at Pulwama, well inside Indian Territory. To retaliate, on February 26, 2019, the Indian Air Force did a precision air attack on the militant's main training camp at Balakot, deep inside Pakistan and destroyed their training facilities and killed around 300 trainees. This bold decision was taken by the central leadership, and the bold action was taken by the Air Force also shook up Pakistan's military leadership.

With China, the Prime Minister had tactfully dealt with odd border clashes, especially in 2018, when the Chinese army occupied Doklam, on the Indian side, close to the tri-junction of India –China-Bhutan; finally, the Chinese army withdrew. In May 2020, the Chinese occupied the Galwan Valley, with two division strength facing Eastern Ladhak. At the Galwan Valley, the Indian army pushed the Chinese away, and now, there is no direct contact. However, the presence of a large force facing Eastern Ladhak is a threat to India.

On 'homeland Security', the states with coordination with the centre have not brought in the long pending 'Police Reforms'. The functioning of the police force has been affected due to the lack of modern firearms, sound communication system with the latest technology and task-oriented vehicles, including helicopters/drones. The Intelligence system needs improvement with the latest technology, spread across all the sensitive areas, with effective coordination with other Intelligence agencies. These aspects have been neglected by all successive governments and need urgent action.

'Communal Harmony' and 'Human Rights' have not been given importance by all successive governments; these aspects also affect the internal 'law and order' situation. Religious barriers, Caste system, feudal system and above all, the vote bank politics have added to the volatile situation.

'Climate Change' and 'Environment Protection' have also not been given importance by all successive governments. The present NDA government has brought in solar energy and electric vehicles, a good move in the right direction.

The people of India would like to elect a government to carry on the good work the previous government has done and carry out a course correction on the fault lines and move ahead to serve the people. For this to happen, one year before leading to the elections, at the centre, state and district levels, electronic media channels should make the candidates in the field to come to an open forum and state their views on important issues affecting the people. The best way of making the candidates to do this is by pitching the candidates against each other so that the viewers, who are the prospective voters, know the candidates' views on various issues concerning them and how they intend to go about dealing with the issues; thus, the voters would know which candidate is best for them, then only people will vote for the best candidate. This should be done by qualified and experienced anchors that have no political affiliations.

If the candidate is standing for election more than once, the candidate should be asked what all he/she has contributed with proof till filing their candidature, and why they could not fulfil their manifesto fully on which they were elected earlier, and what are the course corrections and changes they would like to bring about, if elected again.

The media channel anchors can frame the questions the best way they feel and allow the people to draw their own conclusions on the candidates. THIS IS THE BEST WAY FORWARD. Otherwise, the people would not know who to vote for from the candidates in the field. This is one of the main lacunas, and the electronic media can play an important part, and the people of India will be very grateful to them.

During the debates between candidates, questions should be asked on the economy, with special emphases on development, growth and creation of Jobs, education and health, with special emphases on how to bring the people below the poverty line into the mainstream; national security, with special emphases on relationship with Pakistan, China and security of the Indian Ocean, and homeland Security, with special emphasis on terrorist attacks, drugs, rape and lynching; Communal Harmony and protection to the minority communities; Climate Change and Environment Protection.

The nature of questions on the issues will differ from one level to the other. At the Gram panchayat level, the questions should be mainly on land records and social issues. At the Block level, the questions should be on using the funds for development, administration, law and order and social issues. At the district level, the questions should be on using the funds for development, administration, law and order, education and health, and social issues. At the State level, the question should be on governance, policies and structural changes, economy, development and growth, job creation, education and health, administration, homeland Security and Intelligence, social issues, Climate Change and Environment Protection. At the centre level, the questions should be on international relations, national and homeland Security [including Intelligence], governance, policies and structural changes, economy, development and growth, job creation, education and health, administration, social issues, Climate Change and environment.

These questions will make the candidates more accountable and transparent, and above everything, the candidate's mindset will be channelized towards serving the people. NO MORE MUD SLINGING ON RIVAL PARTIES AND CANDIDATES. HAVEN'T THE PEOPLE OF THE COUNTRY HAD ENOUGH? IN ANY CASE, WHO WANTS TO LISTEN TO THIS RUBBISH?

Let us see the state of the union and the various subjects of importance that the candidates should be familiar with if they have to come into public life to serve the people and guide the media anchors on the nature of the questions to be asked.

Economy

The politician's main function is to create a better life for the people of the country; if the people have to live a better life, they should have a job, commiserating with their qualification and experience, earning enough to look after themselves, their family and educate their children. For this to happen, the political leadership should concentrate on development and growth to enable required Jobs to be created and protect the present Jobs.

It is Jobs that will bring up 60% of the people into the middle class. This 60% include 20% under the poverty line, 30% marginal and 10% from the low-middle class. Out of the remaining 40%, 20% are already in the middle class, 10% in the high-middle class and 10% well off.

Just mentioning creating Jobs in a colourful manifesto with flowery language will not do. Development and growth should be the main objective, and everything should revolve around them. THIS SHOULD BE THE STARTING POINT. With focusing on development and growth, the trajectory of the economy will go upwards to a level that will not only bring Jobs but also cater for the 'National Security and homeland Security', which are the other important parts of our existence. Therefore, the fundamentals of a sound economy should be clear to the politicians at the macro-level, leaving the specialist to deal with it at the micro-level.

Now, let us see the background of the economy.

Prior to 1991.

Pre-independence, which is before 15 August 1947, for about half a century, the GDP growth was 0%; this was during the British Raj. Agriculture was the main source of income, and primitive methods were used; there was no manufacturing of goods as all the resources, including gold, were taken to the UK and manufacturing took place there; the finished goods were brought to India and sold.

After gaining independence, in the 1950s and '60s, the GDP growth was 3.5% to 4%, in 1970's it was 3%, and in 1980s, it was 5.5%, the average from 1950 to 1980s was 3.5%. This was during Pandit Jawaharlal Nehru-Indira Gandhi-Rajiv Gandhi's era. This was mainly due to Pandit Nehru following Karl Marx's socialistic economic approach with central control that choked the private sector, followed by Indira Gandhi's 'licence-permit raj' that further throttled the private sector and encouraged corruption among the politicians and the bureaucracy, and Rajiv Gandhi continuing with his mother's economic policies. All three leaders did not pay heed to the low growth path for four decades that required fiscal reforms. The only development that took place was during Nehru's era with the first and second five-year plans that was commendable, especially the first one. During Indira and Rajiv's era, the emphasis was on giving foibles to the poor to better the vote bank instead of emphasizing development and growth that would have created Jobs for everyone. Further, licensing and excessive regulations to protect the licensing arrangements had crippled the country.

The run-up to the 1991 Crisis

As a result of the unsound economic policies prior to 1991, India faced a debt default. There was uncertainty, and India's international credibility was perhaps at an all-time low. Just prior to this, the State Bank of India had sold 20 tons of confiscated gold to secure a loan of $250 million.

In crisis management, the first lesson was to avoid the earlier mistakes. The second lesson was the realization that the central bank has to play a critical role in the crisis, especially when there is political uncertainty and that the stature of the RBI governor and the central bank matter.

The economic turning point in 1991.

Financial sector reforms are just one element of the economic reforms. 1st part of the reforms was to correct our mistakes that were made, and the 2nd part was to improve our systems and policies.

Under Prime Minister P V Narasimha Rao's stewardship, crucial economic reforms were carried out, and the economy was put on an upward trajectory. The 'licence-permit Raj' was removed and replaced with a market-orientated economy. Even international relations were orientated towards economic considerations. Liberalisation was the turning point, and India integrated into the global economy.

The reforms moved into a more competitive economy that enhanced growth, productivity, and employment. Over time, the reforms constituency has enlarged significantly. There are better road connectivity, improved telephony, automobiles, improved power availability and more freeing up factors of production, such as land and labour. Administrative reforms needed attention, even today.

During Prime Minister H D Deve Gowda government that followed but was short-lived, in the 1997 Budget, the big take away was the simplification of the tax rates to just three slabs, i.e., 10, 20, and 30 per cent. The finance minister, P Chidambaram, initially felt that the rates of 10, 20, and 30 may be too modest for a country like India, which still had several people living in poverty. On the suggestion of the staff in the Finance Ministry, a few options were put up to the then Prime Minister, H D Deve Gowda, who opted for the lower and simpler tax rates of 10, 20, and 30 that was accepted by everyone. In addition, the Voluntary Disclosure of Income Scheme [VDIS] was launched that secured tax collection of ₹12,000 crores. Simplification and lowering of excise and customs rates over a long period helped in import/exports; this helped the economy further.

Luckily, the NDA government under former Prime Minister Atal Bihari Vajpayee who subsequently came to power, followed the economic reforms further and brought the GDP growth to 8.1% during its last full year, i.e., when they left the government in May 2004. A sudden rise in the GDP growth was due to the economic process that Prime Minister Narasimha Rao had launched in 1991 and later, the acceleration of the process by Prime Minister Atal Bihari Vajpayee [1998-2004]. The Rao-Vajpayee reforms could actually translate into 8% plus growth. The best years for economic growth were from 1991 to 2004. With the economic fundamentals put on the correct track, the private sector expanded, and as a result, the people of India gained as more Jobs were created, with a scope of more Jobs to come. Atal Bihari Vajpayee had brought in significant changes in the telecom sector, roads, and highways sector.

The early reforms of the 'P V Narsimha Rao's government' had stabilized the exchange rate, inflation and current account within two years and returned the aggregate growth rate to its pre-crisis levels. But a sharper break in the growth rate came only in 2003-04 after the economy had time to adjust more fully to the Rao-Vajpayee reforms. Reforms take time to show results; one has to give time to the economy to adjust.

Economic Slid Downwards.

With the baseline of 8.1% GDP growth, created during NDA [1999-2004] and the earlier reforms taking proper shape, the UPA government under the then Prime Minister Manmohan Singh maintained 8% GDP growth in UPA-1 but brought down the growth rate to 5% during its last full year, i.e., by the end of UPA-2 tenure in May 2014 [the growth rate of 5% was later corrected to 6.9% [a drop of 1.2%]]. This was due to the government allowing the overall Budgetary expenditure to expand without regard to revenue, resulting in large fiscal deficits. Emphasis was on the social expenditure but did little to sustain the high growth essential to grow revenue at a fast pace. The economy that seemed unstoppable and had grown at an average rate of 8.1% during the first three years of the UPA-2 rule dropped down to culminate into an economic crisis. Apart from the growth rate declining, inflation increased to 10%, current account deficit to 4-5% and the Rupee depreciated to 13% during the preceding three months; not a very healthy sign.

Apart from the mismanagement of the economy, the denial of clearance to major projects on the environment or other grounds and rampant corruption at the political level involving a small part of the bureaucrats, like 2G, Coal and CWG scams, affected the economy. Unfortunately, some bureaucrats with a good reputation and unimpeachable integrity were caught in the crossfire, hence, froze the top bureaucrats from taking any decisions; there was complete policy paralysis. So deep was the freeze that a definite change under the present NDA Government has still not fully restored the confidence of the bureaucrats.

The worst action by Manmohan Singh's government was the legislature on retrospective taxation that was counterproductive; it drove the potential investors away from India. Even the developed countries encourage inward investment by creating workable business ethics, but a developing country like ours did not give any importance. Further, the difficulty in land requisition greatly undermined domestic and foreign investor confidence.

There were no checks on public banks; they lent vast sums of money to fund poorly conceived projects, and to add to this, they further permitted 'reconstructing' of poorly performing loans, not once but several times. Reconstructing Bad Loans on the brand of an individual or company, hoping to recover within a reasonable time and space is ok but what do you do when the returns are not forthcoming over a long period beyond the redlines. The answer is to stop further reconstruction and demand for compensation by asking for their assets, through the courts if necessary, so that the bank does not lose out and the money of the investors is protected. In most cases, depending on the brand names backfires. Two cases that are flashing across the media are Vijay Mallaya's 'Kingfisher Airlines', as well as Nirav Modi's, and Mehul Choksi's 'Diamond Jewellers'. They have both faulted very badly and are facing court cases. They are many such cases under the ED scanner.

The Weak Spots

From 1947, successive governments had addressed poverty, but the implementation of various schemes for the poor was not effective till the last 3 to 4 years, as the cash did not reach the grassroots level, there was corruption at the distribution level. Opening of bank accounts and direct bank transactions by the present NDA government helped, and the money is reaching the poor.

There is corruption at the 'Public Distribution System' of rations because of the nexus between the staff and the owners of the grocery shops that has not been plugged. The owners of grocery shops give funds to the local politicians to fight the election; they get their support, and nobody in the administration can touch them.

As a result, poverty that kills and continuously hurts hundreds of millions of Indians, has not been eradicated. As per the latest statistics, more than 5 lakh Indian children die of Malnutrition every year, meaning 10,000 each week; 38% of Indian children are stunted at a very young age, forever denying them a fulfilling life, intellectually and physically. The only ways to uplift poverty is to emphasise on education, skilled education, healthcare and creating Jobs and more Jobs so that positive effect reaches the lowest level.

Only 5% of the Indian people pay individual Income Tax, 45% of the private sector is in the unorganized sector that employs the maximum number of people, and both pay no tax, and the wages are very low as compared to other countries; there is still plenty of black money in the market. All these four factors are not good for the overall economy.

The Public Sector Banks [PSBs] have let down the people of the country by giving loans to businessmen/business houses without checks and further re-constructing loans not once but several times and failing to recover the Bad Loans that resulted in banks unable to give further loans; thus, affecting the credit market. The inefficient functioning of the 'Non-Banking Financial Services [NBFSs]' has also affected the credit market.

Public Sectors are not doing well. Some Public Sector firms running at a loss are in the process of being sold to private agencies; Air India is leading the way to be the first public sector company to go private. In other cases, where the loss is not much, efforts are being made to have Private-Public Sector participation, with even increasing Private Sector share to 51%.

The Present Government's Achievements

The present NDA Government has controlled the inflation to a low level, corruption has been dealt with an iron hand, Banking reforms and the insolvency and bankruptcy code have put banks on a path to recovery from the high burden of NPAs, the fiscal deficit is contained at 3.4% of the GDP, FDI inflow has been $239 billion over the last five years, and path-breaking structural reforms of the GST has been carried out. Once the states agree to include oil and real estate in the GST, there will be more GST collection.

In addition, the Budget spent on the social sector has helped the people - 'the Swachh Bharat mission' has reached 98% of rural India; 5,45,000 villages have become open defecation free. Under the 'Pradhan Mantri Awas Yojana', 1.53 crore houses have been built; electricity has been provided to 2.18 crore houses; 143 crore LED bulbs have been distributed, health cover has been improved, with the world's largest health cover programme- 'Ayushman Bharat' that has already benefitted 10 lakh families.

The present government has brought the GDP growth from 5% [later corrected to 6.9%] when they took over from the UPA government in 2014, to 7.7% as in March 2018 and 8.2% as in June 2018. When the government completed their 5 years tenure in 2019, the GDP was around 7%, with the economic fundamentals in place.

However, in the first quarter of 2019-20, the GDP growth dipped to 5%, and in the second quarter of 2019-2020, the GDP growth has further reduced to 4.5%; the government is concerned and is taking a course correction in the economy, and the GDP growth should see an improvement.

In economics, everything revolves around GDP growth, which will create other benefits, like a higher standard of living and higher per capita income; more income will increase savings and Investments.

The government will get more revenue to implement crucial welfare schemes that will benefit the 20% of the population below the poverty line and 20% marginal.

GDP will also allow the private sector to expand further that will provide more Jobs. The Jobs are in the private sector; government Jobs are limited.

With the growth atmosphere, FDI flow will increase, and India will be on the world stage as a very important player.

Domestic and foreign investment has dipped; India's taxation is high, and the crucial reforms on land and labour have not been done; even the infrastructure is not up to the mark. exports are below the expected per cent as India's cost and tax rates are high and not in line with the Asian countries to be competitive.

The public banks NPA have affected the credit market; NPAs are being reduced, but it is too slow; consumption is low, people don't have money to buy as in the job market, wages are low; therefore, demand is low, manufacturing is low and key sectors are suffering; the farmers are still under stress. These entire factors are affecting the ecosystem and the GDP growth.

The Governments- Reliefs

To increase investment and exports, the government has reduced the Corporate Tax to 22% for existing companies with an income of up to ₹400 crores and 15% Income Tax for new companies that will open by March 31, 2023. Effective Income Tax will come to 25.17%, from 34.9%, for existing companies and 17.01% for new companies. The reduction of Corporate Tax will benefit 99.3% of the companies; however, 0.7% of the companies with above ₹400 crores of income are left out. India is inching towards the global level with effective Corporate Tax from 17.07% [new companies] to 25.17% [old companies with ₹400 crores income], as compared to US-21%, China – 25%, Vietnam-20%, OECD –average 21.4%.

Old and new companies will also be exempted from Minimum Alternative Tax [MAT] of 18.5% imposed on all profit-making firms that declare lower tax. MAT on firms that do not opt for exemption-free 22% tax slab cut to 15%.

In addition, the surcharge imposed in the Budget on capital gains from the sale of shares or units of funds is withdrawn. Foreign investors will enjoy this benefit too.

Corporate Service Responsibility [CSR] for start-ups – scope of 2% mandatory CSR spending is extended to include incubators, set up by the government and PSUs and contributions to IIT's, National Labs and Autonomous bodies doing scientific and medical research. This will promote innovation.

All these steps will boost domestic and foreign investment, help 'Make in India' manufacturing units, and increase India's competitiveness.

Multiple structural changes have been made by the government, and the Indian economic growth will be higher in 2020 than in 2019 because structural reforms take time to start paying off.

Independent monetary policy and fiscal discipline have halved inflation. The GST has cut indirect tax categories from 100 to 5 and doubled payers to 12 million.

Insolvency and Bankruptcy Code [IBC] brought in by the present government has helped in recovery from loan defaulters. The recovery of ₹42,000 crore from loan defaulter Essar Steel is the first one; this demonstrates the power of policy when the executive, legislature and courts together take on vested interests, precedence, and history. Bank recovery from 200 larger defaulters is to follow.

Instead of carrying out Banking structural changes to privatize most PSBs and keep a bare minimum PSBs [including SBI], the government has merged weaker banks with stronger banks intending to make the merged banks into one strong bank and bring in more efficiency in functioning and delivery. Earlier mergers failed to give the desired results. Privatizing most of the PSB's would have been a better option. However, the government is topping up the Public Sector Banks by 70,000 crores in 5 years; this will help the banks to give credit to MSMEs that will generate more Jobs.

The government has earmarked Rs 100 thousand crores for building the infrastructure over a period of 5 years; this will increase the consumption of cement and steel, develop more ancillary units, and bring in more Jobs.

The government had spoken of creating Industrial Corridors among a group of villages to generate Jobs for the major portion of the rural labour that are now dependent only on Agriculture, but no ground work has been done in this direction.

The government has yet to take bold steps on land, labour and administrative reforms that are crucial.

All these will improve the ecosystem, and India can look forward to achieving a double-digit GDP. Once the GDP improves, Jobs will come and wages will increase, and if this improves, consumption will increase, and the demand for goods and services will increase. As a result, the GDP will increase further and more, and more Jobs will come, and wages will increase. The unemployment rate will come down, and more people will be able to look after themselves, their families and educate their children.

The unemployment is 6.1%, based on the inputs from the organized sector. This does not give the correct picture of the actual people unemployed, as most of the Jobs are in the unorganized sector that has not been taken into account. If they can take this data into account, then the unemployment percentage will be lower.

Over the last few years, we have seen the public-private partnership model is in progress. Some major projects, like airports, were built on these bases; there has been a focus on improving our cities and the challenges of urbanization which is very important.

Certain sectors of the economy showed weaknesses because they had been in crisis at inheritance, and sector-specific adjustments typically take longer than those related to the overall economy. Change in policies has taken place since 2014, and the annual growth of around 8% that India saw from 2003-4 to 2011-12 is poised to return.

Due to the increase in the international oil price, the boost in the US economy [levied of tariffs on goods imported to the US] and the dollar becoming stronger, and the effect on the world market, including European Union and China, the Indian economy has been affected, and the Rupee has become weaker.

The finance minister has stated that the government will maintain a 3.3% fiscal deficit to keep the gap between revenues and spending in check, the key measure to the state of public finances. So, economics is fundamentally sound.

Inflation is under control due to the easing of food prices. Temporarily, the inflation has gone up due to heavy rainfall that has destroyed the crops. Tax collection has increased but not to the required level, and divestment from state-run companies [target of ₹80,000 crores] is being maintained, but no tangible monetary benefits have taken place; nobody wants to buy Air India in its present state. Both GST and demonetization have started yielding results in the economic governance only but not monetarily. GST slabs have been reduced to three, aiming to further reduction to two, and the process of filing tax has been simplified. Once the states come on board, oil and real estate will be included in the GST.

India's 'Ease of doing business' ranking has risen to 63 from 139; slowly, the confidence of the bureaucrats is being restored. Now, people within India and abroad have confidence in the central leadership handling the economy.

P V Narasimha Rao's government had improved foreign relations based on trade with all countries, including Israel and ASEAN countries; Atul Bihari Vajpayee's government also followed the same approach, and now, the present government under PM Modi is following the same approach on a bigger scale. Now, people within India and abroad have confidence in the central leadership handling the foreign trade. The Indian people also have hopes for Modi.

The way to go forward

No country becomes economically strong and becomes a global economic player without savings and Investments, exports and a two-digit GDP growth. India has to enlarge its exports tremendously, increase savings and Investments, and raise its GDP to a double-digit. This calls for policies to generate a virtuous cycle of raising exports, savings and investment, and GDP.

Based on creditable data, the government should work out the overall expenditure and the likely realistic revenue that can be generated. While working out the expenditure, the government should also determine where they can cut down the expenditure on schemes for welfare measures, subsidies, running the government itself, including huge expenditure on politicians, etc., that are unproductive and outdated. This will give the actual expenditure and the required revenue.

In spite of cutting down expenditure, if the revenue likely to come to the government is less, then the following action should be taken on a war footing -

- First, unproductive outdated schemes for welfare measures and subsidies should be given a second look and further cut down drastically. Families with more than 2-3 children and the creamy layer of the backward Caste should be kept outside the preview of welfare measures and subsidies.

- Second, the expenditure on running the government should be to the bare minimum.

- Third, the expenditure on maintaining politicians should also be curtailed to the bare minimum, in terms of their pay and allowances [including pensions], accommodations, communication facilities, their security, personal staff and foreign visits. No country spends so much of the money on their politicians as a developing country as India does.

- Fourth, though the tax base has been expanded by more than 60% in the last five years, more effort is required to enlarge the tax base further. The unorganized sector should be tackled by 'Voluntary disclosure of Income Tax Schemes [VDIS]' and allowing them to spend part of their earnings to expand their present business and also invest in other business- giving incentives is the answer.

- Fifth, to increase the GST collection to the actual level, the government should pinpoint the defaulters and take necessary action to recover what is due to the government; this can be affectively done by establishing a technology platform to point out the defaulters at the earliest.

- Sixth and finally, all government ministries, institutions and organizations at the centre and state level should fast-track the payment of outstanding dues to various agencies, contractors, and vendors; this will spur investment and boost growth. Some officials hold up payment till a bribe is given. These officials should be taken to task.

The government at the centre and state should spend more on Infra-structure projects so that consumption of raw materials increases and automatically, ancillary units are set up to support the projects. This will generate a number of Jobs, and more people having money will increase consumption, resulting in higher demand.

To avoid the Public Sector Companies from eating into the exchequer coffer and turning the tide by getting huge funds into the government hold, a bold disinvestment target should be achieved by having a time-bound plan for the strategic sale of the affected Public Sector Companies and follow with a periodic progress report. Companies running at a loss like Air India should be sold off at the earliest; marginal companies should be run with public-private participation at 49/51%. Companies running at a profit should be allowed to run with effective management and be under periodic scrutiny with employees facing a test of efficiency. Any money the government gets from de-investment should be spent only on development projects.

So far, Air India has not been de-invested as there are no buyers. The selling off of Air India needs a realistic approach. At this point in time, Air India is a loss running airline, and with the competition in the international and domestic routes, turning it into a profit-making airline is asking for the moon. This is the reason why no buyers have come.

The buyers will see if they can get the airline at a reasonable price with no government share in it, with internal and external flights that are commercially profitable, with a viable fleet of aircraft, a minimum operating staff/ technicians and offices/guest rooms required.

In case no buyer is in a position to buy the whole airline in its present form, i.e., international and domestic, then sell that part, which was covering the international routes, i.e., before the merger, and run the remaining part covering the domestic routes and later, sell the domestic part separately. Ultimately, it is better to sell at a lower price and go at a loss, rather than running the airline in its present form and still go at a loss.

The buyer may not take all the surplus aircraft, the non-operational offices/guesthouses all over the world, and miscellaneous items like wall paintings/statues, etc. Surplus aircraft and miscellaneous items can be sold separately to other buyers even at a lower price, and the non-operational offices/guest houses can be closed. Give a golden handshake/ VRS to the staff/technicians not likely to be taken in by the buyer.

Finally, if nothing works out, give that part of original Air India back to 'Tatas' at a reasonable cost, as the country had snatched Air India from them, in a very unfair means or allow the staff/technicians of Air India, including the retired personnel/children to take over as an independent consortium without any interference from the government. It will save a lot of money for the exchequer/taxpayers.

The same realistic approach can be applied for other non-profitable Public Sector Enterprises, which hold a large piece of land that can be sold separately.

The money received from the de-investment of PSUs should be strictly used for building the infrastructure that will bring more Jobs that will increase the consumption that will trigger the demand and ultimately bring in Investments.

Exports

In global exports, India's share is only 1.7%; no country has grown fast without buoyant exports that give high productivity Jobs, leading to becoming a middle-class society. Indian exports have hardly grown for the last five years. This is because India is a high-cost economy that cannot compete with its Asian peers. The high cost is due to high-cost land, labour, capital, electricity, railway freight rates, air freight, corporate and Income Tax rates. For higher export growth, all these rates have to be lowered to the Asian level.

The aim should be to get into the Asian market first and be competitive with China, Vietnam, Thailand, Indonesia, Malaysia, Singapore, South Korea, and Bangladesh. They all have lower costs and faster export growth, and later get into the global market and be competitive with the USA, Japan, European Union, UK, and Brazil. Then only India can become the number two biggest economy, USA and China being the number one.

Investments

The domestic and foreign investors find India's environment not favourable for business, though India has improved its ranking in 'Easy to Do Business' to 63, from 77, Investments in India has suffered because of higher rates that are disincentives. As a result, many Indian businessmen are moving to low tax havens like Singapore and Dubai [many billionaires have already left in recent years], a great loss to the country.

Reforms

Land Title – Legally in India, "property owners" are occupiers who happen to have a "title document" that merely records a transfer of title with the imprimatur of the state. It registers the deed of transfer only, not the authenticity of the title itself. As a result, title holders have a presumptive title, not conclusive ownership. Banks rarely treat property documents as sufficient collateral for giving loans. Apart from pledging their property, borrowers have to show additional assets. This leads to capital starvation, unable to leverage all the land that their citizens own to jump-start the economy. In India, only 3% of all private and public land is leveraged for capital as compared to the US, where conclusive title and clear boundaries allow 40% leverage, unlocking a $15 trillion of low-cost capital.

Remedy – First, India should move from loose property description by patwaris to digital GPS boundaries tagged to a unique owner. Second, the state should guarantee the title rather than registering the deeds. Third, property document should be transferred in a demat format, like the shares of a company in the stock market.

Even by an estimate of 40% of capitalization, India will unlock around or more than $4 trillion capital over a decade. Farm families will move out of poverty, and many small-micro businesses will be created with capital-fuelled activity, creating many Jobs.

A large pool of capital will also help start-ups and large enterprises that can even become global industrial leaders.

India's growth rate and prosperity will depend on empowering farmers and micro businessmen, and giving importance to the land title are very important.

India needs new land laws to slash land prices and acquisition costs, new labour laws that reduce effective cost through flexibility, lower fiscal deficits to reduce interest rates, electricity reforms to end high industrial rates to subsidize farmers, rail reforms to end high freight rates that subsidize passenger traffic, lower taxes on aviation fuel to lower air freights, shift to direct cash transfers to farmers to lower agricultural prices; and make all these competitive internationally.

India should bring down the various rates to the Asian level to be competitive. This includes the import duties, Corporate Tax rates, and the Income Tax rates. The import duties have recently been brought down in line with Asian norms of 10%; the Corporate Tax rates have recently been brought down to 22% for large companies with revenue of ₹400 crores and 15% for new companies. However, they are still not in line with many Asian countries where the Corporate Tax has fallen to 15 - 20%. The peak Income Tax rate of 42.75% is out of line with rates in several competing countries and does not attract foreign investment because of the high rates. Most of the foreign portfolio investors organized as trusts are exiting for countries with lower rates, causing a crash in the Indian stock market.

Reducing India's Corporate Tax rates has been a good move to spur up investment; however, more reduction is required to be in line with the Asian countries. Except for import duties that are 10%, the remaining rates are high and not in line with other Asian countries

The peak Income Tax rate of 42.7% is out of line with rates in several Asian countries. Foreign portfolio investors organized as trusts find they have to pay 42.7% tax; many countries require their pension funds to be organized as trusts and invest in fast-growing economies because of high taxation; these trusts are exiting India, causing the market crash.

Constant changes in income-tax surcharges and import tariffs represent tax policy driven by lobbying during the election period. The aim should not be for winning the vote bank but on economic considerations. Even incentives should not change the goal post at political whims and fancies. Attracting large foreign investment to boost investment requires stability and predictability in tax rates.

In booming markets, contracts are sacred, and changes in rules do not affect old deals made under different assumptions at that point in time. Populist government change to suit business houses funding them; one example was the changing of e-commerce rules to benefit Reliance at the expense of Amazon and Flipkart.

After the last interim Budget of July 05, 2019 - foreign investors have fled the stock market as they see a rising momentum for expanding job quotas and extending them to the private sector. As per the Supreme Court's judgment, the job quota for the weaker section of society cannot exceed 50% to preserve some space for merit. The present government has proposed an additional 10% job reservation for the poor across the board in the public and private sector. Even domestic investors are leaving the country to start their business elsewhere.

The Chief Minister of Andhra Pradesh , Jagan Reddy, has reserved 75% of Jobs in industrial and infrastructure ventures for state residents. The Chief Minister of Madhya Pradesh, Kamal Nath, has also reserved 70% of Jobs in the private sector companies for state residents.

Labour

The present government, instead of undertaking radical reforms to enhance labour flexibility, has enacted National minimum wages, over and above the minimums already laid out by various state governments. The National minimum wage will be higher than wages in the most backward states; this will rob backward states of one advantage they have over advanced states, which is low wages. Low wages are an incentive for investors, and this advantage is lost. Let investors come to backward states and establish themselves and grow; wages will automatically increase. Allow the states to decide on the minimum wages as per their economic conditions.

A very few companies quitting China want to shift to India, but most of them want to shift elsewhere because of the higher rates, quota system and high minimum wages.

Budget

Through fiscal and monetary discipline, inflation has been brought down from double digits to low single digits. During the post monsoons period, inflation had temporarily gone up due to heavy rainfall that destroyed the crops. Higher inflation hurts the poor the most.

Fiscal constraints mean the government lacks the required money to kick start flagging investment, so it seeks more from private and foreign investors, but that requires a conducive competitive climate.

The Budget seeks to attract massive foreign Investments; the government proposes bidding by multinationals for subsidies to set up mega factories in high tech areas, like solar energy, silicon fabrication and mass storage batteries.

Though the Budget has addressed both fiscal prudence and growth, it lacks the increase in savings and investment, exports, and GDP [even to 8%].

To some extent, it boosts rural consumption through support to farmers and the rural economy by providing direct income transfer to the middle-class taxpayers through tax rebates to entrepreneurs through ease of doing business.

Farm Loan Waivers

The impact of Farm Loan Waivers has a great impact on state finances. Since 2014-2015, many state governments have announced Farm Loan Waivers to relieve distressed farmers struggling with lower income in the wake of repeated droughts. A holistic review of the agricultural policies and their implementation, as well as evaluate the effectiveness of current subsidy policies with regard to agro-inputs and credit in a manner that will improve the overall viability of Agriculture in a sustainable manner. Farm loan waiver by the government implies that the government settles the private debt that the farmer owes to a bank. This amount eats into the government's resources that either affects fiscal deficit or the government has to cut down its expenditure. A higher fiscal deficit implies that the amount of money available for lending to private businesses will be lower, and the cost at which this money would be lent would be higher. State governments prefer to cut capital expenditure because by doing so, productive assets such as more roads, buildings, and schools, etc., don't come up, which undermines the ability to produce and grow in the future.

Budget - 2019

Aiming to push consumption, the Budget proposed additional interest reduction on affordable housing home loans and relief on purchasing e-vehicles. Reduced GST on electric vehicles to 5% from 12% to promote the use of electric batteries for transportation that will control pollution and also reduce the consumption of subsidized fossil fuel. In a push towards electric mobility, the government proposes to extend the Income Tax benefit of 1.5 lakhs on interest on loan taken to purchase electric vehicles to buyers. No customs duty on parts for exclusive use in e-vehicles to promote electric mobility.

The stand-up scheme will be extended up to 2025. Funds worth ₹10 lakhs to ₹1 crore will be given to entrepreneurs to buy items ranging from scavenging machines to robots. The scheme had benefited many women and SC/ST entrepreneurs. Banks have been asked to provide loans to at least one woman entrepreneur per branch to set up a Greenfield enterprise.

Provided Budget for ₹1.95 crores rural homes for the poor and total deduction of ₹3.5 lakhs on interest on loans taken by first-time buyers purchasing a house up to ₹45 lakhs. Both will provide a boost to the housing sector. Not only will it create more skilled and unskilled Jobs, but it will create demand for other ancillary industries downstream.

Nil tax till ₹5 lakhs will give the people more money to save and invest.

Provided Budget for Jal [water] mission to provide drinking water to all citizens, means less water-borne diseases thus saving money on treatment.

To force people to keep their money in the bank, proposed 2% TDS on cash withdrawal of over 1 crore a year from a single bank to encourage cashless transactions and transparency. TDS of 2% on withdrawing 2 crores and 5% on above 5 crores; TDS in both cases can be later claimed.

The recent Budget of the government has been sound, keeping the fiscal fundamentals in mind. However, it will not increase consumption that will lead to demand, subsequently leading to investment. It will also not increase exports as tax rates are still high and not in line with the Asian Tax rates, thus not competitive. The government has very little fiscal space to stimulate the economy; borrowing from the domestic market, in terms of gold bonds, etc., that ties the government down, and from the foreign market, in terms of foreign bonds, which is risky as there is no chance of structural change if things go wrong. The move of the government has been in the interest of the country; however, what matters most is the quantum and handling of such borrowing and the role of the central bank; the RBI is the country's debt manager, though the government is in the process of forming a separate debt management office. The Budget has not done much for the GDP growth, and much more has to be done, to even touch 7%.

Though the government committed de investment of public sector companies running at a loss to bring in 10,05,000 crores, unless the government plans to do so in a phased manner, with a quarterly monitoring process, the intention will remain on paper.

Revenue

The government gets its revenue yearly from direct taxes from individuals/companies, from indirect taxes [GST], from the Public

Sector Enterprises, and periodically from the surplus money with the RBI.

If the revenue is less than the expenditure required, the government should first take the following action – cut down expenditure on un-productive and outlived schemes and commitments, enlarge the direct tax base, enlarge the indirect tax base [GST] by making it simple and easy to file and having only two slabs of 5% and 18%, try to shrink the unorganized sector to a great extent, by giving tax incentives, sell the non-profitable public sector enterprises at a galloping speed. The government should not depend on the RBI's surplus money; they should treat it as a bonus to be used for development. Borrowing from the domestic and foreign market should be the last resort.

More revenue is generated if businessmen invest in India and Indians abroad also invest in India instead of going elsewhere. Land, labour and administrative laws, and taxation in line with the global market and norms, and separating economic offences and criminal offences, if everything is a criminal offence, then nobody is going to get into business in India; spending time in the filthy Indian Jails scares everyone.

The government has proposed to raise the FDI cap on aviation, media [animation and AVGC] and insurance [100%] to allow FDI's to increase their stake beyond the stipulated 24% cap to up to sectoral foreign investment limits. This will increase Jobs in these sectors.

The government looks to ease local sourcing rules for foreign investment in the single-band retail sector; this will benefit high tech companies like Apple and Rolex who plan to open their own outlets; this will further encourage FDI and growth in the industry even more in India and spur the growth of the Indian economy.

With the tax rebate on income below 5 lakhs, the tax relaxation on capital gains with respect to investment in a second property and benefit from the relaxation of tax on a notional rental income of a second self-occupied property, the lower-middle-class taxpayers will have disposable income. This will help consumption, savings, and Investments.

With an increase in allocation in MUDRA loans, the entrepreneurs will receive more.

With tax-free profits for affordable housing development getting a one-year extension and tax on notional rent on unsold inventory being available for two years, the real estate sector gets special attention.

In India, capital is a far scarcer factor of production than labour. But one of India's most enduring paradoxes is that its corporations invest in the most capital intensive technologies. We need reforms that would nudge our corporations to spread the nation's scarce capital over many more workers.

The traditional economic thinking was based on consumption-led economic growth. The international experience suggests that a sustained high growth rate needs a catalytic-virtuous cycle of savings, Investments and exports supported by a favourable demographic phase.

Investment, especially private investment, is the key driver that drives demand, creates capacity, increases labour productivity, introduces new technology, allows creative destruction, and generates Jobs.

The single biggest constrain to ease of doing business in India is the ability to enforce contracts and resolve disputes – 3.5 crore cases pending in the judicial system.

$5 Trillion Economy

To achieve a $5 trillion plus economy, the three most essentials that must be dealt with is the tax system, laws, and overhaul. These three factors work in their own sphere to achieve their individual objectives; however, they don't realize that in doing so, they may cause damage to the national policy objectives.

There has to be a change in the attitude towards the private sector, particularly the big business houses, affirmative good rather than evil. China has grown to a $13 trillion economy only because of private enterprise. China's garment exports were $110 billion in 2017, while India's was $17 billion, the gap is huge.

The task of achieving a $5 trillion plus economy has to be shared equally by states. Both centre and states encouraging private investment to make India the second-largest manufacturing nation and making tax and regulatory laws function in unison and designed to become growth-oriented.

The current size of the economy is $2.7 trillion; to achieve a $5 trillion economy, the growth rate should be 8% over the next 5 years. This has been achieved earlier, and there is no fundamental or structural block to securing this ambitious and credible objective. However, growth cannot be sustained at 8% without private investment and exports. The need to revive is the virtuous cycle of investment, Jobs, productivity, exports, consumption, and growth.

Investors look for macroeconomic stability and a supportive regulatory and policy environment. They invest when the inflation is under control, the fiscal deficit is within prudential limits, and the external account is broadly in balance. They want better infrastructure for connectivity and efficient functioning, and the easing of supply-side constraints. This means land acquisition within a reasonable time frame, flexible labour laws, and an efficient capital market. They also want competitive Corporate Tax, with a simplified, transparent, and fair mechanism for dispute resolution.

The UNCTAD projects India's GDP growth to be 6% this year. The drop in export intensity of economic growth over the last five year period signalled an erosion of competitiveness. Consequently, opportunities arising out of the shift in manufacturing production lines out of China on account of the US-China trade war have so far bypassed India. In Asia, Vietnam and Bangladesh have been the main beneficiaries. The recent lowering of Corporate Tax rates in line with emerging market peers will not by itself ramp up the competitiveness if India's cost of setting up and operating a business remains high. Land acquisition and labour flexibility need legislative changes; both are important factors considered for investment decisions. Red tape is a source of invisible costs; bureaucratic and regulatory processes need to be made investor-friendly; like in China, setting up a single-window system to get all government clearances will speed up establishing a business enterprise. GST must be streamlined, and the process to file tax returns made simple. Radical education reforms are needed to harness the enormous potential of the Indian youth. Any regressive steps that hold up or not conducive to business should be avoided, like retroacting tax amendments, tax terrorism, job quota for locals, treating economic offences as criminal offences, etc. If the government, under Modi's leadership, can create a favourable business atmosphere, foreign investors will flock to India. The recent meeting between PM Modi and the American corporate giants was the right move; the results on the ground will depend on their Investments.

One of the boldest reforms in the last 20 years has been the cut on corporate profits from approximately from 35% to 25.2% for existing domestic companies and 17% for new manufacturing companies established before October 31, 2023, provided the companies don't take any exemptions.

For existing companies, the tax rate is now below or equal to those in Japan, South Korea, China, Indonesia, and Bangladesh, though higher than those in Taiwan, Thailand, Vietnam, and Singapore. For new companies, the tax rate equals that in Singapore but below those in other countries mentioned.

The government has simplified the corporate profit tax system and thus eliminated numerous sources of bribes, harassment, and tax disputes.

Similar reforms are required for personal tax. Aligning the top personal Income Tax rate to the corporate profit tax rate at 25%, with all exemptions eliminated, would curb corruption, harassment and minimize tax disputes.

The government should reduce the personal Income Tax rates so that the taxpayers have more money in their pocket that will increase personal consumption. Further, the government should assure the taxpayers that higher declared incomes in future tax returns will not form the basis of investigation of past reported incomes. This will increase the tax base that will offset the effect of the reduction of tax rates.

The government should carry out labour laws to ensure that the workers get proper wages and, if they are fired, they should at least get some compensation through monetary assistance that will help until they get another job/self-employment, say- 45 days of wages for each year worked.

The government should also carry out pro-growth reforms, like strategic sale of public sector units [PSUs], monetization of infrastructure assets such as highways, airports, seaports, railway stations, and power transmission lines, and sale of unused government-owned urban lands to get more revenue to make up the loss in cutting the Corporate Tax. PSU sales and monetization are on the government policy agenda; the government now must pursue this agenda vigorously.

By doing the above, the government will avoid slipping on fiscal consolidation; it will maintain the aggregate demand; it will enhance the efficiency of PSEs, infrastructure assets and urban land; and it will signal its resolve to move ahead towards a $5 trillion economy.

Finance Ministry

The most important is the Finance Ministry working in coordination with other ministries at the centre and states that deal with land, labour, and administration. India hasn't paid any attention to the administration that creates bottlenecks, and without proper administration, nothing can move properly with efficiency and effectiveness.

The tax authorities have a single-minded focus on achieving their revenue targets. There are ridiculous tax demands that have led to numerous litigations; India has 2% of global trade but has more transfer disputes than any other country. Taxation on businessmen above the norms is bad, but tax terrorism is worse. The businessmen face debts, low market behaviour and tax terrorism that blocks the selling of their shares to pay off debts in extreme conditions. When the market is low and further goes low, and there is no chance of recovery, the lenders put pressure for their money to be returned, and if the entrepreneur is unable to sell his shares to pay back the debts due to tax authorities putting an embargo, the entrepreneur is under tremendous mental pressure and may even commit suicide. This is not fair, and tax officers indulging in tax terrorism should be taken to task.

Our regulatory and labour laws, particular at the state level, still require multiple licenses and permits; the land acquisition law requires that industry be set up in 48 months. Due to the populous government's policy, no sugar industry can survive if the regulatory raw material price is more than the market-driven selling price of the final product. This has crippled the entire sugar industry.

Slowdown

Growth has fallen to 5% from 7% in the first quarter and below 5% in the second quarter of 2019-2000. This slowdown is due to the combined effect of the cyclical global downswing and serious structural flaws that are pulling down long term growth. exports, which revived in 2018, after 5 years, are falling again; manufacturing growth has sunk to just 0.6%, investment has slumped; the Bad Loans of banks are shrinking too slowly, and the current slowdown is threats to expand them again; the crisis in non-Banking financial corporation's arising from the collapse of IL&FS is still not over. Foreign investors are fleeing from India, and the Sensex has lost 3,000 points.

A small economic revival package provided by the FM will give short-term relief, but major structural reforms can only tackle long-term growth.

Though poverty has fallen drastically, and India is the 5th largest economy in total income, in terms of capita per income, India is very low, 145th in the world ranking, out of around 178 nations.

Instead of looking towards the vote bank, if the government under Modi's stewardship can take bold reforms in taxation, land, labour, and administration, to encourage savings and Investments, and promoting exports that will bring the required Jobs, the government would have achieved a lot for the people of the country and the NDA government and Modi will be remembered for posterity.

The steady decline in India's quarterly GDP growth rate since the beginning of the last financial year was preceded by a drop in export intensity of economic growth over a five year period. The opportunities arising out of a shift in manufacturing production lines out of China on account of the US-China trade war have so far bypassed India; the main beneficiaries in Asia have been Vietnam and Bangladesh.

The recent move to lower Corporate Tax rates to levels aligning with emerging market peers will not by itself ramp up competitiveness if India's cost of setting up and operating a business remains high. The way forward needs clear legislative changes to impart flexibility in areas such as land acquisition and hiring as they influence investment decisions. Cutting of red tape [invisible cost], investor-friendly regulatory processes, streamlined GST and radical educational reforms to unlock the enormous potential of India's youth will help. Avoiding regressive steps that hold up a business such as retrospective tax, job quotas for locals, faulty NRC in other states and political raid raj that make businessmen run away from India.

Now, the NDA government, with a massive victory in the last May 2019 elections, again under Modi, is hoping to reach a $5 trillion economy by 2025. Let us see how the future unfolds before the country goes into the next elections in 2024.

The drop in GDP growth to 5% in the first quarter of 2019-2020 and further drop to 4.5% in the second quarter of 2019-2020 has worried even the IMF; though India has taken a number of structural changes, there is a drop; structural changes take time to adjust and have tangible effects. In the midst of a significant slowdown, the IMF feel it is mostly cyclical, not structural, because of the financial sector issues. The answer is to have continued sound macroeconomic management.

Most high-frequency indicators suggest that weak economic activity has continued into December 2019. Private domestic demand expanded by only 1 percentage in the quarter. This is attributed to the abrupt reduction in non-bank financial companies [NBFC] credit expansion and the associated broad-based tightening of credit conditions appear to be an important factor, and weak income growth, especially rural, has been affecting private consumption.

Income relief might have only a limited impact on consumption, as only 5% of the population pays tax. Instead, a greater push to schemes like the PM Kinas, National Rural Employment Guarantee Scheme, or a universal basic income to cater for a larger population that is under stress and stimulate demand to contain the slide in growth.

Government should de-invest Public Sector Units running at a loss even at a lower price and quickly spend this amount meaningfully in the development of infrastructure to bring in more Jobs and increase consumption to bring about a push to the economy to the required magnitude. Structural changes would probably help the economy, with a focus on Agriculture and power-sector reforms.

For the engine of growth, the leading indicators are the sale of automobiles, two-wheelers, air conditioners and refrigerators. What do all Indians consume; there are five things - food, clothing, and one house minimum in our lifetime, healthcare, and education. The richer; after buying a house and a car, they want to go for holidays abroad, have their healthcare in Singapore, and want their children to study abroad.

The economic slowdown is due to structural problems.

To increase productivity – the government has to make smart policies that are more effective to achieve in the medium term.

At present, the growth rate is 7% that has not brought enough Jobs to cater for the educated population growth.

The rate of population growth in India is alarming, and very soon, India will bypass China and become the largest population in the world. To cater for the growth in population, India will have to grow economically at a galloping speed, this is not practically possible, India can grow at 10%, the present government is determined to make the crucial reforms to achieve this target, will the opposition, especially the Congress allow the reforms to be passed in the parliament?

The unemployment rate will always be a concern unless India controls their population. The family planning ministry had always advocated 2 to 3 children. Since the early '70s, initially, there used to be a number of advertisements to make families aware of the benefits of having small families, but now the move has died down. India should now be strict and give educational benefits to families with 2-3 children only and cater for Jobs for them.

MGNREGA was a good scheme as a short term measure, but in the medium term, the government can't run the world's fastest-growing economy on employment support; it must create employment.

Jobs have to be created in the rural and urban area to have an even spread throughout the country. manufacturing capacity should be Beefed up, where the maximum population lives to avoid migration to other places where most of the unskilled migrants become waiters, watchmen, drivers, and scrap dealer's, they cannot live with dignity. Unskilled migrants should be given skilled education with which they can take up reasonably good Jobs and live with dignity.

8.1 Agriculture Sector

The state of the Agriculture sector is not sound for the last two decades. 60% of the people in India live in rural areas and depend on Agriculture for their livelihood. They provide food for the rest of the country, whereas in the United States of America, only 3.3% of the population are employed in Agriculture and produce enough for the whole country with a trade surplus in Agriculture; a trend that has been going on for at least for the last 50 years. Comparatively, India has too many people cultivating too little land; this was observed way back in 1880. The USA has the advantage as the farmers are rich and own vast pieces of land stretching over miles and miles, and the farmers depend on mechanized farming. Whereas in India, the majority of the farmers have small landholdings without any mechanized equipment. Even the tilling of land is done by bullocks, and the sowing and harvesting are done manually and above everything, dependence on the rainfall. It is the only few rich farmers who do mechanized farming and depend on deep tube wells for water.

There is agricultural distress in many parts of the country, especially in the Deccan Plateau, covering Maharashtra, Andhra, Karnataka, and Tamil Nadu, where many farmers are committing suicide. This calls for urgent and immediate relief to farmers.

The main reason is lack of water due to less rainfall or drought conditions where there is no water or excessive rainfall/hailstorms where crops are destroyed. The farmers cannot get returns on their Investments and are unable to pay back their loans that they have been taken for hiring equipment, buying seeds and fertilizers, hiring farm labour, and rent payment if the farmer has taken land on rent, and payment for electricity for drawing water from the ground or canals/rivers. Most of the farmers take a loan from the unorganized sector at a huge interest of up to 42%. Farmers find it difficult to sell the produce, as the middlemen dominate the market and dictate the price. In most regions, except Punjab/Haryana, most of the small farmers have to depend on the bullock cart due to bad roads and non-availability of proper transport to cart their produce to the markets; this adds to the cost.

What pushes the farmers into a debt trap in the first place? Most of the farmers do not earn enough from the agricultural produce to repay the loans. They cannot meet even their essential consumption expenditure, let alone expenditure on education, healthcare, marriage, and other social obligations; often forced to borrow from private money lenders. Farm loans and personal loans get them into a debt trap.

Farmer's distress is also due to lack of control over the business. Nobody knows what the unsubsidized rate is. There is a producer, transit, and consumer rate, and this destroys the business model.

Dependence on Agriculture alone is not sustainable; there has to be some additional income. A number of members of the farmer's families and farm labours shift to the towns and cities for Jobs. Most of them live in slums, and the infrastructure in the towns and cities cannot cope with the additional population pressure.

Apart from helping the farmers by subsidizing the farm inputs and building canals and reservoirs for water, the government should make a sincere effort to shift the surplus farm labour to the industries, as was done by all the developed countries.

This can be achieved by building Industrial Corridors within reasonable reach of a group of villages, where Micro, Small, Medium Enterprises [MSMEs] can come up and provide Jobs. Small and affordable living accommodations with civic facilities, educational institutions and health facilities should be made available.

In addition, the Industrial Corridors should have banks to provide loans to the farmer community with reasonable interest and easy processing and markets with online facilities to help the farmers to sell their produce. For the storage of produce, the government should build storage facilities, including cold storages for perishables produce, to enable the farmers to sell their produce when they get a fair price.

The roads from these villages to the Industrial Corridors should be built, and the government should provide public transport from the villages to the markets, at a reasonable fare. Power, preferably based on solar energy, and a filtration plant for drinking water should be provided.

The enterprises should include food processing/canning-bottling plants for domestic consumption and export. Veterinary coverage for Animal Husbandry should be made available with an institute to guide the farmers on modern methods of breeding goats, Cows and buffalos for milk and meat and pigs for pork. Horticulture, herbal medicines, and fisheries can also be added. These will create more Jobs and more income for the farmers.

Proper roads should be built from the Industrial Corridors to the nearest highways and railways that will eventually link to the cities. As time passes, these Industrial Corridors would slowly enlarge into Small Townships and may grow further.

For encouraging MSME's in rural and urban areas, the government should open one window system for obtaining sanctions as it is done in China.

Due to the division of the farmland, on the death of the family head, the holdings are divided between the heirs, this results in the holdings becoming smaller and smaller, and the farmers with small holdings do not benefit, as farming is not viable, as the cost of production goes up.

Over 86% of landholders in India are marginal and small farmers [up to 2 hectares]. Their crops are vulnerable to weather aberration; chemical fertilizers and pesticides are harming soil qualities. Falling Agriculture productivity is serious. Waiving farmer's loans should be short term. It is viable for them to switch to new technologies. Digital Technology reaches many smallholders through easy-to-use platforms, considering their educational level.

Long term measures should curb the land fragmentation, provide alternative efficient farming methods and online selling of farm produce to 'big Basket', etc., to avoid middlemen. As a safety net, the farm loans should be covered by getting the maximum farmers under crop insurance; crop insurance won't make much headway unless the technology is also used.

The small and marginal farmers are the most hit, and the only solution is to get them into cooperative farming on the Israel model. Israel's co-operative farming concept has been a great success; they have even converted deserts to green pastures. They are masters in converting wastewater and seawater to potable drinking water. They have also gone for precision farming, in which they use drones to monitor the growth of individual plants in terms of water and fertilizers required for each plant. India should follow their concepts to reduce the cost of production and management of the farms more effectively and efficiently and make up for the water shortage.

Cooperative farming, apart from producing cereals and pulses, farms should include producing vegetables and fruits, horticulture [flowers and herbal plants], livestock, poultry, and fisheries. A multi-producing farm has the advantage – if one produce loses out, the others make up the loss.

Encourage the agro-industry – wine from grapes, cheese from milk, sauce from tomatoes, jams, canning of vegetables, fruit and meat products like mutton, pork, and Buffalo Meat.

Earlier, the UPA government and now the NDA government have been resorting to measures such as loan waivers which are short term measures, without paying attention to the underlying crisis they seek to mitigate. In the long run, giving loan waivers schemes are not good for the health of the banks and unfair to the people who have kept their hard-earned money in the banks that was used to give loans. The investors would lose the interest they would have earned otherwise. Further, loan waivers will only upset Bank's credit culture; this would even harm needy farmers.

In real estate, the returns are 300%; in luxury items, it is 200%; and in consumer items, it is 100%. Likewise, agricultural produce should at least give 200% returns on the total cost of production for the farmers to live a decent life. Today in the rural area, a family of husband, wife and two children require at least 25 to 30 thousand Rupees per month, provided they have a house and conveyance of their own, to live a normal life. This comes down to ₹3 to ₹3.6 lakhs per annum.

The present NDA government has formed the 'Agriculture Insurance Company of India Limited'. Under this company, the government has implemented two Crop Insurance Schemes – Pradhan Mantri Bima Yojana [PMBY] and Restructured Weather Based Crop Insurance Scheme [RWBCIS] from the year 2016 to 2018, many farmers growing kharif and rabi crops have benefited.

Prime Minister Modi, in his last Independence Day speech, appealed to the farmers to cut the use of fertilizers and pesticides, as these inputs are spoiling the health of the soil, thus affecting the overall productivity. He got the support of one of the largest pesticide producers in the world, 'Bayer'.

To maintain soil's fertility, science can help. Ultimately, we need to make sure that the farmers can look after the plant by, ideally, doing it by using little crop protection inputs, with quality and not quantity. If the plant becomes ill, it is treated well in time with the proper inputs of a required scale. Constant use of inputs will negatively impact, like an overdose of medicine to a patient. In India, there is a large quantity of older products, some toxic generic products, are used. Switching to less but higher quality products will give better yield. The use of minimum fertilizers also reduces the cost.

One of the ways forward is research in the area of synthetic, biological fixation, where we are looking at a biological approach to synthesize microbes so that they can absorb nitrogen from the air. If the research is successful, this will eliminate the use of synthetic fertilizers and also help in reducing greenhouse gas. Basically, we will have a biological solution that we can apply to the seed, which will help nature do nitrogen absorption by itself.

Other ways are to use crop protection inputs; here, we use a combination of Digital Technology and sensors that help a lot. A sensor finds the area that requires attention well before the problem spreads, and the Digital Technology helps in the application of inputs only to that area where there is a problem. This will also significantly reduce the amount of required inputs [pesticides].

With fertile land and enough output, ultimately, the results will show that we don't require that much land for Agriculture; what we need is to make sure that the land required remains sustainable. Part of the land that is freed can be used for other purposes for living, such as harnessing rainwater, Animal Husbandry, horticulture, fishery, etc.

Total small and marginal farmers are 1.7 crores, out of which 72 lakhs are indebted farmers. Out of the farmers with 1 acre or less land, 28% take loans from banks, coop banks, etc., and 72% take from money lenders. Out of the farmers with 1.5 acres, 67% take loans from banks, coop banks, etc., and 33% take from money lenders. Of the total small and marginal farmers, 47% take loans from banks, coop banks, etc., and 53% take from money lenders. Medium and big farmers [5+ acres], 93% take loans from banks, coop banks, etc., and only 7% take loans from money lenders. The main reason why farmers, especially the small and marginal, do not go to banks, coop banks, etc., is because there are too many procedures, and the bank officials take a cut. They prefer going to money leaders who sanction the loans faster, though they charge a heavy interest.

The cooperative farms should be managed under a committee, with centrally obtained input data regarding the weather, soil study, market analysis to find out, what to grow, at what time and how much to grow. Centralized and mechanized farming should be carried out, and resources like equipment, seeds and fertilizers, and farm labour are pooled. Water management, including drip irrigation, should be a top priority.

The government should continue giving subsidized seeds and fertilizers, free electricity, and in addition subsidized premium for insurance cover and tax rebate on the purchase of tractors and other mechanized equipment to encourage this concept. A team of farmers from each cooperative farm who work at the grassroots level should be sent to Israel to spend some time in their farms to study their management.

Self Help Group - The Shrimant Adivasi Bachat Gat Gavanpada, the self-help group, was set up as an attempt to promote traditional and organic farming techniques in the tribal-dominated region, which faces perennial water shortages.

To tide over agrarian distress, a self-help group with 40 tribal farmers from Peth, a remote tribal area in the Nashik district, was set up. They diversified by sowing organic brown rice, Jasmine flowers, and mangoes of almost every variety on a commercial scale.

90% of the population is tribal, exclusively growing rice, tur and ragi as a means of sustenance. They adopted a multi-prone approach of producing a kharif crop, horticulture, and fruits- a novel way to hedge their losses and make money. A composite farming concept, in which if you lose on one produce, you make it on another produce.

Apart from using the latest agrarian techniques to improve productivity, the group is also using novel marketing techniques to sell their produce.

The 40 farmers have planted 20,000 Jasmine vines in the villages of Karanjali and Hingdari in Peth Taluka, 200 km north of Mumbai. When the flowers are fully grown, they are centrally collected, and one of the group members takes them to Nashik to sell in the market, and the proceeds are equally distributed to the group members. They earn more than what they get from the traditional crop.

A Jasmine vine, once planted, stays productive for over 12 years and is in bloom for eight months a year, producing 100 to 150 gm of flowers each. A farmer gets ₹300 to ₹1,200 per kg of Jasmine based on the quality of the flower.

The farmers are using farm tourism to augment their income by holding mango festivals, where people can visit the farms and eat as many mangoes as they want, free of cost, but if they wish to take back with them, they have to purchase at a set price.

Yashwant Gawande, after retiring as a state transport bus driver, decided to set up the self-help group. He read about how Israeli farmers were able to pack in 700 to 800 mango trees per acre of land as against 40 to 50 that he planted earlier and followed their concept. He also used their technique of planting multiple crops alongside his mangoes.

Seeing the benefit of the above group, if more such groups come up and the farmers see the benefits, this can lead to full-fledged co-operative farms with multi -produce being developed. Self Help Groups can be the starting point.

Artificial Intelligence [AI] can boost Agriculture productivity – information is collected by drones or satellites and then analysed; a simple satellite image or drone photograph can correlate to millions of data points. Using algorithms and machine learning, these data points help farmers select crops and timing the application of insecticide, fertilizers, etc., aggregating on a wider scale; this data can inform policymakers to finalize procurement and warehousing requirements, etc. Over time, analysis of this data can improve India's farm-related policies, etc.

India lacks efficient Agro-exports - China is the largest producer of onions; however, Chinese onions have few takers in South Asia; the people prefer Indian onions that have the pungency which Chinese onions don't have. In India, a political party in power can lose the next election as Indian cuisine is incomplete without onions.

The Netherlands, size of the state of Kerala, accounts for 20% of the world onion trade, ahead of exports of onions by all major growers -China, Mexico, India, and the United States. India can export onions in a good year, like in 2018, but in a bad year, it cannot export as whatever is produced is consumed domestically, as happened in 2019.

The Dutch also dominate 50% of the world's cut flower/bouquet trade. They are also the world's top exporter of tomatoes, peppers/chillies, cucumbers, and pineapple, and many other agro products that they do not consume domestically in large quantity. They also export a lot of milk/milk products and beer.

A country need not be large to be a major grower or exporter; Netherlands, Belgium and Israel are raking it in high-efficiency, hothouse-driven growth.

China, India, and the US are the world's three largest food and Agriculture produce generating nations. The US is the largest exporter because of its vast area, efficient production, and smaller population [less consumption]. China exports far more than India because of improved efficiency; its total output is double that of India, but the Netherlands is the real export superpower because of its efficiency.

India grows poorly and consumes most of what it grows. If India can improve its efficiency with western expertise, it can be a major grower and exporter. India can export more spices [pepper], rice [including basmati rice], Kashmiri apples and almonds, mangoes, seafood [including tinned] and Buffalo Meat [including tinned],

The pricing of commodities depends on demand and supply. If the demand and supply are equal, then the pricing is correct, if the demand is more than the supply, the prices go up, and the effect is on inflation that will go up and affect the overall economy. Either the farmers produce more, or the government resorts to imports to make up the shortfall to meet the demand.

Likewise, if the supply is more, the prices will go down, and the farmer's profits are reduced and at times may not make up what they had invested. This is the worst situation for farmers. In this case, the farm produce should be moved to other states where the supply cannot meet the demand, or the government should buy the surplus farm produce and store them with their reserve stock and make an effort to export the surplus stock to other countries. The farmers should also go for 'E' Marketing' within the state grid, and the government should tackle the international/national grid.

Recently there was a surplus of tomatoes, and the farmers, to get a reasonable price, had to throw a great part of their produce on the roads. If a tomato processing/canning-bottling plants were available, tomato juice/puree could have been processed and canned/bottled, which would have earned the farmers more revenue, especially during the off-season.

Laying down the Minimum Support Price [MSP] by the government only helps the farmers when the government buys the farm produce. However, in the open market, the farmers normally sell their produce less than the MSP, as the middlemen dictate the price, and the farmers are forced to sell to them as there are no storage facilities. The government also dolling out money to clear the farmer's debts is a short term measure. But for a long sustained measure, depending on the 'market mechanism' is the best answer, and the government should meet the farmers halfway. In any case, a loan waiver will not help marginal farmers in the long run.

The UP government has recently waived the loans of about 94 lakh small and marginal farmers in the state. This waiver applies to commercial and cooperative banks and entails a fiscal cost of ₹36,359 crores. TN has followed by extending the waiver to all agriculturists on the orders of the Supreme Court; this applies to cooperative banks only and will cost the government ₹2000 crore to compensate cooperative banks in the state. This has opened a 'Pandora's Box'. Later, other states like Maharashtra, Punjab and Karnataka followed. This does not address the loans taken by farmers from unorganized banks, which give loans with an interest of around 42%. This can only be done if unorganized banks are forced to come into the formal Banking system; otherwise, there is no control over them.

Instead of loan waivers, relief and liquidity to farmers are better proved through an efficient crop insurance system. In this respect, the Pradhan Mantri Fasal Bima Yojana [PMFBY] and Restructured Weather Based Crop Insurance Scheme [RWBCIS] is a good start. In addition, if modern technology is pressed into service with satellite imaging, GPS devices and drones to assess farmer's damages and settle insurance claims speedily, it will help the farmers tremendously.

In September 2020, the government carried out reforms with two overdue Farm Bills. Farmers [Empowerment and Protection] agreement on Price Assurance and farm Services Bill, 2020 and the Farming Produce Trade and Commerce [Promotion and Facilitation] bill, 2020. The aim was to bring structural reforms in the agricultural-sector, by allowing free trade outside the preview of Agricultural Produce Marketing Committees [APMC].

Followed by the 'Essential ComModities [Amendment] Bill', which does away with the rural government's power to impose stock limits or impose trade restrictions like export ban, aiming at deregulating comModities such as cereals, pulses, oilseeds, edible oils, onion, and potatoes. The bill amends the Essential commodities Act, 1955. The bills also streamline contract farming with regard to Farmers [Empowerment and Protection] and Agreement on Price Assurances and Farm Services Ordinance- 2020.

The bills will allow the farmers to sell their produce outside the 'Mandi' mechanism to anybody who pays the maximum rate. The farmers can go for contract farming where the investor tells the farmer what to sow and how much, and the investor buys the produce. This way, the farmers are sure of the market.

Maharashtra Farm Organisations have welcomed the bill, whereas Punjab and Haryana have certain reservations; they feel that the farmers will not get the MSP, and the corporates will take over the farm sector. The MSP mechanism will be retained, with the government buying from the farmers at the MSP rate; only 6% of the farmers benefit from the MSP. Private players coming in will invest in the rural infrastructure that will help the farmers. The bills have a positive impact on farming, and the farmers, on the whole, will benefit.

By the Essential commodities Act, 1955, the government could control the production, supply and distribution of that commodity and impose a stock limit. The key change seeks to free agricultural markets from the limitations imposed by permits and mandis, that were originally designed for the era of scarcity. The regulation is only done under extraordinary price rise, war, famine, and natural calamity of severe natures. But now, the situation has changed, and India has become an exporter of several agricultural products. The move is expected to attract private investment in the value chain of commodities removed from the list of essentials, including investment in cold chains and storage facilities for perishable items, as most of these items were under the ambit of the Essential commodities Act, 1955.

The recent Budget has provided an income transfer of ₹6,000 per year to 12 crore small farmers [₹72,000 crores per year]. With this scheme and an increase in MSP and more allocation to MGNREGA, more money will be in the hands of the farmers, and rural consumption will increase. A pension scheme of ₹3000 per month, after the age of 60, is proposed for unorganized sector workers with a monthly income of ₹15,000.

Direct support transfer, increase in MSP [when the government buys], and MGNREGA [for unskilled labourers] will help, but as a long term measure, development of Industrial Corridors among a group of villages to create Jobs for the farming community and also give administrative support to the farmers, and encouraging the farming community to go for cooperative farming on the Israel model, by giving incentives, which will increase productivity and better management, should be the top priority. This way, 60% of the Indian population in the rural area will benefit.

The land will be required for irrigation projects and for the 'Industrial Corridors'. To get land from the farmers for a cause that will benefit the farmers' community, either change the alignment of the planned canal, even if a longer detour has to be taken where the cost will go up, that should be catered by the government, or the government should pay the market price with incentives to the owners; the market price should be the speculative price of the land after the irrigation systems/Industrial Corridors come up. It should strictly be a commercial transaction, and then, only the farmers will sell their land. In addition, as incentives, one flat [with two rooms, kitchen, and bathroom] in the industrial corridor and one/two Jobs for the members of the owner's family in the irrigation department/administrative set-up in the Industrial corridor are provided. The landowners will only sell their land when they find that they and their family members benefit, and their future is secure.

Land acquisition reforms should be carried out at the earliest. labour Reforms to protect the farm labourer's interest and also to protect the farm owner's interest should also be carried out at the earliest. The reforms will also help in the relation between the owners and the workers in the industrial sector.

Water is the main requirement, and shortage of water has been one of the main issues as 57% of the farmland depends on the rains.

Since India is a vast country and it is not practically possible to be able to provide water everywhere, a certain amount of improvement is made by channelizing the excessive water from the rivers and lakes during the monsoons by building a series of networks of canals to reach the needy areas, but it does not cover the whole water needy areas. On a war footing, the state governments of affected states should construct more canals, build more bunds/reservoirs to harness the rainwater, encourage the use of sprinklers and drip irrigation for judicious use of water, plug leakages and restore ponds and lakes that are in an unhealthy state due to human and animal waste being dropped into it, and build re-cycling of wastewater plants in all villages.

In the recent drought situation in Andhra State, trains carrying water [water trains] were used, and water was drained out into catchment areas around the drought-affected region. This could be done along the existing rail tracks only; the government should consider building a network of rail tracks with water tanks/reservoirs at reasonable distances around the likely drought-affected areas to cater for emergency situations. This will help in bringing water to the needy farmlands.

With the latest science and technology available to treat wastewater, it should not be difficult to build treatment plants in a drought-prone area. For this, a huge amount of money is required. Cutting down of non-essentials schemes will provide the huge sums required. Even the developed countries are using re-cycled water; it is not only used for Agriculture, industries, and non-drinking purposes, but the technology has advanced to make recycled water potable. Singapore provides this potable water, and it is the best drinking water.

The present government, in the last three years, has built two lakh water conservation projects under the 'Jalyukt Shivar Abhiyan' in drought regions. The scheme has yielded very good results and has helped make villages drought-free and raise the underground water levels. More projects need to come up with the utmost priority.

A strict policy on water management should be followed, especially where there is a scarcity of water, Firstly, High water-intensive crops, like sugarcane, should not be allowed to be cultivated, and instead, the farmers should go for a change in crop pattern, like cultivating horticulture, growing seasonal vegetables/fruits which are short term and market-linked that give quick returns to the farmers.

The sugarcane lobbies are strong, with the politicians controlling most of them, and they are unwilling to reconsider going for alternative cultivation. In drought-prone regions in Marathwada that get an average of 600 mm of rainfall, cultivation of sugarcane is forbidden, but the farmers cultivate sugarcane. Higher yield per hectare with minimum use of water should be the new Agriculture model.

Harnessing the rainwater by building bunds around low-line areas in all villages, growing trees around the drought-affected areas to improve the vegetation that will attract the water-bound clouds are some measures that the local villagers can do by forming task forces and executing under the guidance of the 'Zilla Prashad's and supervision of the village 'Sarpanch'. A film on the way Shri Anna Hazare achieved bringing water to the farmers of his village, 'Siddl Rayelgaon [Maharashtra], should be circulated to all the 'Zilla Prashad's' and 'Sarpanch's to be shown to all villagers. If the villagers of Siddi Rayelgaon can do it, why can't other villages?

In advanced countries, like the USA, special aircraft carrying water are used to douse out a wild forest fire; the same technique can also be used to drop water in drought-affected areas.

Aircraft can also be used to spray chemicals that draw water clouds from areas where there is likely to be heavy rains to areas where there is likely to be less or no rain.

Way back in May 2016, the Indian Meteorological Department had predicted that the country must be prepared to face more frequent, intense droughts over the next three decades. In an agrarian economy that depends on the monsoons, inadequate rainfall depletes the ground water and affects the storage of water in dams. To get over the shortage of water, India should encourage sustained farming and the use of integrated technology with conservation efforts.

India has to give importance to the awareness of the effects of Climate Change. By burning fossil fuel, we emit dangerous greenhouse gases that are causing global warming, leading to extreme climate events like floods and droughts. Even Cows emit a lot of gases that cause global warming. The year 2016 has been recorded as the hottest year since 1901. The town of Phalodi in Rajasthan state has recorded a temperature of 51 Celsius, the highest ever recorded in the country.

As global temperatures increases, Earth's water cycle intensifies even more, causing extreme drought conditions. The same extra heat that evaporates water from the oceans pulls moisture even more quickly from the soil. More water also evaporates more quickly from the soil, making drought deeper and longer. Forest fire also adds to drought.

The Indian Central Water Commission Bulletin of April 2016 reported that the water storage in the 91 major reservoirs in the country dipped down to 37.92 billion cubic meters, which is just 24% of the total storage capacity of these reservoirs.

In the Southern part of Australia, the people of the cities and towns have been surviving the drought from 1997 to 2010 by sound urban water planning and management. These measures included the change of washing machines, toilets, cooling towers, shower heads, water taps and streamlining the industrial processes to do more with less water. Australia invested large sums of money in water conservation and efficiency. By the time the drought ended in 2010, one in three Melbourne households had a rainwater tank. A number of retention ponds were built to contribute to the urban water supply. Highly treated sewage water was used to irrigate farm fields. They also reduced the water use to 41 gallons [155 litres per person.]

Drought-tolerant varieties of crops developed by the Indian Council for Agricultural Research [ICAR] and the State Agricultural Universities should be grown in large quantity in the rainfall regions. They range from wheat, rice, maize, sorghum and even cotton in different climatic conditions?

Just digging more and deeper bore wells is not the answer. Technological intervention to examine integrated groundwater –rainfall interactions will be useful to identify critical locations in the rain-fed regions for additional support through groundwater without affecting the resource adversely. The Internet of Things [IOT] laboratory at the *Interdisciplinary centre for water Research, Bangalore, is currently developing and deploying such sensors. They are trying to make them affordable to the farming community.*

Agriculture growth can be achieved by putting dairy in the lead role. UP- as per the labour Bureau report-2015-16, Agriculture employs the largest workforce of 47%, and the growth rate is 2.5% per annum during 2000-01 to 2014-15. UP is located in the Gangetic plains that have the most fertile soils and the best water conditions in the country. Almost 78% of the state cropped area is irrigated against the figure of 47% for the country. The states Agriculture growth has the potential to grow at 5% per annum. This can be achieved by putting the Cow [dairy] in the lead role; this will assure income to farmers and provide employment to 70% of the female workforce; this will also cut down rural poverty.

UP's dairy sector requires more milk processing units. With Amul and private sector dairies and funds from NABARD, many dairy medium-sized processing plants can be set up to process 30% of UP's milk production in the next 5 years. Current levels of processing through the organized sector are less than 12%. UP produces 17% [over 25 million tonnes annually], but it is lagging behind in processing. As a result, the farmers don't get a good price for milk, whereas Gujarat processes half the milk produced by the organized sector.

Wheat and rice- UP accounts for 30% of wheat and 13% of rice, but marketing is poor; a robust procurement network system is essential; farmers are selling 10 to 20% below the MRP.

Sugarcane- pricing needs to be rationalized. Sugarcane prices should be linked to sugar prices; the molasses market should be freed, the nexus between the liquor barons and politicians should be broken to get the best price for sugarcane farmers.

UP also have abundant vegetables and fruit, especially potatoes and mangos, solar-powered cold storages for potatoes and harnessing solar power in fields, and solar-powered irrigation pumps can be sustainable solution to augment farmer's income. Innovative farming techniques, such as high-density mango orchards [350 trees per hectare] and even ultra-high-density orchards [1,675 trees per hectare], can increase the yield and incomes of farmers.

Food processing plants- very little in India. Should take a leap forward, quality and latest technology processing are necessary for the export of the surpluses.

60% of house construction is in rural areas. Landless manual labour moving out of Agriculture can be easily deployed in construction.

2/3rd of all salaried Jobs are in rural areas. The Jat's of Haryana, the Patel's in Gujarat and Maratha's in Maharashtra want Jobs with the government or government-owned organizations.

Create non-agricultural Jobs. At present, 3.5% of rural households currently have private salaried Jobs, as per the Socio-Economic Caste Census. India can be a competitive agricultural exporter with its year long sunshine, fertile land, good rainfall, and cheap labour. There is significant growth potential.

Jobs can be created by- Food processing, the production of consumer appliances, labour-intensive exports, like, leather goods [middle class dropouts can be trained in three months]. India's total exports are less than the procurement by a large US retailer.

In the past, industrial revolutions have been built on cheap labour exiting Agriculture. A wiser approach would be to provide the enabling environment – good law and order, roads, electricity, telephones [and data], cheap but marked-priced credit, fair markets, and easy government interfaces, and wait for the entrepreneurial instincts of our people to do the rest.

Fertilizers

Direct Benefit Transfer [DBT] - a subsidy to be paid to the companies only after the purchase of fertilizers by the farmers. Installation of point-of-sale [POS] machines in all the two lakh odd fertiliser retail outlets in the country connected to a central server would capture every sale transaction along with details of the buyer [who is buying and how much]. This will eliminate big farmers who are not entitled and unscrupulous plywood makers who use urea for cheap binding material and avoid pilferage by hoarders who sell urea at a greater price.

Data generating and identification of deserving beneficiaries is the first step, but it should be followed by the next logical stage of the subsidy getting credited directly to the bank accounts of the beneficiaries identified.

There has to be a control on the price of fertilizers; otherwise, the industries can price the fertilizers at will. Though the subsidy is transferred to the farmers, if the price is not controlled, they will have to buy less quantity with the subsidy they receive.

Fertilizer price has two components, one is the retail price, which is fixed, and the other is the subsidy, which is variable. Irrespective of the international urea price fluctuating, the farmers get to buy the urea bag at a fixed cost of ₹284. With the new Direct Benefit Transfer [DBT] regime, which would be reversed. The price of a urea bag will become variable, while the subsidy component will be constant. In 2008, when the international urea price reached the $500 per ton mark, in India, the urea retail price was ₹239 per bag. At present, the international prices are half, but if it goes to the 2008 level, the farmers will have to shell out ₹1200 per bag.

To get the DBT benefits, the farmers will have to register with land records that are very difficult to procure; to help the farmers to procure their land records, the procedure for this purpose should be streamlined. Worst are the tenant farmers whose land is in the name of the owners; they should be asked to produce the owners land records together with the tenancy agreement papers/ rent payment receipts. Further, the farmers have to pay the full price initially and be reimbursed subsequently; this means that the capital expenditure and credit requirement for the farmer will increase. It is the credit part that is the main cause of farmer's suicide.

To avoid farmer's suicides, firstly, credit should be given by organized banks at reasonable interest, and the gap between the initial payment and the subsequent payment of subsidy should be reduced to the minimum. Going for cooperative farming will help with the farmers keeping an amount in the central kitty for taking credit for this purpose.

Depending on the soil and crop selection, like wheat, rice, pulses, potatoes, etc., the nutrients requirement is different, so is the quantity required varying. So, the subsidy will vary accordingly. This aspect should be kept in mind.

Organic Farming should be encouraged to bring down the cost of fertilizers and insecticides. Apart from keeping the soil fertile, organic food is good for health.

Beef

The banning of Cow Beef, including bulls, has brought a great economic loss to the people in this business and job losses to a number of labourers connected with this business. This situation can turn round if they turn into a massive Buffalo Meat business, including processing and canning of Buffalo Meat for exports. This change round will take place if buffalo breeding farms are established on a large scale.

The ban has affected the tannery business as leather is not readily available; the leather goods export is hit badly. The alternative will be to go for more synthetic leather goods; the government should give substantial incentives for the manufacturing of synthetic leather for both the domestic market and exports.

Gaushalas or Pinjrapoles [Cattlc Shelters]

Gujarat State – during the year 2015-16, a total of 936, out of which 371 were government aided and maintained with 2,47,220 animals, out of which 99.84 lakh were cattle, the State spent a huge amount of money; this amount could have been used for education and healthcare.

Maintaining Cows above their useful years will require more fodder; they will be forced to divert land to fodder production at the expense of producing other agricultural commodities.

Maintaining a large number of Cows and bulls without any useful needs is a disaster for Climate Change as they give out gases that increase the overall temperature.

There are social issues, economic losses, job losses and huge economic pressure on state governments to maintain old Cows and bulls. Social issues can be resolved through dialogue, economic and job losses can be balanced by going for alternative openings, but the huge economic pressure on maintaining old Cows and bulls at the expense of eradicating poverty needs to be considered in seriousness. One view is that when the Cows and the bulls become non-useful, they may be allowed to be slaughtered and cremated with proper Hindu rituals. After the skin is removed, that will be useful to the tanneries. This may be accepted by the majority of the Hindu community. The Muslims, the Christian and 20 to 30% of the Hindus may still like to go for the Beef part; this may be allowed after the Hindu rituals are performed.

Animal Husbandry

Buffalo Meat

When Cows/buffalos are slaughtered, the flesh part of the Cows is known as the Beef, and that of the buffalos is known as meat. Since Hindus consider the Cow to be the 'Gau Mata' [Cow Mother] and pray to the Cow, in fact, in most of the temples of worship, an idol of the 'Gau Mata' is installed at the entrance. Hindus by and large pray to anything that helps them in their livelihood; when a child is born, he is given his/her mother's milk for six months and then switched on to Cow's milk, so the Cow is considered as the child's mother; thus, the Cow is called 'Gau Mata' and has a religious symbol.

Most of the states have banned the eating of Beef, but eating Buffalo Meat is allowed. As a result, the domestic demand for Buffalo Meat has increased; as per the latest data, India, and Brazil each account for nearly 20% of the world's total Beef exports, Australia in the third spot with 15%. India exports mostly Buffalo Meat. India does not officially export Cow Beef; the 20% includes a small part of Cow Beef that is officially banned in India. The bulk of Indian Buffalo Meat is exported to Vietnam, Malaysia, Egypt, Saudi Arabia and Iraq, rest to Algeria, Angola, and Russia. China does not officially import Buffalo Meat directly from India but gets Indian Buffalo Meat through Vietnam. The Indian Buffalo Meat exported is primarily used in the processed and canned food industry. If this industry is promoted in India, the Indian farmers can thrive.

Milk

In the 2013-14 census, out of total production of 132.64 million tons of milk [excluding goat milk], 70.44 million tons or 53% was accounted from buffaloes. The balance of 62.19 million tons of milk or 47% was from Cows; this included 33.89 million tons of milk from crossbreeds' containing the genetic material of 'western breeds like Holstein Friesian, Jersey and Brown Swiss. The indigenous cattle, the real Gau Mata, contributed only 29.31 million tons or just over 1/5th of India's milk products.

Buffalo milk is now preferred as the milk has 7% fat content and 8% solids non-fat contents and gives a better price than Cow's milk. Farmers prefer breeding buffaloes, and the population of buffaloes is increasing at 8.5% compared to Cows that are at 3.5%.

Cows give optimum milk for 7 to 8 years and live for another 5 to 6 years giving less milk but uneconomical to maintain. After the production age [7 to 8 years], the farmers sell to butchers, traders who resell them to slaughterhouses.

Out of 20 Cows, they maintain an optimum balance by replacing 5 to 6 old Cows with new stock every year, and maintain the cows already in milk, those that are pregnant/dry, calves or young heifers which are going to produce in future.

The states under BJP governments - Maharashtra, Gujarat, Uttar Pradesh, Haryana and Karnataka and the states under Congress -Madhya Pradesh, Rajasthan, Chhattisgarh, contribute a total of 56% of the milk.

Summary

The Agriculture sector can improve and subsequently become lucrative if India encourages co-operative farms on the Israel model and farms go for composite farming, producing kharif and rabi crops, vegetables, fruit, horticulture, and Animal Husbandry, and as well as fisheries; if there is a loss in one, the others make up. The co-operative farms go for organic farming to lower the cost of fertilizers and insecticides and maintain soil conservation and further provide organic food for better health.

The government should develop Industrial Corridors to provide Jobs, education, including skill development and healthcare to the farmer community, administrative support to the farmers, in terms of organized banks, markets for their produce, and storage facilities, including cold storage, and institutions to promote growing vegetables, horticulture, Animal Husbandry and fisheries.

Each state should support one or two co-operate farms as examples, and when the farmers see the benefits, everyone will chip in. Similarly, each state should develop one or two Industrial corridors and when the rural people see the benefits, they will offer their land for more Industrial Corridors to be developed.

8.2   Manufacturing Sector

The main problem in India is generating Jobs, and with the Indian population expanding at a high rate, a higher number of Jobs are required. It is never-ending. It is the manufacturing sector that brings more Jobs, and this sector in India is the weakest. The unemployment rate is 6.1% based on the inputs from the organized sector. The Jobs in the unorganized sector should be worked out to get the real picture of unemployment to plan for the future.

The population has to be controlled to a family of two/three children. Illegal migration has to be checked. The quota for education and Jobs need a relook, and in any case, the creamy layer of any backward community should be barred.

Growth brings Jobs and raises the per capita income. The present growth rate is hovering around 7%, and the per capita income is around ₹12,000 P.A, not a happy situation. The growth rate should be 10-12%, and the per capita income should be at least sustainable. Nations with high per capita income enjoy the highest rank on the indices of human development and happiness. At present, India's ranking is 222, very low.

Manufacturing growth has sunk to just 0.6%. Only major structural reforms can tackle the fundamental flaws slowing down long-term growth. The main reason why manufacturing is not picking up is that it is very costly, due to the time taken to get the formal government sanctions, due to a number of sanctioning authorities and the corruption at every level, difficulty in getting land which is the starting point in establishing any industry, and due to lack of proper land laws, long procedures to get a bank loan, non-availability of sufficient skilled labour force and labour problems due to lack of labour laws.

India is a large country, and there is tremendous scope for domestic consumption of goods. With a huge population settled/working abroad and with the present government reaching out to foreign countries on trade, the demand for Indian goods will grow, provided the quality is better and cheaper than the Chinese goods that have flooded the international market, including India.

Why is the market for Chinese goods striving - they are cheaper as they follow a single-window system to get all the necessary registration/clearance for land acquisition, building construction, electricity/water connections, municipal support; there is no corruption. Bank loans and a disciplined labour force are available. The time to start an enterprise is short, and the overheads are less. Further, the Chinese goods come into India clandestinely, through Indo-Nepal and Indo Myanmar borders, without paying any octroi tax.

The only way to stop Chinese goods from coming into India and competing with them in the international market is by producing goods that are competitive and cheaper than their goods. To achieve this, a single-window system to get government sanctions/clearances, the government creating Industrial Corridors/areas by buying land at market price and leasing out at a reasonable price, asking banks to make it easier for entrepreneurs to take loans, passing the land and labour laws and the 'Lok Pal' bill to curb corruption. The system for 'online' sanctions/clearances should be created to avoid corruption by middlemen/government staff.

China had its town and village enterprises, and most of the rural industrialization came via manufacturing.

The greatest thing that happened in India is the golden quadrilateral. Now we should go for mass, rapid transport. With transport, more people from the village will commute to the city and have access to opportunities in both places.

Job for Dropouts

At the bottom of the pyramid are at least 60% of the children who are dropouts of class 5, 8 and 10; we have to find suitable Jobs for them. With the development of skills, they can become bedside attendants, sewing machine operators, security guards, drivers, cooks, and waiters. India will have the highest number of old people in the world very soon since communicable diseases are not as much as they were in the 80s or 90s. These old people will require care, and that will become a huge demand area.

What India needs is people who can pick up a skill and start a business in a village or taluka in one and half years and employ people.

The government should promote good quality worker housing colonies like Singapore.

Micro, Small, Medium, Enterprises [MSMEs] need to understand that they cannot build a sustainable business by paying workers crude wages, not having them on the payroll, paying them in cash as there is a very real possibility of pushback from them; they should pay the minimum wages.

Job creation depends on how the MSMEs flourish, and as years go by, these enterprises will grow to become large industries and employ more people.

The service sector is becoming really big in India, across cities, towns, and villages.

For manufacturing to pick up, three reforms are necessary – Land, labour, and administration. Every enterprise starts from the availability of land, without which nothing can move forward. labour needs protection from the owners, and the owners also need protection from labour. There has to be mutual benefit and working understanding, without which the required productivity will not be achieved. The administration has to be sound and efficient, without which a lot of bottle necks will be created that will affect productivity.

The Rajasthan government, under the then Chief Minister Vasundhara Raje, in 2014-15, amended four labour laws that spurred the states MSME sector and brought industrial peace in the state. For the last 4-5 years, there has been no labour unrest in Rajasthan. If the same took place in other states, there would be no labour unrest in the whole country.

The amended four labour laws were – [1] The Industrial Disputes Act of 1947; Employers now could entrench up to 300 employees without permission from the government, this was capped at 100 employees earlier; a worker should raise an objection regarding discharge, dismissal, retrenchment, or termination within three years while there was no time limit earlier; the trade union can be formed only if it gets 30% of the total workers as members, up from 15% earlier.

[2] The Contract labour [Regulations and Abolition] Act of 1970; was made applicable only to companies that employed more than 50 workers, up from 20 workers earlier.

[3] The Factory Act of 1948; complaints against the employer about violation of the Factories Act do not receive cognizance by a court without prior written permission from the state government.

[4] The Apprentice act of 1961; the stipend for apprentices was 'no less than the minimum wage'.

The Economic Survey of India praised the Rajasthan government, holding it up as a role model for the rest of the country. Comparing the Compound Annual Growth Rates [CAGR] two years before and two years after the law was passed, the survey noted, "It can be clearly seen that for all the variables, CAGR post labour reforms in Rajasthan has increased significantly vis-a-vis the rest of India." As a result, the number of firms with 100 employees or more have increased at a significantly higher rate [from 3.65% to 9.33%] in Rajasthan than in the rest of India [4.56% to 5.52%].

If the other states had carried out the amendments, the number of firms with 100 employees and above in their states would have increased, and more Jobs would have been generated.

The MSMEs are the backbone of manufacturing where the maximum Jobs will be made available, and the state governments should give all support to it. Reforms in the land, labour and administration should be carried out at the earliest. Efforts should be made to transfer the surplus Agriculture labour to the industrial sector.

On September 23, 2020, the central government went ahead with passing amendments to the labour Reforms in three labour code bills, which will provide social security for workers in organised and non-organised sectors as well as remove hurdles for winding up companies. The reforms will improve industrial relations, occupational safety, and social security; the welfare of the workers in the country are looked after while also providing a transparent system to suit the changed business environment. The reforms will provide "universal social security" to the workers by expanding the ambit of the Employees Provident Fund Organisation and Employees State Corporation of India; there will be a "social security fund" to cover 40 crore workers in the unorganised sector. The new labour code universalises minimum wages and timely payment of wages. Overall, the reforms will spur economic growth.

The reforms will also allow firms with up to 300 workers to fire workers without government permission. This will motivate investors to set up large factories in the country, and by setting up more factories, more employment opportunities will be generated.

8.3   Banking Sector

Banks

Indira Gandhi's government issued an ordinance on July 19, 1969, to nationalize 14 banks that had deposits of over ₹50 crores, ignoring the views of the Finance Minister, Morarji Desai and the industry. Since banks are linked to economic development, her government wanted the banks to extend facilities to backward areas, Agriculture, small-scale industries and, in addition, Banking operations to cover a larger social purpose.

The fundamental obligation of banks is to the depositors, a commercial enterprise driven by a large social purpose and political considerations is completely off the mark. The political pay-offs are evident when the government retains control over these lenders, like repeated instances of waiver of farm debts.

Since the government is the major shareholder, it has to constantly find resources to capitalize and strengthen banks, given that the returns on such investment are now negative. As a result, to limit the fiscal deficit, the government is being forced to push the Indian Central Bank to transfer a good part of its reserves.

Vajpayee led government did make an attempt to change from the past, and the then Finance Minister, Yashwant Sinha, was to introduce a bill in Parliament seeking to lower the government's equity in banks to 33%, this would enable banks to raise fresh capital without any dilution of management control. The proposal was jettisoned by the opposition, and later, the UPA government that succeeded it, through the law, reinforced sovereign control over state-owned banks.

Since the nationalizing of banks, 50 years have passed, but Banking has been seen as an enterprise driven by social purpose and political considerations, not depositor's interests. This needs to change.

The government has to keep in mind the fundamental issue of governance, the incentive structure for bankers, dual control, and the separation of ownership by distancing the government from the management of the banks.

To change, the government should divest shareholding in most banks and retain control on the State Bank of India, India's largest bank.

Reforms and Structural changes should be taken to help the bankers to make the credit floating smoothly again, with minimum risks to taxpayers and to the broader economy. Nationalizing of Banks require a new look.

Public Sector Banks, in general, have let down the economy of the country in a big way by writing off 'Bad Loans' to the tune of crores and crores. The investors have lost confidence in the Indian Banking system; this is bad for any economy. Public Sector Banks have been giving loans to individuals, companies and agencies on their brand names or influence from politicians. Banks were giving loans/re-constructing the current loans to individuals/companies/agencies for 'Non Performing Assets' to enable banks not to go in the red/Bankruptcy reforms. There were no checks and balances at the CEO's level or at the 'Board level'. A number of CEO's and Board members have been placed in the banks with political influence. There was a nexus between the politicians, bank officials/board members and the corporate; otherwise, how is it that the checks and balances laid out in the Banking system were not strictly followed.

With no credit available in the market, the MSMEs suffered the maximum. To tide over the financial crunch in the public sector banks, the government is topping the banks by Rs 70,000 crores in the next five years for bank capitalization to absorb the past losses and recreate lending ability. This will enable the banks to give credit to 'Micro, Small,

Medium, Enterprises' [MSMEs] that can promote manufacturing, thus, provide more Jobs. This is a short term reprieve to the banks.

For years, the worst banks had been put under 'Prompt Correction Action' [PCA] by the RBI, meaning they could collect deposits but do very little commercial lending; however, their lending record was so bad that they were high in non-performance loans.

To make the PSBs more economically sustainable and better managed, the government has merged a number of weaker banks with the better managed stronger banks; the total number of Public Sector Banks [PSBs] is now down to 12 from 27 two years ago. The merger will improve the management of weaker banks and make the group more economically sustainable.

For long term sustainability, bold structural changes are required to prevent PSBs from sliding downhill again. A bold structural change would be to reduce the number of PSBs to the minimum; say to three/four banks, including SBI, and privatize the other banks, starting with the corrupt banks that caused a huge loss to the investors and the banks with the maximum NPAs that were written off, also creating a huge loss to the investors.

In the merging of weak banks with stronger banks, the danger is that the weaker ones may sink the strong ones. Earlier, the merger of Punjab National Bank with the troubled New Bank in 1993 created problems and failed to bring in significant synergies.

Earlier this year, Bank of Baroda, a strong bank, was merged with two weak banks, Vijaya Bank and Dena Bank, but post-merger performance showed little improvement, and their share fell to ₹92 from ₹150.

The former RBI Governor, in his note to the Parliaments Estimates Committee, had pointed out that a large number of Bad Loans originated during the period of 2006-08 when growth was strong, most of the Infra-structure projects, like power projects, were completed in time and within the Budget. Bank lending to industry, excluding individuals, Agriculture, and Food Corporation of India, jumped 30%

to 35% year on year during this period. Normally, during such times that the banks make a mistake by not doing their own due diligence and when growth does not move as expected, Bad Loans are created.

The global crisis with the collapse of Lehmann Brothers, the jolt felt by the Indian economy, the fiscal policy mistakes that followed poor coordination among regulators and the wrong lessons learnt, dogged India.

The rise in GDP growth suddenly stopped under UPA-1 [2004-2009]; this was due to UPA-1 expanding the social expenditure but did little to sustain the high growth, so it is essential to grow revenue at a fast pace. UPA-2 [2009-2014] did a lot of damage to the economy. This was due to the denial of clearance to major projects on environment or other grounds. Rampart corruption at the political level involved a small part of the bureaucrats, like the 2G, Coal and CWG scams. Unfortunately, some bureaucrats with a good reputation for unimpeachable integrity were caught in the crossfire, hence, froze the top bureaucrats from taking any decisions, and there was complete policy paralysis. So deep was the freeze that a definite change under the present NDA Government has still not fully restored the confidence of the bureaucrats.

Further, the legislation on retrospective capital taxation was counterproductive; it drove the potential investors away from India. The difficulty in land acquisition greatly undermined domestic and foreign investor confidence.

There were no checks and balances on public banks; they lent vast sums of money to fund poorly conceived projects, and to add to this, they further permitted 'reconstructing' of poorly performing loans, not once but several times. Reconstructing Bad Loans on the brand of an individual or company, hoping to recover within a reasonable time and space is ok but what do you do when the returns are not forthcoming over a long period beyond the red-lines. The answer is to stop further reconstruction and demand for compensation by asking for their assets through the courts if necessary, so that the bank does not lose out and the money of the investors is protected. Mallya's 'Kingfisher Airlines' and Nirav Modi's and Choksi's 'Diamond Jewellery' set up have faulted very badly, and both are facing court cases. Recovery is not possible, as both have left the country and to get them back to India to face prosecution is a huge task.

The Government needs to bring 'Banking Reforms and Structural Changes' to regulate, to bring in efficiency, creditability, transparency and to check corruption/ make the regulatory systems more effective to monitor the Banking loan system at crucial stages/reduce the number of public sector banks to the bare minimum/ take firm action on recovery of Bad Loans, to win over investor's confidence, without investment the banks will cease to exist.

The Banking regulator has put its foot down against the considered opinion of the board of private banks; it may be indicated that things are not going in the right direction. One of the key responsibilities of the board is to oversee the senior management, which is not being done. The boards of the private banks are acting as the handmaidens of the management, rather than acting as the custodians of the various stakeholders. The Bank boards should be independent of the bank management, and overseeing the quality of financial reporting remains an important responsibility of the board. Board overseeing is needed on the quality of the loan asset portfolio, as under-reporting of NPAs and other stress assets influences the integrity of financial reporting. On the contrary, in the recent case, where the board of ICICI issued a statement of unconditional support for its former CEO, despite evidence seeming to paint her in an unflattering light.

Lending intended to keep the original loan current and hope that time and growth will set the project back on track. The more time the growth takes to grow, the more the interest, and if the project does not take off, then the promoters land up as debtors, and the banks are unable to collect the debts. In this case, the banks should attach the promoter's assets and make good the losses, but the banks take an easier path of writing off the bad loan, causing loss to the bank.

In the fiscal year of 2018-19, bad debt recovery was expected to rise nearly 2.5 times to ₹1.8 lakh crore, but NPAs were on the decline because recoveries have picked up, not just due to resolution in the National Company Law Tribunal but also because debtors fear that they are likely to lose the control of their companies if they cross the red line. Many loan defaulters were paying up as they feared being rendered ineligible to run or bid for their company if banks initiated insolvency proceedings in the NCLT.

RBI's asset quality reviews had made significant concerns about the quality of loan portfolios and their reporting. Correct financial reporting of a company is the responsibility of the Bank CEO, who has the best information on the company, bank auditors, bank audit committee, the bank board oversee the reporting and the RBI supervisor monitors that the procedures are strictly followed.

In the wake of the global financial crisis, on the government asking, in October 2008, the RBI issued a statement that the Banking system was 'safe and sound'. After the discloser of the PMCB fraud, on October 04, 2019, the RBI again reiterated the same; quite a few eyebrows were raised.

The PMC scam went undetected for 11 years, despite the RBI requiring all regulated entities, including cooperative banks, to submit details of all transactions and accounts to it since February 2016. It is a concern to see how banks and NBFC's could hide the full extent of their Bad Loans. The scam points to the involvement of the bank's top brass, who hid the real extent of Bad Loans by floating fictitious accounts belonging to dead account holders to hide the loans awarded to the bank's single largest borrower, the real-estate firm-HDIL. RBI allows not more than 15% loan to a single lender; in the case of HDIL, the bank had given 74%. The former PMC chairman, S Waryam Singh, had cross-links across both the bank and HDIL and had held a 1.19% stake till 2017. The fraud was between the top management of the bank and the borrower; there was forgery, falsification of records, under-reporting. Unfortunately, the RBI took notice of the fraud when it came to light. Though, a forensic audit could have detected the scam. The depositors are the biggest losers.

The wrongdoings at the PMC Bank suggest laxity in RBI's regulatory oversight. The RBI is now working out revamping its regulatory and supervisory structure and has proposed to create a mechanism for sharing to detect fraud-related information.

Raghuram G Rajan, the former RBL Governor, had sent a list of high profile cases to the PMO urging that the government bring at least one or two to book. These high profile promoters have tremendous political influence, and one can conclude that necessary or sufficient action was not taken. Till now, not a single defaulter has been brought to book; the whole system has been ineffective in default management. The government needs to explain why these defaulters are still free.

Ambitious bankers slow down the government's decision-making process, and slow to moderate economic growth contributed to the mounting of Bad Loans. Alleged unfair allocation of coal and fear of investigations slowed down the decision making both in the UPA and subsequent NDA governments.

Until the Bankruptcy Code was enacted, bankers had little ability to threaten promoters, even incompetent or unscrupulous ones. Now, the promoters are frightened that they may lose their firms.

In 1991, the committee headed by M. Narasimha, former RBI Governor, first made out a case for pruning a number of government or state-owned banks by restructuring of Indian banks, with 3 to 4 large banks including SBI that could be positioned as global banks, besides 8 to 10 with national footprint or presence, rather than having over two dozen state-owned banks.

In July 1969, the government nationalized 14 banks that had a deposit of ₹40 crores. At that time, the political situation in India demanded that Banking facilities should be extended in an increased measure to backward areas, to Agriculture, to small scale industry, and Banking operations should be involved in social requirements. This was the beginning when the social control of the banks kicked in.

The government controlling a large number of PSBs, in the initial stage, did pay off politically. The Banking facilities reached the backward areas, especially the rural areas, which helped to reduce regional disparity and boosted economic growth. At the end of 2018, state-owned banks alone had built a network of branches/franchises of over 90,000 [including 29,000 in rural areas] from 8262 bank branches in 1969 and over 1.45 lakh ATMs. As compared to 28,805 branches by private banks.

But in the long run, the politicians started telling the management to give loans to their supporters who were not entitled. This is where the whole problem of NPAs and writing-off and waiving off loans to farmers started and reached a point when the PSBs had no money to give credit, thus affecting the ecosystem.

The fundamental obligation of the bank is to the depositors. The government should have only nationalized few banks and with SBI's catered for the social needs and allowed the maximum private banks to flourish.

Now, with competition, rapid technological changes and innovation are transforming the way banks operate, and in addition, the government is struggling to cope with competing demands such as funding infrastructure projects, social sector programmers and delivering public goods. As a result, private banks have taken away a great share that would have come to the PSBs, if most of them were privatized.

In December 2018, the former RBI governor, Urjit Patel, blamed his predecessors at RBI for not taking away the 'punch-bowl' from the 'credit binge party'. He has also accused various governments of using PSBs to pump the economy and shunning reforms. He also highlighted how Bad Loans figures in India are among the highest in major economies, and much-needed reforms still evade PSBs, which account for most of the mess. Further, there was dual regulation of PSBs by the RBI and the government'; RBI did not have full power over the PSBs.

A time has come when the government should carry out a major structural change and privatize most PSBs, keeping 3 to 4 PSBs, including SBI. Even in these few PSBs, the government should not be the dominant shareholder; 33% is adequate, except for SBI, which is strictly a government-run bank. The aim should be to achieve more credit floating and protecting the depositor's money; this can only be done without political interference.

After nearly 27 years, the government has taken a bold step of proposing the amalgamation of three public sector banks; Bank of Baroda, Vijaya Bank and Dena Bank; the respective bank boards will now consider and approve the proposal and prepare the scheme of amalgamation to create a large bank, worth ₹14.82 lakh crore, with over 9,600 branches across the country; this will be the third biggest bank in India. This will help Dena Bank, the weakest of the three and currently under the Reserve Bank of India's Prompt Corrective Action [PCA] framework and has been barred from extending fresh loans. The government felt that instead of amalgamating three weak banks, it is financially viable operationally to amalgamate one weak bank with two strong banks. Apart from IDBI, which LIC is in the process of taking over and Dena Bank, there are nine more banks currently under the RBI's PCA framework; they are – Bank of India, UCO Bank, Central Bank of India, Indian Overseas Bank, Oriental Bank of India, Bank of Maharashtra, Union Bank of India, Corporation Bank and Allahabad Bank. Amalgamation helps in pulling in the management and having one CEO, pulling in the Human Resources and technology, regional outreach, more market reach, the scope for expansion of more branches across the country and more products to the customers.

India needs efficient, competitive banks that do not burden the exchequer and support the industry when the economy is on the upswing.

BJP, Congress, Sena and NCP leaders, who were the heads of cooperative banks, swapped most of the old currency for the new notes during the demonetization.

The Indian Banking system went into a spiral with too many bad debts due to Public Sector Bank's mismanagement. There were interferences from individual politicians to give loans to a particular firm/individual, even without collateral support. With a large number of Bad Loans, there was no credit flow; this affected the MSMEs. The government had to bail out these banks, which was a sorry state.

For a country to have an efficient credit system, the Banking system should function independently under the board of directors who would keep the investors interested in the mind and make a profit to the bank by giving loans. The guidelines given by the RBI and the government should be kept in mind, and there should be no interference from any politician.

Above everything, the PSBs should be reduced to 3 to 4 –including SBI, at the earliest for any change for the better. Using the taxpayers' money to bail out banks is not acceptable.

8.4   Infrastructure

Like Singapore and Hong Kong, India should make capital cities, as a financial, trading and business hub, with business-friendly laws and regulations. The city itself should be governed by an independent body so that they have more freedom. Crowded cities should be avoided; an area within reach of a commercial seaport should be selected and developed into this city; one city should be close to Mumbai, one city near Vishakhapatnam, and one near Kochi. These cities should be connected with world-class airlines to boost trade and tourism to provide more Jobs. Capitalist cities will require a lot of infrastructures.

For any developing country, especially an inspiring country like India, the government should invest a lot of money in building the infrastructure. Apart from developing the infrastructure, the adequate investment will help in high growth and provide more Jobs.

Generally, it is said that we need three things for higher growth; these are infrastructure, infrastructure, and infrastructure. This will help both cyclical and structural factors. Late I G Patil indicated in the early 2000s that we should aim at 6% GDP growth only till we improve the infrastructure. YV Reddy also mentioned that infrastructure could be a constraint for higher growth.

A lot of improvement has taken place in all infrastructure sectors, but we are lagging behind South Asian countries and China. However, in this situation, the government has to pump up the investment by disinvesting the unproductive public enterprises, reducing non-merit subsidies, removing exemptions, increasing tax-base and shifting from revenue to capital expenditure. These are some ways of raising government expenditure without increasing the fiscal deficit targets.

The government is encouraging public sector enterprises [PSEs] to invest more and is trying to clear the pending bills for the corporate sector and MSMEs so that they have more money to invest. The government is also encouraging Public and Private Participation [PPP]. The private sector role is equally important.

The government has set aside Rs 100 crores for infrastructure projects in the next five years. This will help in the development of roads, railway, airports, and seaports, thus, bring in more Jobs. These projects will increase the consumption of cement and steel.

The government has also set aside ₹50 crores for railway infrastructure over a period of 12 years and has proposed to use the Public and Private Partnership to unleash faster development and completion of tracks, rolling stock manufacturing and delivery of passenger freight services.

Apart from Investments, there is an urgent need to carry out structural reforms in land acquisition. Spending on infrastructure will have multiplier effects on the overall economy and help demand and Jobs. During 2004-05 and 2011-12, the construction sector was an important source of job creation. This sector has to be revived in order to create higher growth and more employment.

Water for Agriculture and drinking should be the first priority; Agriculture needs water very badly, and the health of people depends on drinking pure water. The rivers in India are polluted with industrial and domestic waste dumped into it. The rivers need to be cleaned by dredging out the waste; a wastewater filtrated plant should be installed at the end of all canals leading to the rivers. The possibility of connecting rivers that overflow during the monsoons with the rivers that have less water should be explored. A canal grid system to cover drought-prone areas should be constructed. The locals should build rain catchment areas.

Nuclear plants to provide electricity across the country should be explored. Solar energy is being encouraged by the government. Once the people realize that solar energy is clean energy and saves a lot of money, they will automatically get involved.

Rural roads and highways are being constructed, and the present government has done a lot. However, public transport needs to be looked into.

Industrial Corridors should be developed where Micro, Small, Medium, Enterprises can come up to provide Jobs for the families of farmers and farm labourers; where affordable accommodation for workers and their family can come up, where educational institutions and hospitals can come up, internal roads and civic facilities can come up, and a market for farm produce, storage facilities, including cold storage can come up.

Railways have to improve a lot. Main civilian seaports, Mumbai, Chennai, Kolkata and Vishakhapatnam, and smaller civilian seaports like Cochin, Mormugao [Goa] and Kandla were built during the British raj. After gaining independence, the government has expanded these seaports and built more facilities, but it was done haphazardly. The government has built a civilian seaport – Nava Sheva, on the mainland, opposite Mumbai seaport, for commercial vessels. The navy has their part of the seaport adjacent to the civilian seaport for their ships and is well planned and maintained; the Navy has built a new seaport at Karwar for their western fleet.

As a social obligation, the government should build hostels for working women, houses for the poor workers and old homes throughout the country.

The present government has taken the initiative of cleaning the Ganges and making it into the river-way for transportation of passengers and goods. This same initiative should take place in other rivers.

Private and Public Sector participation in building the Infra-structure should be encouraged with private [51%] and public [49%]. The returns on the Investments are low and take a long time to make up the Investments; otherwise, the private sector will not come forward. Further, anyone investing in a scheme like this will be having other lucrative businesses; the government should consider giving incentives, like tax concessions in their other businesses.

8.5   Energy

Oil and coal are crucial for India. India is dependent on the Middle East for 95% of oil, and though India has the third-largest coal reserves in the world, it has to be dug up; we are dependent on outside for coal. Coal India Ltd. cannot cope with the demands, and the privatization has not made much of headway, initially due to scams.

In the 1970s, India nationalized coal to enable the public sector to optimize coal production. Presently, in underground mines, India's output per man shift [OMS] is 0.8 tonnes against 40 tonnes in Australia; in open cast mines, India's OMS is 16.6 tonnes in 2017-18, against 75 tonnes in Australia.

Private production was allowed but only for captive consumption. In 2018, full commercial mining was allowed, but no auctions took place.

In August 2019, FDI was raised from 25% to 100% and allowed through the automatic route.

The present government is encouraging renewable energy, like solar systems, which depends on the sun and windmills that depend on the winds to generate electricity. Nuclear energy for electricity has hit a roadblock due to local protests.

The energy sector needs more attention. India's coal secretary, Subhash Chandra Garg, has stated that India must urgently expand its coal production from 600 million tonnes a year to a billion tonnes a year to meet the minimum energy needs. A massive amount of coal is needed to generate thermal power till new electric storage technology comes in. Coal is also needed for processing iron. The coal secretary has advised auctioning massive world-sized coal blocks and not small ones as was done in the past year.

To avoid projects stalling halfway, environmental, and tribal clearances should be obtained well in advance. Railway links are essential; this aspect should also be looked into.

Gas

Once the Chabahar seaport in Iran is operational, bringing gas by sea will help India in gas energy.

India's exclusive economic zone is $2/3^{rd}$ of the landmass, and there is plenty of scope for exploration of oil, gas, seabed mineral and fish. Efforts should be made in collaboration with foreign firms, as they have the latest technology and the know-how.

Ministry of Home Affairs, Earth Science, Petroleum, and many more have to deal with energy, and there has to be coordination between all these agencies. At present, they are all working in isolation, and as a result, the claim for extended continental shelves haven't been claimed.

8.6   Human Resources

India is producing a number of graduates not up to the mark from average universities/institutions who are just unemployable. India needs a totally new education system that brings out academic excellence, with world-class institutions and world-class research to fit into the Jobs in future. The quality of education has to start at the school level [Government and private]; the government municipal schools need more attention. The politicians focusing on more quotas in the educational institutions and Jobs for their vote bank are doing a disservice to the people supporting them and will doom India to failure in the near future.

The UPA government brought in the 'Right to Education'. It was a good move but failed to produce academic excellence. Side by side, if they had improved the standard of government-run free municipal schools to cater for the people at the lower level, it would have paid huge dividends. Whereas the private schools are a shade better, but everyone cannot get into these schools as they have to pay the fees, and only a handful of the poor and lower-middle-class can afford it. The advanced private schools are good, some are very good, but the high-middle-class and the rich can only afford it.

A better policy would be to improve the standard of municipal schools, and after a student passes $10^{th}/12^{th}$ standard, sidestep the students to some skill training by which they can pick a job and earn their living and some of them who are keen, side by side take up higher education by attending night classes/correspondence studies that will help them to get a better job. For this, community centres should be organized, with all these students as members and where guidance and counselling can be provided. Even for the middle class and higher middle class, guidance and counselling are necessary. Everyone becoming a graduate is not necessary; sidestepping into skill education and picking up a job improves the living standards. Even working and side by side attending night schools/ corresponding studies, one can pick up a better job.

For example, an apprentice in mechanical engineering who, side by side, goes for further studies in mechanical engineering and has passed the 'Associate Member in Mechanical Engineering' [AMIME]' examination is preferred to a fresh student who has passed 'Bachelor in Engineering' [BE]. The apprentice is preferred as he has practical experience in addition to AMIME, which is equal to BE.

For the poor, the concept of peeling off after $10^{th}/12^{th}$ standard and going for skill education, picking up a job to earn a living and side by side, and later going for higher studies should be encouraged, rather than everyone trying to become a graduate. India has the maximum number of graduates but without skill education. Jobs are available, but not enough people with academic and skill excellence.

In the 2000s, India achieved world-class in four sectors, software, establishing BPOs, Pharmaceuticals and Automobiles. Apart from the economic liberation in 1990 and the effect of it, the achievements were attributed to the availability of academic excellence. In the 2010s, not a single world-class sector was added as the availability of academic excellence slowly died down. [The main reason is India's education system that is not good enough; the country produces a greater percentage of graduates who are just unemployable].

The politicians are focusing on creating larger quotas in educational institutions and Jobs instead of giving priority to academic excellence. The need of the hour is changing to a totally new educational system that emphasis on academic excellence, world-class research, and world-class institutions.

If India does not improve the skill and the economic gap, the scale of FDIs needed in India will not come, and more Indians will acquire companies abroad.

China has become a world leader in technologies of the future, such as 5G telecom [Huawei], solar panels [Jinko Solar], and storage batteries [BYD]. India is far behind. China has forged ahead because of its emphasis on academic excellence. It has good universities, good research facilities in the world and produces the largest academic papers published in journals. To top it up, China offers world-class salaries to attract world-class academicians. India has a long way to go; just saying that India is the fastest growing economy and becoming a world economic power is not enough, we have to work hard towards achieving this goal by changing the educational system. The sooner, the better.

Teaching should be sufficiently adapted to the pupil's needs. Students should be divided into three groups – Above average, average, and below average. Every class should have three rooms with three teachers.

Teacher's being absent is rising, this is not good for teachers- students ratio; what has worked better was to employ them on short-term contracts [which could be extended if they showed good results] and incentivize them to teach.

Children should be grouped and taught on the basis of their learning levels and not according to age or grade, constantly improving their learning outcome.

The impact of math games among pre-schoolers, game based curricula might work better when they are integrated with age-appropriate lessons in primary schools.

With large classrooms and overworked teachers, there is very little happening by way of learning. On the contrary, by grouping children according to their learning levels and giving targeted instructions, one could get them to their right level.

Nearly 74% of the students in Delhi government schools are lagging behind in reading levels. The best method is to divide the children into two groups, i.e., readers and non-readers, based on an assessment. Special classes using material specifically designed for them are held for the non-readers for an hour every day. Similar classes are held for those who are not performing in maths.

The three Language formula has been accepted by most Indians. Hindi should not be forced, especially on the southerners, as they lose out.

The municipal schools run by the states have to develop their infrastructure and create an atmosphere of learning; bring in trained teachers, with better pay and allowances, and periodically the teachers should attend advanced method of teaching capsules. Parent-teachers meeting must be held. Most of the government schools give mid-day meals. However, the quality of meals needs improvement.

To give a feeling of belonging, the schools should have a uniform and a school flag, and an inspiring school song. The students should be divided into houses with names of inspiring figureheads to motivate them. Apart from studies, the school should encourage sports, extracurricular activities, like debates, drama, and hobbies, along with conducting social events. Conduct talks on code of conduct, manners, hygiene and sanitation, and road safety should be conducted with student's participation, without any examinations. Adding Meditation and yoga and showing movies on general subjects, like exposure to the animals, aquatic species, vegetation, wonders of the world, etc., without any examination will be a good change from the normal curricula.

Skilled and higher education should be made available for only two/three children per family. Likewise, reservation of Jobs should also be for only two/three children per family.

Most of the students from poor families come up the hard way and psychologically are affected, some very badly, due to circumstances and the environment they live in. Late Father Eddie Fonseca, former Principal of Ornella School, Pune, for 11 years felt that these affected students would only come into the mainstream if they were taught with love and affection. When he interviewed new teachers, he would ask them if they would teach with love and affection, and if they said that they would, he would select them. Before he took over, the school had a very bad reputation, with students behaving very badly and with very low marks.

However, within his tenure, he brought up the school to a high level; the students were disciplined, excelled in studies, games, and extra-curricular activities. Father, himself was a good hockey player and was in the school team. The old-timers will remember the famous inter-school hockey finals; Ornella School was pitched against St Vincent's School, Pune. The match was like the cricket match between India and Pakistan, exciting and watched by a large crowd. In the end, Ornella School won the match and came into the limelight.

The students at Ornella School, under Father Eddie Fonseca, have done very well in life - one became a priest, one became an Air Marshall in the Indian Air Force and was awarded a Vir Chakra in the 1965 Indo-Pak war, some were successful in government Jobs, private-sector Jobs, in running their business and in the field of education – it was Father Eddie Fonseca who brought happiness in their lives. His motto – "Teach with love and affection, then only the students will learn and do well". A reflection on the life of Father Edmund Fonseca was compiled by Valentino Casper in his book, 'Will You Love My Children'. Father Edmund Fonseca, a towering personality, has had a profound influence on several lives, including that of the author Valentino gasper. Every person managing and teaching in Government Municipal Schools, where the students are from the lower strata of society, should follow Father Edmund Fonseca's method of dealing with deprived people if proper education has to reach everyone. Having 'Right to Education' is welcome, but what about the method of teaching.

In the secondary school [5th to 10th class], there are a lot of dropouts due to no support from the family and the students themselves are not interested in studying any further, but they cannot be left at that stage; for them, skill development is the answer where they can pick up Jobs and come up in life, be independent, help their parents to educate the other siblings.

Similarly, the dropouts at the higher secondary schools' stage [11th and 12th class] and at the college stage [3 years], and students, after graduation, should be given skill development to enable them to take up Jobs and come up in life and be of help to their parents and help other siblings.

Only bright students should be allowed to go for post-graduation [Masters]/PhD.

At every stage, talks on hygiene and sanitation, general law, code of conduct, and traffic rules, with student's participation should be conducted to make them better citizens, without any examinations.

Inspectors of schools/colleges should guide the teaching staff and give suggestions and recommendations in teaching and the administration of the school.

The New education policy [NEP], announced by the government on August 05, 2020, was long-overdue; the policy addresses some of the concerns and is welcomed. It is based on two committee reports-the TSR Subramanian Committee of 2016 and the K Kasturirangan Committee of 2019. The challenge before its framers is to respond to the knowledge economy and at the same time to reckon with a milieu in which pedagogy has become deeply politicised.

The highlights – it proposes extending the Right to Education to all children up to the age of 18 years. It talks about improving foundational literacy and numeracy and underlines the importance of pedagogical and technological interventions to scale down the learning crisis. It proposes a range of measures that aim to make education more experiential, holistic, discovery-oriented, learner-centred, and enjoyable, including making the mother tongue or the local language the medium of instruction till 5th standard, thereafter, in Hindi/Sanskrit and English as an optional subject. Vocational subjects [local skilled needs] are added in middle school. The southern states feel that Hindi is imposed on them. This requires clarification.

The children will be given more choices of subjects, and there will be no hard separation among arts, humanities, and science. In higher education, it envisages the breaking of boundaries between disciplines and transforming institutions into large, multi-disciplinary universities and colleges. The policy recognises that vibrant campus life is essential for high –quality teaching and learning process.

India's digital divide has been highlighted and deepened by the COVID pandemic. Disparities between rich and poor, urban, and rural, show up strikingly in access to digital tools. Technology is a force multiplier in some cases; in others, it is inaccessible. This is beyond the NEP.

Elections in Colleges are being politicized by the political parties, and as a result, there is a lot of violence on college campuses, which is bad for any educational institute. Elections for electing the students' president and vice president who nominate other office barriers to coordinate the aspects of running the college other than teaching and administration, like passing general orders and instructions, organizing sports, extra-curricular activities, social events and maintaining discipline and keeping the living accommodation and outside clean. Politics is nowhere in their charter of duties.

What is happening in JNU and similar universities is a bad example, and the political parties are to be blamed for the mess. The poor students with scholarships should be given only three chances to graduate, pursue post-graduation/courses, or complete a PhD.

And if they fail, they should be transferred to a skill development institute to pick up Jobs. They will be able to be of some assistance monetarily to their parents and be in a position to educate the other siblings; this is how the family will grow. At the stage of learning, these students should remember that their and their family's well being should be the centre of their concerns and not the political situations in the country. After 18 years, they can always vote for the candidate of their choice.

Freedom of Speech is being misunderstood; it is not absolute. People feel that it gives them the liberty of saying what they feel; it comes under the preview of the law of contempt. One hears politicians telling the defaulters they are free to say what they feel and that they will come and support them; this gives a wrong impression.

Debates should be encouraged, and topics of general interest like Climate Change, Environment Protection, physical and mental fitness, etc., should be covered. Topics on religion and politics and controversial topics that create a division between people should be avoided.

The East Asian economies success story was based on four fundamental policies, land reforms, export-led growth, high savings, and human capital formation. India is lagging behind in all four, except high saving, but that too is slipping.

For the long term, the most constraining factor on economic growth is human capital formation. A healthy, literate, and skilled populace is vital in manufacturing, services and modern Agriculture and is essential for India to grow at a rate of 7 - 10%.

The World Bank report of 2018 shows that India ranks 115th in the Human Capital Index [HCI], below every South Asian country, except Afghanistan and Pakistan. It appears that the World Bank did not take the present government's education and health schemes into account; if taken into consideration, maybe the ranking would not have been so low.

At the core of human capital formation are school and university education. Presently, India's schools, colleges and universities are not up to the mark and are not producing good students. There are private schools and government schools that excel, and there are colleges and universities that provide reasonable higher education. But the vast majority of our educational institutions stand nowhere globally. Our children who go to excellent to reasonable institutions; many go to Europe and the USA for higher studies and excel abroad because the educational system there is superior.

Our educational system is inferior because, in most institutions, the infrastructure is poor, the campuses are under-provisioned and maintained; the principals lack management of proper education; absentees of teachers affect the process of education; language and mathematical skills are very poor.

Indian university students are also poorly trained and skilled; most cannot write a coherent structural essay. Whatever language they are educated in, their competencies are poor.

In higher education, as in schools, infrastructure, teacher's being absent, shambolic teaching, unprofessional management cripple the education experience. Indian employers report that our graduates are not employable; they don't have modern skillsets and have to be retrained at work. Education reforms to include skill at the graduation level is necessary.

A study by the National Council of Applied Economic Research [NCAER], a non-profit think-tank of economics, notes that 75% of businesses globally expect the process of automation and technological upgrading to mean that workers will be required to develop and learn new skills in order to meet the evolving demands asked of them by their employers.

To benefit the maximum, business leaders, non-profit and government leaders need to join and come together to identify, develop, and scale solutions that connect more people with economic opportunities and share in India's growth.

The workplace of the future will be quite different, and in order to succeed, the best approach would be to bring this effort to India and apply it to the best practices of what is working in India and elsewhere. In this field, J P Morgan is helping from around the world to succeed in the workplaces of the future by supporting education and skills investment that aligns with the business needs of India's growing economy, and India should take full advantage.

India has the largest and youngest workforce population in the world, and they have to be prepared for what the Jobs of the future will look like. Great opportunities are in retail, healthcare, and technology.

A number of non-profit organizations are introducing multi-skill training in schools, bringing job readiness to industrial training institutions, providing college students vocational training programmes and technical certification courses to improve their opportunities in the labour market.

Education and training should align with the skills needs of growing industries.

Vaishnavi Londhe, a young woman, took up a course in fabrication when in school through the vocational and technical skill provided by Lend-a Hand-India, a non-profit organization. This training helped her in landing a job at a manufacturing workshop. She now supports the family and is pursuing additional studies, which is preparing her for the skills required by the workplace for the future.

For human capital formation, India requires schools and universities of a good to an excellent standard. We have good to excellent private schools, especially the Christian run schools and some of these schools run by Jesuit priests, who are qualified to impart education, but they are a few. There are some Christian SSC schools that are funded by the government; the standard of these schools are not very good because of the quota system. The standard of the schools run by the municipalities that cover the majority of the population are very poor.

We have Deemed Universities, like Symbiosis International, Amity, Bharati Vidyapeeth, Indian Institute of Science, DY Patel Education Society, Manipal Academy of Higher Education, etc., that are of a good standard, but there are a few. The standard of the IIMs and IITs are good, but again, they are very few. The government universities that cover most of the population are very poor, barring a few.

India has two categories of educated people, one of excellence that can compete internationally in education and the other, a vast majority with poor learning achievement and low employable graduates.

Presently, schools are the biggest crisis in India and have been for a long time and are also the biggest gap between India and East Asia. Skill deficiency of workers is well known; 23% of Indian workers have formal skill training compared to 70 to 80% in other countries.

Promotion of technology and knowledge economy will add to growth, low human capital will not. In order to have structural change from Agriculture to non-Agriculture and from unorganized sector to organized sector, education and skill development are needed. Women labour participation is low and declining; raising women human capital and participation rates can improve economic growth. 35% of India's children are suffering from Malnutrition, this has to be addressed with urgency, and otherwise, India may not achieve high human capital and productivity.

The central government has recently released the National Education Policy, 2020.

8.7 Healthcare

Providing proper healthcare to all citizens is the primary responsibility of the state government with assistance from the central government, and healthcare should reach out to everyone, including the underprivileged, like the Dalits, Tribals, Gypsies, Other Backward Caste [OBCs], the third gender people and the differently abled.

For an emerging economic superpower like India, the health of its people is critical for economic two-figure growth. Apart from having a healthy society, the amount of money spent on health by individual families has affected their overall family Budget, and a number of them have even got debts.

The present government, in their last tenure, launched 'Ayushman Bharat', an insurance coverage based on the healthcare delivery model, combining both preventive and curative healthcare with coverage of ₹5 lacs per family per year, vide Pradhan Mantri Jan Arogya Yojana [PM-JAY].

Preventive care is to be delivered through 'Health and Wellness Centre's [HWCs] that provide comprehensive primary care; curative intervention is sought to be addressed by leveraging existing public and private hospitals infrastructure and Human Resources in the country.

Universal Health Coverage [UHC] has clubbed Government and empanelled private hospitals to provide general and ICU beds. The government has also linked primary and tertiary care via the National Health Authority to ensure better coordination across the process of care.

Digital Technology can be used to maintain patient's medical record; use of voice-enabled records to build both ease and reliability of data capture; apart from the hospitals having the medical history, the patients should also have a copy [CD] of the medical history with them.

All states have the Employees' State Insurance Corporation [ESIC], established by the ESI Act, 1948, where every employer contributes 3.25%, and the employee contributes 0.75% of the wages of ₹21,000 and below per month. The employees' have to register with a doctor's private clinic that has been registered with the ESI and get medical benefits. There are a number of these Clinics all over the place. However, this facility is only available to employees in the organized sector and not to everyone.

Delhi state government has started the Mohalla Clinics all over Delhi that provides free medical treatment to anyone from that Mohalla. The Clinics are within reach and are convenient to the patients for small ailments and for first aid for serious cases that have to be moved to a hospital.

However, the state government has not introduced the central governments - 'Ayushman Bharat', an insurance cover based on the healthcare delivery model, combining both preventive and curative healthcare with coverage of ₹5 lacs per family per year, vide Pradhan Mantri Jan Arogya Yojana [PM-JAY].

For everyone, Ayushman Bharat for preventive and curative healthcare, with coverage of ₹5 Lakhs, per family, per year and the Mohalla Clinics for small ailments, is a good combination. Both the schemes can go side by side for the benefit of the citizens. However, the central government's ESI scheme should carry on for the employees in the organized sector.

Food security for people below the poverty line that involves 20% of the population is a good scheme, but implementation is very difficult as there is corruption at the distribution level; the opening of bank accounts and direct transfer of cash would ensure that the benefits reach the poor.

Mother's health during and after pregnancy is very important. The mothers have to be well-fed because if the mother's health is good, the infant mortality is lower, and if the child is well-fed, till the age of 5 years, child Malnutrition will be lower. For a better diet for the mother and child, direct cash transfer would ensure the benefits reach the mother and child.

Pollution has to be checked by taking all the precautions, and pure drinking water should be made available by keeping all the water resources clean.

The people from the poverty level suffer from poor health due to no nutritional food, poor personal hygiene, even soap/towel to wash their hands are not available to them, vulnerability to diarrhoea and dengue, no provision of medicines and vaccination, inadequate education, no Jobs, if working [no proper wages and job security], no proper housing, living in extremely unhealthy conditions [no proper hygiene and sanitation], no proper clothing, especially in extremely cold climates, exploited by the society and psychologically affected], etc. The government has to address all these concerns.

Malnutrition continues to be a serious concern in India and is the cause of deaths of children under the age of 5 years, which contributed to 68.2% of such deaths in 2017.

India has been trying to address child Malnutrition for many decades through various policy initiatives, but the prevalence of stunting and underweight remains high; the rates of decline have been very slow. Stunting and low weight are not just related to intake of food and nutrients but are related to enteric infections, which are linked to water and sanitation. Nutritious food helps, but better housing, clean water and sanitation are essential for a healthy life. Stunting is an inter-gestational problem, and growth retardation starts from the time the baby is in the womb. A malnourished mother will give birth to a low birth weight child, who is likely to grow up stunted.

A pregnant woman needs care from the very beginning till after the birth of the child and beyond till the child stops having mother's milk. Nutritious food, clean water, better housing and proper sanitation, and periodic medical check-ups are very essential.

Nutrition has to reach remote parts of the country. This is sustainable through - Department of Women and Child Development, Education and Health. The care of the mother is done by the health department; the nutrition program is run by Anganwadi-under women, and the child development and school meal program is run by the education department. There is a need to integrate health and nutrition program. 35% of the children are under 5 years, so the task is huge.

Most people are now working due to the economic activities, and with it, the stress and strain, health issues due to fast food/odd timings, pollution and no proper rest, the burden of diseases has shifted from acute to chronic care and added tremendous expenditure. The burden of chronic ailments such as diabetes, cardiac, respiratory disease, kidney failure, and, to top them, cancer is enormous. Breast and cervical cancer account for 40% of cancer cases. Cancer is one of the most expensive diseases to diagnose and treat and usually is not covered by insurance, which drives families to an extreme financial burden. There is a strong need for insurance companies to add cancer insurance component as an option, in which the add on premium would be higher.

Diabetes and its associated comorbidities pose another financial challenge to any proposed universal healthcare model. The manifestation of diabetes in chronic kidney disease imposes a huge cost on the healthcare bill. This results in ₹3-4 lakh expenditure for each patient suffering from End-Stage Renal Disease [ESRD].

Ayushman, in the scheme, points for diabetes are allowed to accumulate points for better Glycaemic Control, weight control, etc., which in turn would lead to improved diet and body fitness by exercising, thus delaying disease progression and thereby saving the cost associated with diabetes linked comorbidities.

At the critical stage, disease management, in general, is very expensive; an incentive point system that can be cashed in for additional overall tertiary care coverage for better health management, is worthy for consideration.

Giving health incentives for early diagnoses and early intervention will further help in the disease not going to the chronic stage and, apart from saving a huge amount, will save a lot of discomfort to the patient.

So far, 4.5 million families have benefited from this game-changing health reform that has paved the way for the world's most technologically comprehensive Universal Health Care [USC].

Doctors in government hospitals are well qualified, so is the support staff. A skewed doctor and support staff-patient ratio is the major cause of trouble as they are over-worked. Apart from controlling the population to 2-3 children per family, to encourage doctors and support staffs to join government hospitals, incentives should be given with higher pay and allowances and perks.

To maintain a high standard of hygiene, visiting hours should be strictly adhered to, and relatives and friends should be reduced to a bare minimum.

We need to increase the seats in government medical colleges and medical faculty and strengthen primary and secondary healthcare facilities. Government healthcare facilities in villages and taluka level or small town need to be improved.

Recently, an intern was beaten up. When a serious case comes with a lot of people, police protection should be called for, and the patient should not be shifted to another hospital at the critical stage to avoid clashes in the event of the death of the patient.

Unpleasant ragging of junior doctors should be stopped; soft skills and some techniques should be introduced to boost their emotional quotient. At the medical student's and PG level, some orientation and counselling should be given to the students.

8.8   Reforms

To achieve reforms or amendments to the existing reforms, the present ruling party should first get their party members, the RSS, allied saffron groups on board and then the opposition. The way the amendments to the GST were handled was a good example. The government got everyone on board by giving compensation to the manufacturing states that were at a disadvantage and constituting the GST council with representatives from all the states to discuss the sore issues/ concerns and come to a reasonable decision. Slowly and steadily, the GST slabs have been reduced to three, and when the states come on board, the slabs will be reduced to two, probably to 5% and 18%. Soon the GST will cover oil and real estate. This is the most constructive way forward.

Reforms in land acquisition, labour and administration are a must. Reforms in Banking and elections funding are also required to control corruption.

Summary

Since the household savings have come down from 36% to 30%, there is no scope for investment from this source, so the government has to make more Investments. The best bet is an investment in infrastructure to increase consumption, which will eventually increase the demand

and will trigger the growth and increase the Jobs that will further increase consumption, and the cycle goes on and on.

The government should carry out land, labour, Banking , and administrative reforms immediately. Privatize most PSBs and keep only 3 to 4 PSBs, including SBI, for better credit flow to the MSMEs, where the maximum Jobs can be generated.

To improve the Agriculture sector, encourage the concept of cooperative farming, with multi-produce on the Israel model and build the Industrial Corridors between a number of villages that will provide Market access and administrative support to the farmers and help in moving the excessive Agriculture labour from the farms to the industry.

The government should carry out educational reforms to improve the 'Human Capital', to produce academic and skilled people who can take up the present and future Jobs.

Oil is very important to the energy sector. Exploration of oil and gas in the seabed should be done in collaboration with foreign firms. Oil exploration requires the latest technology and a huge Budget; the Middle East became rich because of collaboration with foreign oil-producing countries.

India has a bright future economically, provided hard decisions are taken in key areas and bash forward regardless of the opposition, if the opposition has nothing better to offer.

On February 01, 2021, Finance Minister Nirmala Sitharaman had announced her annual Budget for the current year. The Budget was expected to address two problems, to provide a strong stimulus to growth and to cast itself in a framework both creditable and acceptable. On both these counts, it has performed reasonably well.

On the revenue side, the Budget has not levied any new tax, direct or indirect, which has provided great relief to taxpayers. An increase in the foreign holding in private insurance companies and setting up asset reconstruction companies to take care of bad debts of public sector banks has been a good decision. Privatisation of two public sector banks is also a good decision; more privatisation of public sector banks leaving 3 to 4 banks is required to further improve investor climate. Fixing tax devolution at 41% is a good move, but this shouldn't be defeated by increasing the cesses which aren't shared with states, the centre in the true spirit of cooperative federalism, must desist from levying cesses. Due to the fall in revenue, the Fiscal Deficit was 9.5% of GDP in 2020-2021; it is high. Once the Covid problems are over, the road map for fiscal consolidation should be redrawn, and ultimately, 3% should be achieved for a stable economy. The push to build infrastructure will boost economic growth, and this has been a good move. Disinvestment of public sector units that are not doing well has been on the cards in the earlier Budget, but no substantial gain has taken place.

NATIONAL SECURITY

Apart from how well the government of the day has handled the 'economy', the government is judged by how well they have handled the 'National Security'. International relations not only boosts 'trade' that helps the country's economy but builds strategic partners that also help the countries 'National Security'.

Indian foreign policy in the changing world has to deal with Chinese on the border issues and with Pakistan on regaining Pakistan Occupied Kashmir, and managing ties with the US; and trade with all the nations, at a level playing field and procurement of energy requirements, like oil and gas.

In the fast-changing world, the present government, under Prime Minister Modi's leadership, has come with a more aggressive, risk embracing policy. The aim of the policy is to expand space and options, with a combination of greater diplomatic activity, more intensive development partnerships and growing global profile, as essential tools for growing global foreign policy. Technology, connectivity, and trade should be the focal approach. In the ultimate end, the economy drives diplomacy; there has to be diplomacy blended with a hard-nosed and soft-touch approach.

India turned away from Regional Co-operation for Economic Prosperity [RCEP] because some terms were not in India's favour. It is advisable to come to a middle ground formula and become part of the organization. With Brexit being sorted out, India should make a trade agreement with the UK and the EU. Trade with Israel is important, and India should maintain the momentum to gain economically. With India, Trump was more interested in the trade part more than the defence and security part; India has to play a balancing act with the new US administration to also achieve the latter part.

India has moved decisively to shape Indo-Pacific and Indian Ocean policies, bringing both together quite nicely to span multiple geographies and the first upgraded quadrant in 2019, with the US, Japan, and Australia, India has given a new weightage to the grouping. India is openly engaging with the other top Indian Ocean powers- UK, France, and Indonesia. India has a good relationship with the new Maldives government, and the new Sri Lanka government has reached out to India, which helps India's relationship with them. Sri Lanka will be the key to India's successful oceans policy. India has to build a stronger relationship with Indonesia and Myanmar to keep the Chinese away from influencing the Indian Ocean Region.

India and EU have a Foreign Trade Agreement [FTA]; India is looking to go beyond this agreement, towards a deeper economic, security and technology relationship. Europe is the only continent where soft power matters along with a performing economy.

China will remain India's topmost challenge and America, the big opportunity. The informal summits with China have not really worked; Chinese intrusion with a large force into the Galwan Valley in May/June 2000 has created India's mistrust towards China, and when the crisis settles down, India will have to work out a new method of engagement from a position of strength. With the US, India will have to get the Democrats and the Indian-Americans on India's side. Finally, the arbiter of effective foreign policy will be technology. The choice of technology will depend on strategic interest, defence, and space. India can look at multi-alignment.

The military aim conforms to India's political aim that depends on the threat perception to the nation. The defence forces will have a national security strategic perspective plan to cater for the threat perception from land, sea, and air. The political leadership will deal with ties with the US and procurement of energy requirements.

As per the Prime Minister's announcement on August 15, 2019, the Chief of Defence Staff [CDS] has been created, and General Bipin Rawat has been appointed as the first CDS. Being the senior-most armed forces officer and chairman of the Chiefs of Staff Committee [CSC], he will be the military adviser to the Prime Minister and Defence Minister. Apart from his key role in the nuclear command chain, he would evolve a prioritized tri-service plan for force modernization and project fiscal support. This is a big reform in defence management and was delayed for quite some time.

The next major reforms are underway to create five 'Joint Theatre Commands'; Western Theatre Command to face Pakistan, from Indira Cole on Saltoro Ridge in Siachen Glacier region to the tip of Gujarat. Northern Theatre Command from the Karakoram Pass to Kabithu- the last outpost in Arunachal Pradesh. Maritime Theatre Command, merging the Eastern and Western Naval Commands and including the strategic Andaman and Nicobar Islands to face a threat from the Indian Ocean Region [IOR]. Joint Air Defence Command [ADC], headed by the Air Force, by integrating air defence weapons, like aircraft, missile system and radars of the three services. Southern Peninsular Command to guard the Western and Eastern Coastline, including Lakshadweep and Minicoy Islands.

The threat from Pakistan in the first part covers the plains from Kutch to little beyond Jammu, via Gujarat, Rajasthan, Punjab and very vulnerable Pathankot-Jammu border, which involves plain warfare with mechanized forces and Infantry; and in the second part, covers the mountainous region from the extreme north of Jammu to Ladakh, via the mountainous region around north Jammu, Udhampur, Banihal Pass, Kashmir Valley, Zojila Pass, Kargil and Pratapur [both part of Ladakh] which involves mountainous and high altitude warfare, with mountain and high altitude formations. The border with Pakistan requires two theatre commands because of different terrain and different types of warfare. However, for better synergy, the whole border with Pakistan can be put under one theatre command, i.e., Western Theatre Command.

The threat from the Chinese, in the first part, covers Ladakh, Himachal Pradesh, Uttarkashi-Tibet Border and then comes Nepal, an independent nation, followed by the second part, covering from Sikkim to Arunachal Pradesh, with Bhutan in the middle, which involves mountainous and high altitude warfare, with mountain and high altitude formations. The border with China will require two theatre commands [Northern [first part] and Eastern [second part] Theatre commands] because the border is not continuous, with Nepal coming in between. However, for better synergy, the whole border with China can be put under Northern Theatre Command.

Nepal is a friendly country, and India does not have a protected border with Nepal. In case the situation changes, and India is forced to have the Border Security Forces along the Indo-Nepal border, and during hostility, regular troops, the border automatically would come operationally under Northern Theatre Command.

The threat from the sea by any of our adversaries covers the coastline around Southern India and the strategic Islands, like Lakshadweep & Minicoy, near to India, including India's economic zones around the coast; this part requires one theatre command - Peninsular Theatre Command. This command should have the Coast Guards, an amphibious force based on specially trained marines and Coastal Security Force [CSF], like the BSF.

The border with Myanmar and Bangladesh should be covered by Assam Rifles and Border Security Forces. Since there is likely to be Chinese interference in Myanmar and Bangladesh during hostility, they should come operationally under Northern Theatre Command.

Apart from the five Theatre Commands, there is a requirement of two special commands, one- Central Grid Command that includes Intelligence, Propaganda, Information, Cyber and Space: and the second- Joint Special Forces Command. There is also a requirement of two functional commands, one- Joint Logistic Command; and second- Doctrine and Training Command.

Depending on the actual pattern of how the war is progressing, movement of forces strategically from one theatre command to another will take place.

Next, the focus will shift towards service-specific reforms. For the army, the current levels of manpower have to be trimmed to carry out any modernization; and for the navy, the number of ships with air cover required for surface warfare as well the number of submarines required for under-water-warfare; and for the air force, the fighter aircraft and missile systems required to support each theatre command and for the Joint Air Defence.

The army requires armed assault helicopters to destroy the tanks well before they come in contact, the navy requires the third aircraft carrier so that when one goes under major repairs, at least two are operational, one with the western fleet and one with the eastern fleet; the air force requires a total of 42 fighter squadrons to take on Pakistan and China simultaneously, if required.

The CDS favours staggered procurement of big-ticket capital acquisitions, like 114 fighter jets for the IAF and submarines for the Navy; with the submarines getting priority over the third aircraft carrier the Navy has been pushing for. During World War 1, the German U-boats played an important part in destroying British ships in the Atlantic and Mediterranean. To keep the Chinese away from the Indian Ocean Region, the Navy should look at smaller submarines, like the U-Boats, less expensive and with the same Budget, more can be bought, this will enable the Indian navy to dominate the under-surface warfare.

The CDS needs to look into the requirement of armed Apache Assault Helicopters by the army to take on the enemy tanks. The army is in the process of getting only 6 of them, whereas the air force has already got 22. In all fairness to the army and in the interest of the operational requirement, it should be the other way around, and the CDS should weigh what is beneficial to both the services.

Prior to November 01, 1986, the flying branch meant for the army was with the Air Force and came operationally under the army only during training and war. Around 1977, the Military Operational Directorate had done an in-house study of employing armed assault helicopters, piloted by army officers, to take on the enemy tanks well before contact. Late General Hanut Singh, an Armoured Corps officer, contributed a lot to this concept. However, though the flying branch meant for the army was transferred to the army to form the Army Aviation Corps, on November 01, 1986 [after 11 years], two squadrons of armed light helicopters, Modified to fire rockets to take on the enemy tanks remained with the Air Force. Now, to replace the armed light helicopters, the Air Force is procuring 22 armed Apache Assault Helicopters. The establishment of the Army Aviation Corps will not be completed till the bulk of the armed Apache Assault Helicopters come to the army, and this is an operational requirement.

In April 2019, the NSA was appointed to head the newly constituted Defence Planning Committee, and his post elevated to cabinet rank. At present, an officer from the Police Services, who headed the Research and Analytical Wing [RAW], is heading the committee; will he be in a position to understand the threat perception from the land borders, the sea, and the air; there is bound to be a conflict of views/interest between him and the defence brass. It is advisable to have a defence officer to head the Defence Planning Committee.

Officers with homeland security, policing and Intelligence background will understand information warfare, propaganda warfare and psychological warfare, so will the defence officers.

9.1   Pakistan

From the days of the partition to date, Pakistan has been hostile towards India; as one of the renowned journalists put it, quote, "Pakistan is like a monkey sitting on India's back", unquote; over seven decades, India is unable to wriggle Pakistan off its back.

To contain Communism, the USA would have preferred to have a base in India, but very rightly, Nehru did not want to side with the USA, nor with the former USSR [now Russia]. He followed a foreign policy of non-alignment. The USA was forced to go to Pakistan, and a huge amount of funds and Military Hardware were given to them to stop communist expansion toward the Indian Ocean and countries around it. With American help, Pakistan built their armed forces and, instead of using it against Communism, used it against India to occupy the Kashmir Region, part of J&K that has accessed to India

During the same time, the USA had built their base in South Korea to contain Communism from North Korea and China. It provided a huge amount of funds and Military Hardware, with which South Korea built formidable armed forces to guard against Communism and used the balance of funds to bring up their economy, and now, they are bubbling with an economic boom that has brought better lives to their people. Pakistan could have also been bubbling with an economic boom like South Korea, but they preferred to focus on Kashmir, a part of India. Now, Pakistan's economy is in a bad shape, nearing bankruptcy.

India has to protect their border with Pakistan and also protect the people of J&K from the militants sponsored by Pakistan creating violence and bloodbath, with an intention of turning the people against the Indian Government to obtain 'Azadi'.

Pakistan was unsuccessful in 1948 when they sent the raiders supported by their regular army in plain clothes to invade the Kashmir valley, but with Maharaja Hari Singh, the ruler of the erstwhile princely state of J&K, accession to India, on October 26, 1948, and timely intervention by the Indian Army, they could not do so but held on to Muzaffarabad-Kotli-Mirpur belt and the northern area – Gilgit-Baltistan belt, both parts of J&K, now known as 'Pakistan Occupied Kashmir'. [87,000 sq. km]. The part of Kashmir on the Indian side is- 1,01,380 sq. km.

India has to have bilateral talks with Pakistan to get back Pakistan Occupied Kashmir; this can only happen when Pakistan stops terrorism, as talks and terrorism and cannot go together.

In the 1965 Indo-Pakistan War, Pakistan tried to cut off J&K at the Chamb-Aknoor-Jammu area but was unsuccessful. In the 1971 Indo-Pakistan War [when India was liberating East Pakistan], Pakistan tried again to take over J&K but was unsuccessful; India took around 93,300 POWs.

After the 'Shimla Agreement', while the POWs were being sent back, the Pakistan army officers told the Indian officers that they would show them in the fourth round. Most probably, the fourth round will not take place as both the countries are nuclear; minor clashes may take place like the one at Kargil in 1999. But Pakistan army is bent on following a hostile policy against India. India has to be on guard against Pakistan all along the border- [24x7].

During the 'Shimla Agreement' of June 1972, India missed a golden opportunity of getting back the part of Kashmir that is illegally occupied by them and, if it were not possible, at least, get the present line of occupation from NJ9842 extended to the north in J&K, it would have saved the loss of lives on both sides at the Siachen border, where the world's highest battleground is active.

Indira Gandhi agreed to send back 93,300 Pakistani POWs but failed to bring back around 54 Indian POWs who were languishing in Pakistani civilian Jails. The Pakistan army established POW camps, with effect from 15 December 1971; the war started on 3 December 1971, with the pre-emptive airstrike on Indian forward airfields late in the evening; the Indian POWs were taken from 4 December 1971 onwards, when their army started their advance- to 14 December 1971 were put into Pakistani civilians Jails with other criminals and were given prison clothing; they did not follow the 'Geneva Convention' that says that all POWs will be put into separate camps and will be treated as per the convention.

2nd Lieutenant AGJ Switten [later retd. as Colonel] was taken POW on the early morning of 4 December 1971, at Kakian Wala in Chamb Sector and put into Rawalpindi civilian jail. On 7 December 1971, The Indian Army HQ declared the young officer as 'missing believed killed'. The Pakistan army did not make efforts to declare him as a POW and shifted him to the POW camp when it was established on 15 December 1971. In February 1973, a Swiss lady of the 'Red Cross', part of the 'Amnesty International', on her visit to Rawalpindi jail, took a photograph of Switten and on his request sent his photograph addressed to his father- Mr Switten, Light House, Alleppey, India. Mr Switten received the photograph in July 1973 and wrote to the Indian army HQ and MOD; as there was no headway, he spoke to the local MLA, who took up the case in the Kerala assembly and later requested a local MP to take up the case in the parliament. The RAW was put into action, and as per their inputs, there was nobody by the name of 2nd lieutenant Switten in Rawalpindi civilian jail. The Pakistani's had changed Switten's name to Wasim Khan Akram to hide his identity as they faltered in not shifting him to a POW camp.

Switten's father mobilised many people from his native place, Alleppey and had demonstrations in front of the Pakistani embassy, showing Switten's photograph. This caught the notice of one of the leading national newspapers, and they sent a journalist to get feedback from the Swiss lady, who confirmed meeting the young officer and taking the photograph and sending a copy to his father on his request.

Ministry of External Affairs [MEA] requested the US Ambassador to interfere. Finally, Pakistan bowed to international pressure and, to save their face, admitted that they did have a person in Rawalpindi jail having a name Wasim Khan Akram or such name arrested for murder in general area Kakian Wala and if the Indians think that he is one of their army officers, Indians can have him back. Sometime in September 1973, after nearly two years, 2nd Lieutenant AGJ Switten crossed the Wagha border and returned to India. Likewise, there were more POWs who were not transferred to POW camps languishing in Pakistani civilian Jails. The best time was during the process of the Shimla Agreement by insisting on the unit representatives with the Red Cross physically searching the Pakistani civilian Jails for the POWs. In a very sensitive human issue, the Prime Minister failed.

Pakistan has problems in Baluchistan, Sind, and the North West tribal area; the Baluchi's are looking towards India for support. The development in Pakistan Occupied Kashmir, Muzaffarabad- Kotli-Mirpur belt, and Gilgit and Baltistan areas are backward compared to the Indian side of Kashmir, and the people there are suffering and wish to come back to India.

Gilgit and Baltistan area has become more complicated as the Chinese 'One Belt and One Road Enterprise' passes through this area, and there is a presence of Chinese troops for security and providing troop labour. Unless there is an open revolt, India cannot do anything except keeping it under surveillance.

Gwadar Seaport, a Pakistani port developed with Chinese assistance, on which the Islamabad-Beijing axis has pinned its strategic and economic hopes. This is a concern to India.

On July 27, 2015, the militants, sponsored by Pakistan, attacked Gurdaspur and caused damage to property; on January 02, 2016, they attacked again on the Pathankot Air Force Fighter Base, intending to destroy our fighter aircraft, but the attack was foiled by the Indian special forces.

Thereafter, the militants sponsored by Pakistan attacked an Indian Army's rear base at Uri on September 18, 2016, killing 18 jawans; the Indian leadership gave a free hand to the army, and on September 29, 2016, a precision attack by special forces was launched deep inside POK, on 6 to 7 militants launch pads, at a frontage of 150 kilometres, destroying 4 militants launching pads and killing many militants. This shook up the Pakistani military leadership.

After a gap of three years, on February 14, 2019, the militants sponsored by Pakistan again carried out another attack on a convoy carrying CRPF jawans returning from leave, killing 40 of them; the Indian government gave a free hand to the air force to destroy the terrorist's main training camp at Balakot. The Indian Air Force fighter aircraft dropped bombs on Balakot, destroyed their training facilities and killing around 300 militants. This again shook up the Pakistani military leadership.

At present, there are small incidents on the Indo-Pak border, and the Indian army is dealing with it; the Pakistani's now know that if they create problems at the border, India is going to cross the border and create problems for them.

9.2 China

The relationship with China has improved except for the 'Dhoklam' clashes and minor trespassing on the northern border from time to time, at one place or the other. On May 09, 2020, trespassing took place at Nachuk La in North Sikkim and the Chinese were thrown back. In May 2020, trespassing took place at Pangong Tso Lake, and the Chinese intruded into the Galwan Nalla Area in eastern Ladakh. A clash took place between Indian and Chinese forces on June 14/15, 2020, with 22 dead on the Indian side and around 100 dead on the Chinese side. The Chinese have built a permanent camp and an airfield on their side, and India has moved enough troops with weapons and equipment to counter the Chinese. India's supply lines are shorter, the troops are acclimatised, large transport aircraft can land at Daulat Beg Oldi with reinforcements, and India is in a better position than China; however, though there has been a pull-back on both sides to avoid direct contact, the tension in this area will continue.

23 contested areas on the Line of Actual Control [LAC] between India and China were identified during interactions between the two sides over multiple meetings of India-China joint working groups [JWG] in the 1990s, during an exchange of maps for the middle sector in 2000, and comparison of maps for the western sector in 2002, 11 were

identified in Ladakh, under the western sector, four in the middle sector and eight in the eastern sector.

Overall, India has enough troops on the Indo-Chinese border and is in a better position to protect the northern border against any misadventure.

In 1962, China occupied the area of Aksai Chin [300 km] that is part of the Ladakh region of J&K; India has to sort this occupation with China. In 1963, Pakistan had a border agreement with China and handed over parts of the Shaksgam Valley of J&K without India knowing; India does not recognize the border agreement. India has to have bilateral talks with China and get back these territories. At this advanced stage, talking to Pakistan on Shaksgam Valley [5,100 + 37,244 = 42,344 sq. km] is futile.

India doesn't recognize the Chinese 'One Belt One Road [OBOR] Enterprise' that passes through Pakistan Occupied Kashmir/Ladakh that is part of India. 'China-Pakistan Economic Corridor [CPEC] also passes through POK.

OBOR enterprise is a death trap for small countries, such as Pakistan, Sri Lanka and others where Chinese companies had made significant Investments in the past few years. CPEC would also be a death –trap for Pakistan. Chinese companies have constructed many hydro-projects under the CPEC at a very high cost, almost double or triple the usual price. Pakistan would have to repay a huge amount of 7 to 8 million dollars every year, and Pakistan is economically in bad shape. Probably, the Gwadar Seaport may also go to China on a long lease. That is how the Chinese would circle India from the Western, Northern and North Eastern borders; this is a concern to India.

The OBOR and CPEC rely on Chinese workers and supplies rather than giving business to Pakistani companies and workers. In contrast, if CPEC had been a US-Pakistan business partnership, it would have contributed to sustainable growth and expertise that builds capacity for local communities by bringing superior quality and technology, driving productive gains in Pakistan.

Trade between India and China has taken a dip due to the Chinese tariff that is unfair to India. A large amount of Chinese consumable goods are illegally moving into India and causing a huge loss of import duties.

When the world supported India in declaring 'Hafez Saeed' as an international terrorist, they supported the move; previously, the Chinese vetoed the move a number of times. When they saw the world strongly for the move, they joined the world as they would be isolated.

However, China has vetoed India's membership in UNSC and the 'Nuclear Group'.

Recently, China has deployed over two regular divisions about [40,000 in troops], including mechanised forces, along with supporting arms, logistic services, and air force along the Eastern Ladakh frontline and India to counter their move has deployed about two regular Army divisions, supported by tanks and the Indian Air Force, along the Line of Actual Control [LAC]. The Peoples Liberated Army [PLA] has occupied many areas which were earlier considered 'disputed', lying between Chinese and Indian perceptions of the LAC.

The only direct contact between China and India took place in the Galwan area, north of 'Pangong Tso' and close to the mutually agreed 'Line of Actual Control-[LAC]', on 14/15 June 2020, killing 100 Chinese and 22 Indian soldiers.

The Indian Army has gained an advantage by taking pre-emptive occupation of the Kailash range [Chushal heights] on August 29/30 September 2020, overlooking the 'Spanggur Gap' and beyond, including the Chinese garrison at Moldo.

The massing of a large number of troops close to Eastern Ladakh is a threat to India. India has asked the Chinese to withdraw to avoid contact, but the Chinese are adamant about staying put, causing concern to India. The only choice India has is to keep a viable force in Eastern Ladakh, with mechanised forces to counter any Chinese move. It will be a long haul on both diplomatic and military fronts.

9.3   Indian Ocean Region

The Indian Ocean is of strategic importance to India, as 97% of trade passes through the sea. The sea routes have to be protected during hostility and peacetime from militants and sea pirates in the Malacca Strait and near Somalia. The Somalian pirates have caused danger to our shipping.

India has to protect itself from the Pakistani Navy in the Arabian Sea and Bay of Bengal and the Chinese influence in the Indian Ocean and the direct contact through the Arabian Sea with their operations through Gwadar, a seaport built by them to support the Belt and Road Enterprise [the old silk route].

Chinese presence in the Indian Ocean has increased to seven to eight ships at any given time. The Indian Navy is keeping a constant watch, some under the anti-piracy escort group and sometimes doing scientific research, including oceanography. Chinese vessels also enter Indian waters when they have satellite launches in the area. They have been given certain areas for deep-sea mining. In September 2019, a Chinese vessel was forced to retreat after entering Indian Exclusive Economic Zone near Andaman and Nicobar Islands without taking any permission or having informed the Indian authorities. The Chinese vessel was apparently conducting research near Port Blair.

China is building its naval assets at a faster pace than India, but China has got responsibilities on the north, east, and South-China seas and has to protect its oil trade route to the Middle East. India should only worry about the portion of the Chinese Navy that will be causing a threat to India in the Indian Ocean.

As far as the Indian Ocean Region and the Indo-Pacific are concerned, India is ready to work with like-minded nations based on common interests of keeping safe and secure seas, freedom of navigation and rule-based order.

India and several other countries in the region have often taken a stand against China's increased military presence in the South China Sea that is escalating tension in the area. India stands for a 'demilitarized' South China Sea.

In March 2020, India was to host a Multi-lateral maritime exercise, 'MILAN', off the coast of Visakhapatnam, in which 41 'like-minded countries' were going to participate. The US, Russia, France, Israel, Iran, UAE, Australia, Japan, South Korea, South Africa, Saudi Arabia, and Vietnam were among the invitees. China was not invited as India did not want to legitimize their presence in the Indian Ocean. However, the exercise was postponed due to Covid 19.

The quadrilateral coalition of India, US, Japan, and Australia does not have a military role in the Indo-Pacific region at the moment. The intention is to have a stabilization influence, not a military influence.

At the beginning of November 2020, India, USA, and Japan conducted a trilateral exercise, Australia also joined in. Fighter control operations from Indian and USA aircraft carriers through maritime interdiction operations, anti-submarine warfare, diving salvage operations, amphibious operations, counter-piracy operations, X-deck helicopter landings and anti-air warfare operations were successfully carried out.

Thereafter, a trilateral naval exercise between India, Singapore and Thailand was held at the Andaman Sea; it was a non-contact drill at sea format due to Covid -19 restrictions. The main objective –interoperability between the three Navies to enhance multifaceted Maritime operations.

Apart from dominating the Indian Ocean, the Indian Navy has to reach out from the Pacific Ocean to the east coast of Africa, with the navies of the USA, UK, Australia, and Japan, to show the strength of force to the Chinese. A number of joint exercises are being conducted periodically. Chinese have to depend on oil from the Middle East. The Chinese have to protect their interest, but they are using it as an excuse and overdoing it by having full influence in these water expanses.

With the Chabahar seaport being developed by India and Iran on the eastern coast of Iran, the Indian navy will be able to facilitate the movement of trade into Afghanistan and Central Asia. Chabahar is 100 kilometres from Gwadar, and once it becomes operational, ships going to it and coming back can keep surveillance on the activities at Gwadar. Washington gave New Delhi what it termed a 'narrow exemption' to allow access to landlocked Afghanistan, subject to Iran's Revolutionary Guards Corps not participating in the project.

Sri Lanka formally handed over the southern seaport of Hambantota to China in 2017 on a lease of 99 years after it failed to meet debt obligations. China is also trying to negotiate for a seaport in Myanmar. China will be circling India from the sea.

India has an abundance of sea resources around its coast, and the economic zone and its seaports have to be protected. This responsibility is with the Coast Guards and the Marine Police.

The Navy requires three aircraft carriers, one for each fleet and one in dry docks for periodical maintenance/overall. At present, they have INS Vikramaditya [Russian built] and INS Vikrant [Indian Built] on sea trails. The government should give sanction for building another aircraft carrier at the earliest as it takes around 10 to 12 years to build an aircraft carrier.

It takes 6 to 8 years to build ships. In this regard, the Navy has done well but not as well as China; the Indian Navy is competing with China. The submarine fleet is weak; to dominate the underwater, the Indian Navy needs more submarines. India has built a nuclear submarine, and it has been a great achievement. There is a school of thought that if there are financial constraints, why not go for smaller submarines and more in number, like the German U-boats that dominated the underwater warfare and sank many allied ships.

The Chinese Navy made occasional forays in the Indian Ocean Region from 1985 and, for the first time, entered in force into the Indian Ocean Region in 2008, under the pretext of anti-piracy patrol, followed by deploying a nuclear submarine for the same purpose. In 2012, it had started deploying its intelligent collection ships to collect signals, electronic Intelligence and map the ocean floor. From 2013, it has been deploying its conventional and nuclear submarines in the region. It has also roped in its surface action group to demonstrate its operational capabilities in the IOR. Soon it is likely to move in an aircraft carrier. To build its strategic bases, China is investing in major maritime and non-maritime projects in Pakistan and Sri Lanka and looking for an opening in Myanmar. Sri Lanka had to re-pay huge debts to China, and eventually, when they could not repay, they handed their projects to China. Sri Lanka handed over the strategic port of Hambantota to China on a 99-year lease in 2017. The ongoing infrastructure at Gwadar in Pakistan's Baluchistan province would give the Chinese Navy access to the Arabian Sea. In this way, China will circle India from the sea; this move is a major concern to India.

9.4   Cyber and Space Threat/ Intelligence/ Geospatial Cooperation

In March 2019, India launched an anti-satellite [A-Sat] missile to take down an imaging satellite creating a measure of deterrence for vital Indian interests in space that include communications, navigation, earth observation and surveillance satellites.

Indian Intelligence system through satellite/electronic devices and protection against cyber-attack, fake information and psychological propaganda needs attention. We are far behind in our counteractions.

India needs to have mutual Intelligence sharing with other nations around it, like Myanmar, Indonesia, Sri Lanka, and the Maldives, against terrorism in the region.

India and the USA have signed a Basic Exchange and Cooperation Agreement for Geospatial Cooperation [BECA]. This agreement will allow India to use US geospatial Intelligence and enhanced the accuracy of automated systems and weapons like missiles and armed drones. It will provide access to topographical and aeronautical data and advanced products, which will aid navigation and targeting. This could help in coordination between Indian and US Air Forces, as India will receive advanced satellite imagery, topographical and aeronautical digital data in real-time from the US for further enhancing the accuracy of its missiles and armed drones as well as long-range navigation of military aircraft.

This cooperation includes sharing high-end satellite images, telephone intercepts, and data exchange on Chinese troops and weapons deployment long the 3,488 km of India and Chinese LAC.

9.5   Security Problems

The politicians do not understand the security of the military Cantonments where the armed forces are stationed while they are in peace locations. One of the Defence Ministers wanted the armed forces to move out of the Cantonments to places far away from the towns/cities so that the cantonment land could be sold to the builders; he had his eyes on Pune and Delhi as a starting point. He did not succeed. The army started auditing their land holdings and started protecting their land.

A lot of mushroom colonies and commercial hubs have come up around the Cantonments, and the people are forced to use the roads going through the Cantonments, as no broad ring roads were built to join these colonies and commercial hubs. Apart from traffic jams and pollution, manpower is committed to security management and traffic control.

A number of Para-Military Forces and private security agencies wear the rank badges of the regular armed forces, especially the army, and to a civilian and foreigner, it is confusing. Efforts should be made to have different rank badges. It can pose a security problem.

9.6   Military Hardware

The political leadership has to provide the Indian armed forces with the required manpower, equipment, and force multipliers. The Indian Air Force requires 42 Fighter squadrons to face both fronts, and they have only 30 Squadrons. This is not a happy situation, and the government and the opposition should bury their differences and get the required squadrons on a war footing.

As per the former chief of the Air Staff, Air Chief Marshall S Krishnaswamy, who in 1980, as a Wing Commander, was in the evaluation team for Mirage 2000 [first fly-by-wire combat aircraft]. In 1982, 40 aircraft were acquired and in 1982, and there was an option to build 150 of these under license. It is a pity that in 2019, we target the LCA MK-2 to have at least the same capability as that of the Mirage-2000. We could have produced theses at HAL, under license much earlier.

In 1990, we acquired second-hand MIG-21 Trainers to overcome the shortage, and we now plan to buy second-hand MIG-29s, which is superb in its air superiority role, but it does not have the same quality and versatility as that of the Mirage-2000. The procurement of 40 Tejas Mk 1, already in the pipeline and subsequently procurement of 83 Tejas Mk 1A will replace MIG 21. At the end of the day, the Air Force has the responsibility, and the bureaucracy has the power to say yes or no, while the government takes a distant stand- a sorry state.

Initially, the flying branch meant for the army was with the Air Force; this flying branch only catered for the Artillery requirement of directing artillery fire on the depth targets. When the concept of using armed helicopters against enemy tanks and other targets was accepted, the US and the UK armies and even the Pakistani army moved the complete flying branch [army element] to the army for better control and command.

IAF is inducting 22 Apache Attack helicopters armed with deadly missiles and rockets to take on the enemy armour, whereas the army is inducting only 6 Apache attack helicopters from the US by 2022 to take on the enemy Armour and other targets.

These are heavy-duty choppers with precision attacks and operate in hostile airspace with threats from the ground, armed with air to air Stinger missiles, Hellfire Longbow air to ground missiles, guns, and rockets.

The required ground attack helicopters to take on the enemy tanks should be with the army. The Airforce may have the same helicopters for their requirements, but it should not be at the cost of the army.

The Indian soldiers deployed on the borders with Pakistan and China are finally getting the new assault rifle almost 15 years after the army first demanded them. These are US origin rifles, 7.62 x 51 mm calibre, with a longer kill range of 500 meters, only for front line soldiers. In February 2019, 10,000 out of 72,400 ordered were received, and the final batch of rifles were delivered on 15 March 2020. Army got 66,400, Air Force 4000, and Navy 2000.

The bulk of the 1.3 million forces are slated to get Russian Kalashnikov rifles at a later stage. The Korwa ordinance factory in Uttar Pradesh will progressively manufacture AK 203 rifles [6.62x39 mm calibre] in a joint venture with Russia. The rifle is a derivative of the ionic AK 47, with an effective range of 300 meters. The Army will get 7 lakhs, Air Force 29,000, and Navy 13,600; rifles for the Police have also been catered for.

These rifles are replacement for 5.56 mm INSAS [Indian Small Arms System].

The Army fought the Indo-Chinese War 1962 with World War II era 303 mm single round bolt action rifles. Later, India manufactured a 7.62 mm rifle with a semi-automatic reloading system and used it during the Indo-Pak 1965 and 1971 Wars. After several setbacks over the past decades, the army is now pushing ahead with its long-delayed roadmap to induct new Assault Rifles, close quarter battle carbines and light machine guns to arm the infantry soldiers.

2,400 SiG Sauer rifles [7.62x51 mm] calibre guns with an effective "kill" range of 500 metres have already been inducted from the US, and the second lot of 72,400 was inked in December 2020.

Under the "Make in India" project, the Army wants the manufacture of 7 lakh Kalashnikov AK-203 rifles, at the Korwa Ordnance Factory in Uttar Pradesh, with Russian collaboration, to take off soon.

Delivery of 16,479 Israeli Negev 7.62x51mm LMG began in January 2021.

Manufacture of 4.6 Lakh CQB carbines in India is in process.

HOMELAND SECURITY

Jammu & Kashmir

The major homeland Security threats are in J&K, in the Northeast and from Maoists in Central India. The security threats in J&K are due to Pakistan supporting the Hurriyat leaders who want to break away from India, and the Hurriyat have the support of only 15% of the local population in the South Kashmir Valley consisting of 5 districts, they have no support from Jammu, Kargil and Ladhak. The Hurriyat get huge funds from Pakistan to create problems.

Homeland Security in J&K is linked to the National Security at the border with Pakistan as both are affected due to militancy sponsored by Pakistan's in various parts of the country.

With the reorganization of J&K into Jammu and Kashmir regions forming a Union Territory [UT] like Delhi and Pondicherry, with the centre responsible for the internal security, and Ladhak region forming a Union Territory, like any other UT, with the centre responsible for the internal security, it has made the internal security in J&K and Ladhak and Intelligence sharing easier because the National security at the international border is also under the centre.

With Article 370 diluted and the complete Indian constitution covering former J&K, like other states, the governance of the UT of J&K with a legislature and the UT of Ladakh without a legislature, but with the existing Leh district and Kargil district in operation, will be politically smoother as the political powers between various regions, like Jammu and Ladhak have been evened out with Kashmir. As a result, there will be less political disparity. Earlier everything revolved around Kashmir.

The removal of Article 35A will bring growth and development to both the UTs, as land can be bought, and Jobs can be taken up by people from outside Jammu and Kashmir and Ladakh and business from other parts of the country can move in; this will improve the economy and bring in more Jobs to the youth and a better life. Without Jobs, the youth were lured into militancy with money.

In 1965, Dr Karan Singh, the then Chief Minister of former J&K State and son of former Maharaja of Independent J&K, had recommended that Ladakh should be separated from former J&K state; he also felt that there was some good in abrogating Article 370, as it gave equal status to Jammu and Kashmir. He also said the Union Territories of J&K should be upgraded to a fully-fledged state at the earliest.

Once the internal security is under control and elections are held, and there is peace in the valley, the intention of the government of India under the NDA is to revert back the Union Territory of J&K to a state. Ladakh to remain a UT.

10.1   North East

The problems in the Northeast are due to the Centre neglecting the development in this area; the present government is addressing the legitimate demands and removing grievances and concentrating on development. However, more is to be done. The framework agreement with the Naga rebels and the NSCN [IM] should be dealt with statesmanship.

A number of the refugees are also coming into Eastern India from Bangladesh and Myanmar, and this is changing the demography of Eastern India, especially in Assam and the West Bengal States and is a concern to India. If the refugees are not stopped, the Assamese and Bengalis of the Hindu community will become minorities and lose political power, which will create political instability.

10.2   Maoists Problem

The Maoists problem is a social-economic problem. The Tribals feel that for years they have lived off the forests, and now, they should be allowed to continue to do so. They should be dealt with more sensitively; an invitation for peace talks, with an agenda for development in infrastructure, like water, electricity, roads, education, healthcare, and Jobs that will improve the quality of their lives – a missionary approach is required

While dealing with Naxalites, apart from using an effective police force, the political and backchannel route should also be used. It has to be a human approach with firmness, as it is a socio-economic issue. Listen to their concerns and address the issues and take action to benefit them economically by allowing them to carry on with traditional farming and providing them with Jobs, and allow them to come into the mainstream through education and healthcare.

Once they feel that their lives have improved by coming into the mainstream and that they don't have to rely on the forests, they will change for the better, but this will take a long time.

Smuggling

Chinese goods are cheap as compared to Indian goods and are in demand. They are illegally brought to India through Nepal and Myanmar border and have flooded the Indian Market.

Arms are smuggled from China to India's Northeast via Thailand and Bangladesh and reach the insurgent groups in different parts of the country. The arms are further moved to Pakistan and Gulf countries. Most of these weapons land in the hands of terrorists.

Drug Trafficking from the Myanmar border traverse the subcontinent and find their way to Europe and even USA.

Fake currency is also coming into India, causing great concern and security problems.

Border Security

The responsibility of protecting the borders is with the Border Security Forces [BSF] and the State Police. Physical Border Security is a combination of physical obstacles like barbed wire fencing and surveillance censors [including drones], and boots on the ground. This aspect has to be strengthened with drones for aerial surveillance.

India also has a huge coastline that is vulnerable to the smuggling of weapons, fake currency and drugs, and terrorism. The responsibility is with the Coast Guards and the Marine Police, and they require more speed boats with the latest technology in terms of surveillance, weaponry and communication, and real-time Intelligence sharing between the Navy, Coast Guards, and the Marine Police. The state governments should have adequate surveillance towers linked to the coast guards and the marine police at vulnerable places along the coastline.

10.3 Police Reforms [reorganizing and restructuring].

Police infrastructure, its manpower, transport, communications, and forensic resources require substantial augmentation. The government should rethink and bring the police into the Concurrent List. Police problems were simpler and of a local nature when the constitution was framed, but now, the pattern of crime and the dimensions of law and order problems have undergone a sea of change. As per the UNO recommendations, the strength of the police should be 222 policemen per lakh civilians. In India, the sanctioning strength is 180 policemen per lakh civilians, but there are only 138 per lakh. The manpower shortage means that police personnel are often over-burdened, affecting the overall quality of policing. Additionally, police forces are saddled with administrative and structural deficiencies ranging from obsolete weaponry, shortage of vehicles, poor communication networks and technological inputs. Both the police Telecommunication

Network, which is used in crime investigation and transmission of crime-related data, and the crime and Criminal Tracking Network and System, which is supposed to link every police station, are yet to be implemented in certain states.

India has to bring in the 'Police Reforms' that has been pending for a long time. The reforms should cater for sufficient manpower with sound training, bring-in effective 'personal weapons', effective communication, sufficient vehicles to give the force the required mobility and sound Intelligence System, with synergy with other agencies. The government should look into raising 'Sky Police' in big cities, with helicopters and drones.

SOP for better operational coordination between all the agencies, including Intelligence agencies. Stone pelters against the security forces/police should be considered as using weapons to kill and dealt with severity.

To maintain law and order, the police should operate on the 'Buddy system', with 'Quick Reaction Teams' for support. The American TV serial 'Blue Bloods', a story revolving around the New York Police Commissioner gives the way the 'New York Police Department' functions, is an eye-opener; this serial should be shown in the police academy and police training centres.

Terrorists

After the 26/11 terrorist attack in 2008, measures were taken to strengthen the police forces and have enough reserves for reinforcement.

There was an urgent requirement of Beefing up the coastal security and decentralize the deployment of the National Security Guard. Apart from having the National Security Guards [NSG] at Delhi, there is a need to have a substantial NSG at Nagpur or Secunderabad to cover Southern India to cut down travelling time. And since Mumbai, the commercial centre is very vulnerable, there is a requirement of having an element of NSG located at Mumbai to move in as a Quick Reaction Force [QRF].

The recent attack on Sri Lanka shows that ISIS has made an inroad into Tamil Nadu and Kerala and has sympathizers in other parts of the country. It recently announced a separate branch, Wilayah-e-Hind, to focus on the sub-continent; they have bases in Bangladesh and Maldives.

ISIS is attempting to revive militancy in Punjab and disrupt the economy by flooding the country with counterfeit currency.

The police in every state should have Special Forces on the pattern of Greyhounds to deal with any terrorist attack. The country should have laws on the line of the Maharashtra Control of Organized Crimes Act [MCOCA] to deal with organized crimes. The police must get professionals from the IIT's to form a special staff for investigating cyber-crime will help, rather than training a constable for this job.

The National Counter-Terrorism Centre must be set up in all the states. The Unlawful Activities Prevention Act, a law to deal with terror, needs more teeth.

CBI's image needs to be refurbished, an Act should be passed to define the charter and regulate the functioning of the premier investigating agency. At present, the CBI draws its mandate from the Delhi Special Police Establishment Act of 1946 and that the organization was created through a resolution passed more than 50 years ago.

10.4   Criminal Justice System [CJS]

India needs to invest in four wings of the criminal justice system – police, prosecution, judiciary, and prison.

The country is facing a number of heinous crimes such as rapes and murders, the use of force by criminals on bail and the sheer impunity with which they gang rape and burn the women.

One thought that the changes in the law and procedure post the December 2012 Delhi gang rape and murder case would curb future such cases, but rapes are still continuing.

To have an impact on predators, the people want instant justice. The women on the street were happy that the brutal rape was avenged and showered rose petals on the Telangana Police that 'encountered' the four alleged rapists of a doctor on the outskirts of Hyderabad. The clamour for quick justice stems from the fact that our criminal justice system has failed in our country.

When trial takes years and years, and undue delay takes place. The witnesses lose interest or do not attend hearings. Documents are lost, and seized weapons are not traceable. The investigating officers get transferred and thus, cannot monitor trials. The complainant, after pursuing the case for some time, gives up.

The police investigation and presentation by the prosecution need to improve, and the judiciary must rise to the occasion. Sessions courts should finish the case in one go, within a weak/fortnight and not hear the case in a piecemeal manner. They should clamp down on adjournments. Similarly, higher courts must dispose of appeals within a fixed time frame. Expenses for additional judicial officers and their staff should be met by the Centre and State governments jointly. If a rape accused is sentenced, his final appeal should be disposed off within a year.

The police, medical officers, forensic experts, prosecutors should work together as a team; formal interaction sessions between them are essential. Regular training workshops will lead to an exchange of information, knowledge sharing and mutual trust among different wings of the criminal justice system.

As per the National Judicial Data Grid, more than 20 Lakh criminal cases are pending for more than 20 years in the district and high courts.

10.5   Reforms of Jails

The living conditions in Jails should improve. At present, the convicts eat substandard food, drink water with worms, and sleep on bug-infested beds, live in poorly ventilated rooms, use filthy bathrooms. The undertrials are pushed into small jail lockups like sardines, thus crowding the Jails and languish there without any trial for a long time.

When a verdict is given, it does not say that the convict will be provided with substandard food, drinking water with worms, bug-infested bed, poorly ventilated rooms and use filthy bathrooms. Since they are put in jail, the government should provide the basic requirements in life with a reasonable standard. The court verdict should be –'sentenced for …… years prison term but with proper living conditions'.

Jail reforms are also required. Trial of undertrials should be taken up on the fast-track, and those who have been in lockups for more than half the normal sentence due should be released after they attend an occupational skill training for three to six months, so that they can do something useful on being released. A human approach will bring better results.

10.6   Rape Cases

Between 2015 to 2017 statistics, Delhi has the highest rape rate [19.1%] while Pondicherry has the least [0.8%]; Rajasthan is the third-highest for rapes despite its small population. In the global rating, India stands at 94, with 1.8 rapes per lakh female population.

The report of the National Crime Records Bureau [2017] informs us that 1.27 lakh cases of rape are pending in the courts at various stages, with 1,840 of them pending for more than 10 years.

Over the past five years, utilization of funds released by the Ministry of Home Affairs for Nirbhaya fund – only 9% has been utilized; Maharashtra is 0%, the state is among the five worst states for annual average rapes between 2015 and 2017. Similarly, funds released by the Ministry of Women and Child Development have been utilized only to the extent of 20%, Bihar is 0%, the state had 888 rapes [2015 to 2017].

Procedural changes, availability of infrastructure and filling of vacancies of judges in courts is required at a faster pace; the whole approach should be on a mission mode in the public interest.

Nexus between Political Parties and Student organisations.

For a number of years, political parties have made an inroad into the universities, and with this, there is unrest in some of the universities, especially the ones where the communists have a strong presence, like the JNU. In JNU, the confrontation is between the students with a Communist background [more in number] and the students; with a BJP background [less in number].

Though in 2019, the violence and destruction of public property at JNU started over the fee hike and the hostel rent, and the audit of students staying in the hostel, it had a political colour. JNU, at the HRD Ministry's behest, clarified on January 08, 2020, that it would charge only the increased room rent, and the service and utility charges would be paid by the University Grant Commission. Around 7,500 students are studying at JNU; out of this, 3,500 had agreed to pay the increased rent. The right to protest is a fundamental right but without violence and destruction to property, public or private.

The trouble with the attitude of the political parties creating violence in universities is that they cannot differentiate between discipline and violence; if anyone talks about maintaining discipline, they equate the person with 'Hitler' and fascism. Violence leads to the destruction of property, loss of lives and divides the people, whereas living a disciplined life makes the people better citizens and allows them to do well in life.

In India, the schools and colleges run by Christians have no violence because they emphasise proper code of conduct and keep politics out. Politics and studies don't go together.

10.7 Criminals in the Political System

There are too many MPs in parliament and MLAs in the state assemblies with criminal records; they should be debarred from sitting for elections till they clear themselves. These criminals are mostly from influential political families. Able to win should not be the criteria for over-looking criminal records. Getting criminals into politics affects the law and order situation, tarnishes the image of the party and sets a wrong example to the younger generation who wish to get into politics.

States today are incapable of dealing with the slightest disruption in law and order. Central forces are deployed to assist the states around the year. Bringing police into the Concurrent List would only amount to give de jure status to what prevails on the ground.

The Central Armed Police forces are not in the best of health. The government should go into their problems of deployment, utilization, discipline, morale, and promotional opportunities.

With the security challenges increasing, from cybercrimes to terrorism, such lacunae in police infrastructure are unacceptable.

COMMUNAL HARMONY

For any country to progress well to give its people a good life and economically become a global power, Communal Harmony is of paramount importance. India is a huge country with people of seven major religions of the world, like Hinduism [with many Castes], Buddhism [Casteless], Jainism [Shwetamber and Digamber sects], Christianity [Casteless], Jews [Orthodox and Israelites], Islam[Sunni and Shia sect] and Sikhism [Casteless], unlike Europe where the countries are smaller in size and each one having one religion, namely Christianity. In India, religion and Caste have divided the country, and as a result, there are many political power centres within India.

In India, the Buddhists, Jains, Sikhs, Christians, and Jews have harmonious relations with the Hindus, who are in the majority. Most of the differences are between Hindus and Muslims, and it does not take much time to spark off a commotion. Instead of maintaining Communal Harmony, the politicians take advantage and create division between Hindus and Muslims for electoral gains. In many places, the Hindus and Muslims live peacefully, even taking part in each other festivals, till the politicians come in. Politicians should treat all communities at the same level because when they come to power, they represent everyone in their constituency and not only their support base.

Job reservations have created communal distress not only between Hindus and Muslims but also among Hindus by the 'Mandal Commission'. This distress will slowly go if we provide enough Jobs, and Jobs will only come if the country concentrates on the economy.

Refugees coming into India, mainly from Bangladesh and now from Myanmar, are creating problems; they are taking up Jobs meant for the Indian citizens; the people of Assam are affected the most as they would soon become a minority. To maintain the demography of the country and to maintain security, illegal immigration has to be stopped.

The demolition of the 'Babri Masjid' to build the 'Ram Temple' created the riots in Mumbai in December 1992 that has divided the Hindus and Muslims further. There is no doubt that the Muslim raiders, mainly under Ghazni, who came into India, forcibly converted Hindus to Islam and had demolished many temples across the country, mainly the 'Ram Temple' at Ayodhya and eventually, Mosques were built over them. The Archaeological Survey of India surveyed satellite images and confirmed Hindu idols under the 'Babri Masjid'.

The present-day Muslims are not to be blamed for Ghazni's actions and others like him. But the present-day Muslims could have been understanding and given the site for the construction of the 'Ram Temple', and the government should have committed to rebuilding the 'Babri Masjid' close by, but it did not happen. In the Middle-east, for road re-alignment, many Mosques have been rebuilt close by. The Muslim leadership lacked statesmanship and dug their heels, and the 'Kar-Sevaks' forcibly demolished the Babri Masjid, which was condemnable.

In 2019, the Supreme Court gave the verdict in favour of the Hindus and the 'Ram Temple' is being built on the disputed site, and the government has given five acres of land close-by to the Muslims to rebuild the 'Babri Masjid', as per the direction of the Supreme Court.

11.1   Cow Worship and Beef Eating

The Hindus look up to the Cow as the 'Gau Mata' and pray to it. At one side of the entrance to most temples, there is an idol of a Cow. Most of the Hindus are vegetarians; some eat goat meat, pork, chicken, and fish. A fewer percentage started eating Cow Beef/Buffalo Meat when the price of goat meat became unaffordable.

Earlier, there was a ban on the slaughtering of Cows in around 22 states, but the ban was not strictly followed; now, there is a ban on eating Beef throughout India by the present NDA government. There is no ban on eating Buffalo Meat as Hindus do not pray to the buffalos.

Because of the ban on eating Beef, people have started eating Buffalo Meat; they may be very few who still prefer Beef that is illegally sold.

The majority of Muslims and Christians prefer to eat Beef as Beef tastes better than Buffalo Meat. There is a high demand for Beef from Pakistan, Bangladesh, and Middle East countries; Cows are smuggled into Pakistan and Bangladesh in large numbers and Cows are slaughtered en masse, and Beef is air-flown to the Middle East. This angers the staunch Hindus.

Muslims who slaughter Cows are lynched, and Muslims, as well as Hindus, who carry Cows from place to place, are beaten. Lynching and beating are against the law, and everyone has condemned it. This is causing concern and fear among the Muslim community. If a wrong is done, the process should take the legal route. Society has no right to take any action.

A compromise formula will be to give incentives to farmers to run buffalo and goat farms [including canning] for the domestic and foreign market and Muslims to respect the sentiments of those Hindus who don't eat Beef on religious grounds and object to the slaughtering of Cows.

Muslims don't eat pork on religious grounds, and nobody can open a pork shop close to where they live. The other communities respect their sentiments. Muslim servant is not forced to make a pork dish or even wash the vessels used.

11.2   Riots

There are a number of 'Riots' across the country due to religious intolerance; it can be nipped in the bud if the society controls the hotheads in their respective community and if the politicians don't make inflammatory speeches that incite the mobs into violence and destruction of property. The police should deal with the delicate situation carefully and not take any side.

The recent 'Citizenship [Amendment] Act [CAA] seems to have created doubts in the minds of the Muslim community in India by the opposition political leaders and some activists that the CAA will affect the Muslims in India that led to communal riots that have taken a death toll of around 42 people and injury to around 2000 people and destruction to property, In East Delhi on 23/24 February 2020, in spite of Harish Salve, a senior advocate at the Supreme Court of India and a Queen's counsel for the courts of England and Wales, clarifying that the CAA does not affect the Muslims in India.

Illegal migrants into India are deported under the Foreigners Act, 1946 and the Citizenship Act, 1955. This applies to everyone- Muslims, Hindus, Sikhs, Christians, Buddhists, Jains and Parsis.

On August 15, 1947, the Partition of India took place on the basis of religion – Hindu and Muslims; most Hindus from Pakistan crossed over to India, and likewise, most Muslims from the Indian side crossed over to Pakistan. However, there was a small percentage of Muslims who stayed back in India and preferred staying in India, and likewise, there was a small percentage of Hindus, Sikhs, Christians, Buddhists, Jains and Parsis who stayed back in Pakistan and preferred staying there. This prompted the Indian Political leadership to follow a secular, socialistic, democratic government in India. However, 'secular' was entered in the constitution during the emergency in 1975; likewise, the Pakistan political Leadership also sought to follow a secular, democratic government in Pakistan.

In 1988, President Zia-ul-Haq, the dictator of Pakistan, gave more powers to the Mullahs and turned Pakistan into an Islam country, and even brought in the 'Sharia Law'.

Due to the persecution of non-Muslims in Pakistan and Bangladesh, most non-Muslims in Pakistan and Bangladesh came over to India and became illegal immigrants. As these people have no other place to go, to help these affected people, the present NDA government introduced the Citizen [Amendment] Bill in the Lok Sabha on July 19, 2016, and the Parliament referred the bill to a joint committee of both the Houses of Parliament, which presented its report on January 04, 2019, recommending the bill. Subsequently, the bill was passed by the parliament and enacted the Citizen [Amendment] Act [CAA] that has become the law.

The question asked is – why not the Muslims from Pakistan, Bangladesh, and Afghanistan? There is no persecution of Muslims in Pakistan, Bangladesh, and Afghanistan. However, there are clashes among the Muslims, like Sunni's and Shias' and there are many Muslim countries to which they can migrate to.

Another question is – India is a secular country, why can't India take in Muslims too? 'Secular' is for running the country for all the people who are legally already in the country and not keep it open for any tom, dick and harry to come in.

The political opposition and some of the activists are mixing the National Population Register [NPR] with the CAA; they are both for a different purpose. The NPR survey is carried out once every 10 years; the last survey was carried out in 2010. Every country has to know the number of legitimate people living in their jurisdiction for planning the distribution of Budget and resources for various expenditure and welfare schemes, and providing education, healthcare, and Jobs, etc.; it is a governance requirement and nothing to do with the CAA.

To ensure that the people are legitimate, a certain amount of background check is carried out, and for this purpose, a form is created to get the required inputs. From experience, if a column is later added to get the required input to ascertain that the person is actually genuine, and likewise, a column removed that is considered unnecessary, there is nothing wrong in adding/removing a column.

The data in the NPR will help in formulating the National Register for Citizen [NRC], which keeps the record of all citizens, when and if it is conducted, and the NCR also has no connection with the CAA.

The problem is that some of the people, especially at the lower level, do not have their complete records and have not bothered to obtain the missing records, and even if they have the complete records, they cannot find them as they have not kept them in a safe place or have never been told the importance of keeping them.

Since migration has taken place within the country and within a state, some people do not have their parents and grandparents' addresses.

Because of the non-availability of complete documents, the affected people feel that they will be thrown out of the country and feel insecure. The answer is to consider only the minimum documents that identify a person and avoid creating uncertainty.

In the last 5 years, during the NDA government, around 500 plus Muslims from Pakistan and mostly from Bangladesh have become Indian citizens through the normal route, and this can carry on; there is no complete ban.

To maintain Communal Harmony, the state governments should create interfaith Platforms in their sensitive areas where the religious teachers talk about the spiritual guidance their religion gives to their people; even leaflets can be distributed.

The contents below are an extract on the interfaith Platform, from the author's earlier book – 'REPENTANCE', a finalist in the Foreword Magazine- 'Book of the Year', at New York festival -2007'.

Quote– *"When Laxmandas Munshi saw a number of his colleagues rushing after the office hours to attend the Interfaith meetings and heard* *them discussing the good of all the religions during the tea and lunch breaks, he also became inquisitive. One night while Laxmandas was asleep, he dreamt that someone was telling him to go for the meetings. Laxmandas got up early in the morning and decided to attend the meetings. Laxmandas's colleagues were all taken by surprise, when they saw Laxmandas entering the venue of the meeting, as they knew him to be a person who saw nothing beyond Hinduism.*

For the first time, Laxmandas saw all the religious heads on the same platform. They represented the multi-religious and the multi-cultural people of India. No country in the world has this much of different religious representation. The religious heads were dressed in their religious formal attire. After they were introduced to the audience, the Hindu priest first took to the rostrum.

The Hindu Priest started his talk by stating that Hinduism was one of the oldest religions in the world and that the roots date back to Indian pre-historic times. The Priest added that in about 1500 BCE, the Aryans from Central Asia invaded and conquered North India and pushed the Dravidians down to South India. Due to the pressure from the north, some of the Dravidians migrated to Sri Lanka and other islands south of India and to South East Asia. The Aryan culture gradually mixed with the Dravidian culture and the blend of the two cultures took the shape of Hinduism. Hinduism portrays God to be ultimate reality as Brahman but also believes that God is also revealed in other Gods and Goddesses. The Priest further stated that the Vedas are the oldest Hindu scriptures, and they were developed during a period of 1000 years, which is known as the Vedic period from 1000 BCE. By 500 BCE, Hinduism split into various schools of thought. Two of these prominent schools -Buddhism and Jainism – became new religions and split from Hinduism. In fact, one can say that Buddhism and Jainism are offshoots of Hinduism with a little change. The Hindu schools further split into smaller sects. Gurus formed many of the sects. Today, Hinduism includes a great number of schools with a number of sects. Each sect has its own philosophy and form of worship, but they all accept the basic Hindu doctrines that are the basic beliefs about the divinities, personal conduct, and life after death.

The Priest also stated that Hinduism stresses the soul's release from this world and preaches complete detachment from the affairs of this life. The Priest emphasized that according to the Bhagavad-Gita, the best way to gain salvation is through love and devotion to Vishnu.

The Priest emphasized that Dharma is the moral and religious law of Hinduism and explained that Dharma is to fulfil one's religious obligation to society that establishes rules of duty and ethical conduct of all people. The priest further explained how Artha is achieving by worldly success through one's occupation and Moksha is gaining by spiritual release from worldly existence.

In the belief of life after death, the Priest explained that every action of a person influences how the soul will be born in the next incarnation, i.e., if a person lives a good life, the soul will be born into a higher state, if a person leads an evil life, the soul will be born into a lower state. A person's incarnation continues until he or she achieves spiritual perfection. The soul then enters a new level of existence called Moksha, from which it never returns.

Laxmandas Munshi felt that he had lived an evil life by spoiling his daughter, Shobha's life, when she wanted to get married to Michael of a different religion and would be reborn in a lower state in his next life and that it would take a number of lives, before he could achieve spiritual perfection. Laxmandas Munshi was unhappy with his likely future after death.

Then came the turn of the Buddhist Monk. The Monk stated that in 500 BCE, Gautama Buddha, who was once Prince Sidhartha Gautama, founded Buddhism, an off-shoot of Hinduism. Buddha means enlightenment. The Monk added that, unlike Hinduism, Buddhism does not accept the idea of God as creator; the role that Buddha plays in their religion is similar to God in other religions.

The Monk said that Buddhism taught people to devote themselves to finding release from the suffering of life, and through their release, people would gain 'nirvana'. The Monk spoke about Dharma, i.e., the moral and religious law, which governs daily life and shows the way to salvation. The Monk also explained reincarnation, i.e., life after death, as it is in Hinduism.

The Jain Priest then took his turn. The Jain Priest stated that in 500 BCE, nearly the same time Buddhism was founded, the holy teacher Mahavira founded Jainism. The Jain Priest added that Mahavira was the twenty-fourth in the line of teachings of Jainism, and the Jains honour these teachers of Jain principles but do not believe they are Gods and also do not believe in a supreme God.

The Jain Priest explained that Jainism is based on the belief that every living thing consists of an eternal soul called the jiva and a temporary body. The eternal jiva is imprisoned in the body as a result of involvement in worldly activities. To free the jiva, one must avoid such activities as much as possible. Each jiva is reincarnated in many bodies before it is finally freed. After being freed, it exists eternally in a state of perfect knowledge of bliss, similar to Hinduism.

The Jain Priest emphasized on Karma, i.e., good deeds and achievement of 'nirvana' to lead to free themselves from all worldly desires and attachment to worldly things. The Jain Priest further added that as per Jainism, all life is sacred, and no living life should be killed; as a result, Jains do not kill even a fly.

In his turn, the Rabbi stated that Judaism was one of the oldest major religions and was founded by Abraham about 4000 years ago. Unlike the other major religions, Judaism is the religion of one people – the Jews and the religion teaches the belief in one God.

The Rabbi added that it was in 600 BCE that the Jewish Prophets converted Jews to monotheism and that God was known by a variety of names, such as Yahweh [Jehovah], Elohim, and Edonai, and the religion follows the Hebrew Bible or the Old Testament of which the first five books of the sacred book are known as the Torah, which is the basis of Jewish religion.

The Rabbi explained the 10 Commandments that shaped the private and public morality and the most fundamental teachings concerning behaviour towards other people. The Rabbi emphasized that God wants people to do what is just and merciful. The Rabbi added that Judaism teaches that all people are treated alike in the image of God and deserve to be treated with dignity and respect.

The Rabbi further stated that both Christianity and Islam developed from Judaism, and these religions accept the Jewish belief, one God and the moral teachings from the Hebrew Bible or the Old Testament. But clarified that, unlike many other religions, Judaism does not try to convince others to adopt its beliefs and practices. However, it does accept people who choose to convert to Judaism.

Then, the Bishop followed and stated that Christianity believes that there is one God and that God appeared in three ways, that is, as Father and creator, as His son Jesus Christ, and as the Holy Spirit. The Bishop added that Christianity is a religion based on the life and teachings of Jesus Christ in Palestine and that most Christians believe that God sent Jesus Christ to this world as a saviour and that humanity can achieve salvation through Jesus.

The Bishop gave a brief history of the spread of Christianity - after Jesus' Crucifixion in about the year 30 CE, a number of his followers spread his teachings. One of the most important of these followers was Saint Paul. After Saint Paul's death, in about the year 67 CE, Christianity continued to grow in spite of persecution by the Romans. By the late 300 CE, Christianity was widely practised throughout Europe, the Middle East, and Northern Africa. In the year 1500 CE, a religious movement known as the reformists divided Christianity into Roman Catholics and Protestants. Christianity as a whole has spread throughout the world, and today, Christianity makes up the largest religious group in the world. Christians see Jesus as continuation with the God of Judaism, and the life and teachings of Jesus are recorded in the New Testament.

The Bishop explained the belief- that Jesus is the Savoir who died to save humanity from sin and Jesus' death made salvation and eternal life possible for others. The Bishop advised everyone to repent his or her sinful ways and achieve righteousness by obeying God and leading an upright life according to God's moral law.

The Bishop touched on the last judgment; he said that depending on the lives one has led, every person will either be granted happiness in Heaven or be condemned to suffer in Hell.

Laxmandas Munshi was perturbed, as he now knew that he would be sent to hell. Lying on the bed, Laxmandas's thoughts went back to the talks he had heard during the interfaith meetings.

One point that struck his mind was that though Buddhism was an offshoot of Hinduism, it was Buddhism, a classless religion that influenced and spread too far off places like Mongolia, China, Japan, Korea, Sri Lanka, Burma, Malaysia, Indonesia, Laos, Kampuchea, Thailand, Vietnam, and Bhutan, and not Hinduism. He wondered whether it was the rigid Caste system in Hinduism that hindered its influence.

After recovering from the operation, though feeling a bit weak, Laxmandas made it a point of attending the sessions he had missed.

The Imam took to the stand. The Imam stated that Prophet Muhammad founded the religion of Islam in 600 CE and that Islam is the second-largest religious group in the world. The Imam further stated that Prophet Muhammad had preached that Allah is the only God and that he was God's Messenger, as he believed that he was sent to warn and guide his people and to call them to worship God. The Imam added that Muslims consider their holy book, the Quran- the words of God Himself, spoken to Muhammad by an angel.

The Imam gave a brief history of the division of the Muslim community after the death of Prophet Muhammad in 632 CE. The Imam explained how the Muslims were divided into the Shiite community and the Sunni community; the Shiite origin lies in the controversies about the leadership of the Islamic community after the death of Prophet Muhammad. The Shiite had argued that leadership should have gone to Ali, the Prophets cousin and closest surviving male relative, who was also the husband of Fatima, the Prophet's daughter, and the Sunnites supported the election of Abi Bakr, one of the Prophet's prominent disciples as Caliph, the leader or successor.

The Imam further stated that parts of the Quran resemble the bible, the Apocrypha, and the Talmud, and the Quran contains many stories about the prophets that appear in the Old Testament. The Imam added that the Quran also has stories from the New Testament about Jesus, whom it calls the 'Word of God'.

The Imam emphasized on God's will and reality of this world that shaped private and public morality. The Imam also emphasized that God wants people to do what is just and merciful and that the most fundamental *teachings concern behaviour towards other people.*

The Imam concluded by saying that God is just and merciful and wishes people to repent and purify themselves so that they attain paradise after death.

Laxmandas Munshi felt that he still had a chance if he repented and purified himself; God would be just and merciful.

The Parsi Priest then took his turn. The Priest stated that Zoroastrian was founded between 1400 and 1000 BCE by a Persian Prophet named Zarathustra, who taught the belief in one God, Ahura Mazda, who created all things.

The Priest explained that the main teachings of Zoroastrianism is the belief in the battle between good and evil, as Zoroaster taught that the earth is a battleground where a great struggle is taking place between Spenta Mainya, i.e., the spirit of good, and Agra Mainya, i.e., the spirit of evil. The Priest added that Ahura Mazda calls upon everyone to fight in this struggle, and each person will be judged at death on how well he or she fought. Therefore, each person should be dedicated to fighting for good thoughts, good words, and good deeds. The Priest stated that at the end, God would judge each person at death by how he fought well against evil.

The Priest added that Zoroaster composed several hymns called Gathas that were collected into a sacred book known as the Avesta. These hymns are the only record of what Zoroaster believed, in his own words.

The Priest further added that Zoroastrians who migrated to India are called Parsis and that the modern Zoroastrians read from the Avesta, practice traditional purification habits, and attend rituals at fire temples. The Priest concluded by saying that Fire is most important in Zoroastrianism as a symbol of Ahura Mazda.

The Granthiji was the last to speak. The Granthiji stated that Guru Nanak started Sikhism, the youngest religion in the year 1500 CE, as a movement to combine Hinduism and Islam and to have a classless society. The Granthiji added that Guru Nanak, the first Guru told his followers to avoid worldly activities and lead peaceful and righteous lives. The Granthiji added that in 1699 CE, Guru Govind Singh, the tenth and last Guru organized a brotherhood of Sikh soldiers and led the Sikhs in many battles for religious independence.

The Granthiji further stated that the Sikhs follow the teachings of the ten Gurus, the religious teachers and that the teachings are given in their holy book, and as per their holy book, everyone should live a peaceful and righteous life. The Granthiji further stated that as in Islam, they believe in one Divine Power and pray to their Holy Book, the Adi Granth Sahib, as their Divine Power. As in Hinduism, they believe in the doctrine of Karma and in reincarnation. The Granthiji emphasized on karma, i.e., action of thoughts and words, good deeds and code of conduct, a set of moral teachings and values. The Granthiji also explained reincarnation, i.e., life after death.

Now came the turn of the audience. The audience asked a number of questions and all the religious heads in their turn took the trouble of carefully answering and clarifying even some of the most sensitive and awkward questions. A lot of time was spent on explaining who created the earth and life on it, and what happens to life after death.

There were some differences between the religions, like the doctrine of salvation that is taught by all major religions. All major religions stress that salvation is the highest goal of the faithful and one that all followers should try to achieve, but the difference between the religions is in what salvation is and how it can be gained.

Most religions teach that a person gains salvation by finding release from certain obstacles that block human effects. In Christianity, the obstacles are sin and its effects, whereas, in Hinduism, Buddhism and Jainism, the obstacles are worldly desires and attachment to worldly things. Christianity and Islam teach that salvation comes only once and is eternal, whereas Hinduism, Buddhism, Jainism, and Sikhism teach that there is life after death and a person's carnation continues till he or she attains spiritual perfection.

In another case, code of conduct is a set of moral teachings and values that all religions have in some form with a difference, but most agree on several major themes. For example, they stress some form of the golden rule, which states that believers should treat others, as they would like to be treated themselves.

Laxmandas was so engrossed with religion that he paid a visit to the

Hindu temple, the Church, the Synagogue, the Mosque, the Gurdwara, the Buddhist monastery and the Jain temple. Being a non-Parsi, Laxmandas was not allowed to enter the Fire temple. Initially, it hurt him, but Laxmandas respected the communities' sentiments when he was explained that when the Parsis fled Iran to avoid the Muslims suppression and landed in Gujarat, the then Maharaja had told them that he had no objection in their settling down in his kingdom, but they should not convert his people to their religion. The Parsis agreed and since then have honoured their word and have never converted anyone and also forbidden non-Parsis from entering their Fire temple, less they may get influenced by their religion and try to convert.

Laxmandas realised that generally, all the religions centred on devotion to 'God or the 'Divine Power', enlightenment of the soul, achievement of a state of spiritual perfection, leading peaceful and righteous life, the battle between good and evil, the moral obligations which governs daily life and shows the way to salvation, like love, mercy and self-sacrifice, virtues of prudence, temperance, courage and justice, values, truth, brotherhood and kindness, actions towards good deeds, harmony, compassion and humanity.

What struck Laxmandas the most was that no religion preached that their religion was superior to other religions and that their followers were superior to others. All religions wanted that mankind should live in peace and prosperity.

In the end, Laxmandas realized that most of the people, including himself, were not clear about their own religion and knew very little of the other religions, except their name. He also realized that some of them, including him, were under wrong impressions of their own religion and of the other religions. In the ultimate analysis, he found that it was not religion that created barriers between people; in fact, all religions could co-exist with each other; it was the people in the garb of religion that created barriers between people more for political aims that have resulted in bloodshed throughout the world. He found that the inter-faith platform was the best form of making people wiser and bringing them together."

Unquote.

The establishment of 'Interfaith Platforms' in various places will help people to come to gather and understand various religions; this will help people to live in Communal Harmony. The army has facilities at Khadki [Maharashtra] to train all its religious preachers in one place; the state governments should look at the facilities and take some guidance in how to go about it.

11.3   Caste

Among Hindus, Caste has created barriers among various communities. With education, job opportunities available in today's progressive world and exposure to the world at large, Caste has become meaningless. Amongst scholars and thinkers, in the armed forces, in business and in the working class, one finds a cross-section of society from various religions, Caste and colour.

In the ultimate analysis, we all come into this world with nothing and one day will be leave with nothing; the anatomy of the body is similar, and we have a soul. Prejudice against any religion, Caste or colour is baseless.

A number of Hindu religious places of worship have a huge donation in terms of cash, silver and gold, and property in terms of statues and fittings and are vulnerable to thieves and miscreants. Whenever incidents of robbery take place, other religious communities are blamed.

Likewise, a number of churches have donations, property in terms of statues and fittings and are also vulnerable to thieves and miscreants. The electrical fittings and wirings are very old, and with a short circuit, the church catches fire and the wooden furniture and a number of Bibles add to the fire. When these incidents take place, the Hindu hardliners are blamed.

There is an urgent need for religious places to put their cash in banks and invest their cash wisely, like Fixed Deposits, to generate more money to be used for social welfare, insure their silver and gold, have security arrangements for statues in terms of inner security fencing, proper locks on all doors and windows and guards for outer ring security. The electrical fitments and wiring be checked periodically, and firefighting equipment placed at appropriate places.

Some years back, on the Indian-Bangladesh border, some robbers from Bangladesh came over to the Indian side and robbed cash and silver statues and also raped a nun. During the same period, a church was on fire due to a short circuit. Initially, the Hindu hardliners were wrongly blamed; later, the truth came out.

If an incident occurs, a proper investigation should be carried out, and the causes should be determined. The media should not give wrong coverage, and the leadership of various religious communities should not jump the gun and make inflammatory statements.

MINORITY RIGHTS

The Nationality of all the citizens of India, irrespective of their religion, is 'Indian', and there is nothing wrong with being a proud 'Indian'. It is being an 'Indian' that binds everyone together.

It was the British who called India Hindustan, and as a result, the Indians were known as Hindustani, and from this, came Hindutva, the Hindu way of life. The staunch Hindus with a political base are forcing Hindutva on non-Hindus, which seems to create problems between Hindus and non-Hindus.

The Scheduled Caste [SC] and Scheduled Tribes [STs] suffer the maximum as they are socio-economically backward. The only way to uplift them is by imparting education, including skill training and providing healthcare so that they can pick up Jobs. Providing loans at low interest to start off small businesses, cattle farms, breeding fish, horticulture and employing their own people will help them prosper. Enrolling them into the defence forces will give them a jump for a better life for themselves and their family, like the British raised the hill tribe units, like the Gurkha regiments, Garhwal regiments and Kumaon regiments. Apart from the Tribals being good fighters, a good percentage of their population will live a better life, economically and socially and will be able to educate their children for a better future.

The majority of the minorities are socio-economically at the bottom and lower-middle level of the society and badly affected, and like the backward Muslims, most have them have large families. The remaining, very less in percentage, are at the lower-middle level are not affected as they are economically better off and, to some extent, socially connected.

The government should use these people to establish community centres at various places by providing accommodation and funds, as was done in the United States to help the African Americans to come into the mainstream. Once the minorities come into the mainstream, minority rights will automatically be protected.

The community centres should provide guidance and encouragement in education and skill development, health care [including personal hygiene and civic responsibility], and organize social events, sports and promote hobbies.

The SC and ST's are not allowed to enter temple's; in such a situation, the government should give land and funds to build their own temples with priests of their own.

Those of the weaker section who converted to Buddhism live a respectable life and pick up lower-level Jobs; some who have converted to Christianity benefited a lot, they joined the Christian-run schools and got a good education and healthcare, this gave them a jump in society; they picked up middle-level Jobs, and some climbed to the top.

12.1   Manual Scavenging

Manual Scavenging has been one of the lowest forms of treating mankind; it is not only exploiting the weaker section of society but is humiliating, degrading and hazardous to health. A total of 53,598 manual scavengers have been identified between December 2013 and June 2019. The practice was outlawed in 1993, 46 years after gaining Independence. Under the Manual Scavenging Act, it is obligatory for employers to provide safety gear, devices and equipment and ensure prescribed safety precautions are followed before a person is engaged for cleaning of sewers and septic tanks.

The local bodies should adopt mechanized cleaning of sewers and septic tanks, according to the national plan for the elimination of

Manual Scavenging. Super Sucker machines in the range of ₹60 Lakh to ₹3 crores can be used for cleaning the worst clogged sewers in narrow lanes.

A total of 620 sewer cleaners' deaths in 15 states since 1993, most in Tamil Nadu [144] and Gujarat [131], followed by Karnataka [75]. In 2014, the Supreme Court directed that a compensation of ₹10 Lakh to the family of the deceased. Till July 2019, full compensation has been made in 445 cases, partial payment has been made to 58 cases, and 117 cases are pending. The sewer cleaners should have insurance cover with the government paying the full premium.

Madrasas

Most of the Muslim youth study at the Madrasas, which teaches them more about religion and less or nothing on other educational subjects that can get help them to get meaningful Jobs. Madrasas should teach subjects that are job oriented.

The government pumps in a lot of funds for the upliftment of the minorities, but the funds don't reach them as there is too much corruption and misappropriation of funds. The landless labourer's, Dalits and Adivasi's are exploited. Strict auditing of funds should be carried out, and defaulters should be punished.

B N Yugandhar was one of the few remaining 'nationalist policy' reformers; he died in September 2019. He was part of the group that pushed for globalization and domestic reforms in the eighties that saw some light in 1991 reforms under the then Prime Minister P V Narasimha Rao.

He, with his other like-minded thinkers, turned their attention towards strengthening local and community institutions. He played a pioneering role in turning the attention of the administration to local level institutions. His first involvement was in the abolition of bonded labour that was part of the governments '20 point programme'. He was involved with the development of Gujarat states 'Panchayati Raj Reports'. He would stand by youngsters who would go to villages and report misappropriation of funds meant for the poor and exploitation of the landless labourers, Dalits and Adivasis. He acquainted the policymakers with the rural reforms in Korea and East Asia. He was instrumental in integrating the small farmer and landless labourer's project into the district plan and insisted on the Finance Ministry giving it a free fund, albeit of a limited nature for local priority projects, to make local planning an operating system with some resources of its own.

Cauvery dispute – he suggested that the affected states use a formula devised to resolve the conflict over the Mekong basin as a dispute resolution mechanism. Community organizations engaged in sustainable development at the local level to include annual elections, training local leaders, providing technical support, setting up procedures for financial probity, and instituting mechanism to involve the landless poor.

12.2   Uniform Civil Code

The founders of the constitution had hoped and expected a Uniform Civil Code for India, but there has been no attempt at seriously framing it because of the 'vote bank' politics. The Supreme Court, while hearing a matter related to properties of a Goan, described Goa as a shining example with a Uniform Civil Code.

The code is one that would provide for one law for the entire country, applicable to all religious communities in their personal matters such as marriages, divorce, inheritance, adoption, etc. Article 44 of the constitution lays down that the state shall endeavour to secure a Uniform Civil Code for the citizens throughout the territory of India.

All Hindus of the country are not governed by one law, nor all Muslims or all Christians. British, Portuguese, and French legal systems remain operative in some parts. In J&K, until August 5, 2019, local Hindu law statutes differed from central enactments. The Shariat Act of 1937 was extended to J&K a few years ago but has now been repealed. Muslims of Kashmir were thus governed by a customary law that was closer to Hindu law and, in many ways, was at variance with Muslim Personal Law in the rest of the country. Even on the registration of marriage among Muslims, laws differed from place to place. Around 200 tribes in the North East are governed by their own varied customary laws. The Constitution protects local customs in Nagaland; similar protections are enjoyed by Meghalaya and Mizoram. Even reformed Hindu Law, in spite of codification, protects customary practices.

Among the Hindu families in Andhra, Karnataka, and borders of these states with Maharashtra, as per the customary practices in marriage, a boy is allowed to get married to his sister's daughter or the daughter of his father's sister or his mother's brother. Even in the Muslim and Parsi community, cousins are allowed to marry each other. Basically, these marriages take place to avoid dowry or to keep the money and property within the close families. Therefore, such practices and any other practices specific to a community should be incorporated in the 'Common Civil Code' as riders.

Article 25 lays down an individual's fundamental right to religion but is subject to 'public order, health, morality' and other provisions related to fundamental rights, but a group's freedom under Article 26 has not been subjected to other fundamental rights.

For the country to progress, maintaining Communal Harmony is important; there will be Communal Harmony if the majority allow the minorities to practice their rights, and the minorities also don't create problems for the majority.

The opposition political parties should not create problems for the ruling party for vote-bank politics; the recent anti- CAA movement was unwarranted. The activists should be balanced in their movements and not create uncertainty.

The media also should be correct in reporting and avoid creating panic for better TRP.

In the ultimate analysis, Communal Harmony depends on the majority in power, the minority, the political opposition and the activists, and the media.

An ideal situation is when there is mutual faith, mutual understanding, and mutual confidence between the majority in power and the minority, an opposition that is constructive and activists who are practical rather than being critical all the time.

CLIMATE CHANGE

There is a mismatch between the advanced countries and the developing countries as far as carbon emission is concerned. Ever since the industrial revolution, around 90% of carbon emission is the cumulative emission of western, rich, industrial countries and Japan. The USA is the biggest emitter [16.5 metric tons]. Maybe, the new electric battery technology will change that. The developing countries carbon emission is comparatively less, and industrially, they have much to catch up with.

Recently, Greta Thunberg, a 16-year-young girl from Sweden had given a beautiful speech at the United Nations on Climate Change that inspired the world and was one of the possible Nobel Prize winners. Sweden is one of the richest countries, and its annual per capita carbon emissions are 4.5 metric tons, higher than India's 1.7 metric tons. India depends on massive amounts of coal for producing thermal power. India has to seriously plan to generate electricity through nuclear energy.

The climate emergency is a race the world is losing, but it is a race the world can win if we change our ways now. The world is actually facing a climate crisis. We are seeing unprecedented temperature, unrelenting storms, and undeniable signs.

Countries using fossil fuel that emit harmful carbon emissions should reduce their consumption and change to clean energy, like solar and windmill energy. Global rise in temperature to be below 2 degrees Celsius from the pre-industry times.

On September 16, 2019, a special action summit was held on the side-lines of the UN General Meeting, with 60 heads of state or government. It aimed at identifying concrete and urgent solutions. The UN Secretary General told world leaders to come with concrete and realistic proposals to enhance the actions that they are already taking. He asked countries to bring their action plan in line with an objective of reducing global greenhouse gas emissions by 45% by 2030 and to 'net zero' by 2050. He has appealed to the countries to not set up any new coal plants after 2020, stop subsidies on fossil fuels, and levy additional taxes on polluters.

The financial needs specified by the developing countries in their Nationally Determined Contribution's [NDC's] adds up to $4.4 trillion. India requires $206 billion by 2030 to implement only the adaption programmers' in Agriculture, forestry, water resources and infrastructure. The total cost of carrying out all actions in the NDC would cost adds up to Rs 44 trillion by 2030.

The Prime Minister of India had stated that India is doing its best and is not in a position to upgrade its climate action plan till the developed world fulfils its obligation of providing money and technology to developing countries to help them deal with the impacts of Climate Change.

Under the 2015 Paris Agreement, every signatory nation is supposed to finalize and submit a set of time-bound actions that it would take to combat Climate Change.

The first set of action plans, called NDC [Nationally Determined Contribution], was submitted in 2015 and was to be updated every five years.

Management of resources, protection of ecological landscape, the study of environmental degradation, energy security and renewable energy should be the top priority. Environment studies should be carried out to ensure a sustainable and productive future. Subjects related to Climate Change and its impact on the environment should take centre stage.

A lot of untapped natural resources can give us clean energy. Apart from solar energy, we should explore the potential of geothermal energy.

In our fight against global warming, the cities hills will play a vital role. Hills are the lungs; they provide fresh air to breathe by absorbing the city's carbon emission. Hills provide the ideal location for maximum grasslands to grow and flourish; if the grasslands on these hills disappear, the cities might turn into arid land. Tree plantation should be done under the guidance of experts who know what species to plant in what kind of ecosystem.

Two areas that are worrying are the continuing environmental degradation and global warming, which are creating serious problems. The air we breathe, and the waters of our rivers have become highly polluted. Unless this trend is reversed, we will face serious and widespread health problems in the years and decades to come.

Climate Change is one of the most serious challenges facing the human race, impacting the entire world, and it can only be tackled on a global basis. Extreme weather conditions are wreaking havoc worldwide, lethal hurricanes are regularly hitting the American continent; many animals, insect species and plants are becoming extinct, and the melting of glaciers is causing ocean levels to rise. This will wipe out coastlines and small islands of many countries very soon.

One of the main reasons is cutting vegetation for construction, polluted air from factories, especially chemicals, transport based on oil, burning stubble after harvesting and Cows that pass gas in large quantities.

Generating electricity with Solar/ Windmill energy, depending on sun/wind [25% in a year], transport based electric vehicles will help in reducing warming.

In India, there has been an erratic change in the weather pattern, with a lot of rain causing waterlogging in many cities, bringing them to a grinding halt, and destruction of crops, and in some areas, droughts, affecting the livelihood of many farmers.

ENVIRONMENT PROTECTION

The biggest problem in India is the management of solid waste. The management policy requires that wet and dry waste should not be mixed so that only non-compostable and non-recyclable waste with at least 1,500 kcal/kg should reach WTE (waste-to-energy) plants. The people need to be educated in dealing with disposable of wet and solid waste.

WTE plants in India are inefficient in generating energy as their operations are neither strictly maintained nor adequately monitored. Municipal waste in India has a very high biodegradable [wet] waste content ranging from 60 to 70% of the total, compared with 30% in the west.

WTE plants in our cities, using inadequately secreted municipal waste as feedstock, are highly dangerous because of the toxic gases and particles they spew when they burn mixed waste in the process of incineration. There are five municipal WTE plants operational in India with a total capacity to produce 66.4 MW of electricity per day, of which the lion's share of 52 MW per day is generated in Delhi by its three existing plants. The plants in India burn mixed waste; the presence of chlorinated hydrocarbons results in the release of dioxins and furans when the waste is burnt at less than 850 degrees Celsius. Appropriate filtering mechanisms need to be installed to control such dangerous emission. Dioxins and furans are known to lead to impairment of immune, endocrine, nervous and reproductive systems. The plants are operated without the use of activated charcoal that filters out dioxins, furans, and mercury from the emission.

Even when incineration takes place under optimal conditions, large amounts of flue gases, mercury vapour and lead compounds are released, and there is always about 30% residue from incineration in the form of slag [bottom ash] and fly ash [particulate matter], which are also known to be serious pollutants of air and water.

Even the best-maintained plants in the West are said to cause higher levels of cancer and other illness, and that is why WTE plants are being phased out in the West.

Paper, plastic, cardboard, cloth, rubber etc., go to the scrap dealers; this reduces the caloric value of our waste. Low-cost options such as composting and bio-methanation are better.

Most rivers are polluted; people should be educated to keep the rivers clean by not throwing trash into them and periodically cleaning them. A water filter plant should be installed at the mouth of the nalas coming to the river.

Forestry should be maintained and not destroyed. In this, the Indian Forestry Service has to play an important part.

A great effort has to be made to stop the shooting of animals, especially the species that are going out of existence and avoid throwing plastic into the seas and rivers that is affecting the marine-life

Summary

Every candidate standing for election should have some knowledge of all the subjects covered above, then only he can govern properly and serve the people of the country. Just getting elected with family connections or with money power or muscle power and just being a figurehead and governing with his or her henchmen/henchwomen will not help the people and the country.

Making the candidates debate on all the topics on which people's lives depend will allow the voters to elect the best. What the people of the country deserve is a sound, strong and decisive leader.

Once the candidates are elected, they must keep in mind- what Field Marshall Sir Philip Walhouse Chetwode, Commander-in-Chief of British India from 1930 to 1935, said – "The safety, honour and welfare of your country comes first, always and every time. The honour, welfare and comfort of the men you command come next, and your own ease, comfort and safety come last, always and every time."

On commissioning, when the gentlemen cadets pass out of the Indian Military Academy, they go through a door in a slow march. Above the door, the above words are written in bold letters that give the code of conduct as an officer.

These words or words to this effect should also be written at the entrance to the parliament to remind the MPs of their code of conduct as politicians.

There are numerous examples of men in uniform who have followed the words of Field Marshall Sir Philip Walhouse Chetwode; one recent example is of Major General Ian Cardozo [Retd]- during the Indo-Pak war-1971, then Major Ian Cardozo's jeep went over the enemy's minefield, and he was badly wounded on one of his legs since gangrene would set in, he took out his kukri and amputated his leg, he was hospitalized and given an artificial leg.

After many years, when the wooden prosthesis legs were replaced by carbon fibre shaft modular prosthesis legs, the deputy commandant of the Artificial Limb Centre, Pune, rang up Major General Ian Cardozo and asked him to report to the ALC for a replacement to a new technology leg.

True to the spirit of the words of Field Marshall Sir Philip Walhouse Chetwode – "The safety, honour and welfare of your country come first, always and every time. The honour, welfare and comfort of the men you command come next, and your own ease, comfort and safety come last, always and every time." Major General Ian Cardozo told the Deputy Commandant, "First call the affected men and replace their legs and when you are about to finish with the last man, call me." It is people like Major General Ian Cardozo one admires.

Most politicians practice – "their own ease, comfort and safety come above for the Nation and the people."

The men in the Army, Navy and Air Force sacrifice their lives for the Nation and the people. Here is one example - During the Japanese invasion of Eastern India, the British Indian army put up great resistance to stop them at Kohima. After the Japanese were thrown back at the famous "Battle of Kohima"– April 1944 and subsequently the Japanese surrendered; an Epitaph was built at Kohima, with words written on it that read – "When you go home, tell them of us and say, for your tomorrow, we gave our today." All Indians should always remember these words and respect the armed forces.

Even today, the Indian Armed Forces are guarding the borders, the coastline and the airspace against Pakistan and China so that we can go about our lives safely and sleep well.

Prime Minister Narendra Damodar Modi

He is a man of destiny who has risen from a very humble family with values to the post of Prime Minister of one of the largest democratic country. His life took him through the school days, during which he was in the junior wing of the NCC that gave him an ambition of joining the armed forces, but his father dissuaded him from doing so. He was married at a very young age, but he did not consummate the marriage but, by mutual understanding, left his wife to carry on with her teaching ambition and left for the Himalaya's to live a life of his own. He spent three years by himself and wandered around the mountains discovering himself spiritually and the world at large.

After three years, he came back and joined the RSS. Occasionally, he used to meet his Guru based near Kolkata for his blessing. At one point, he told his Guru that he wanted to become a Monk. However, the monk told Modi that he was destined to take a bigger role in doing good for the country and he should go in that direction and Modi did go in that direction to become three times the Chief Minister Gujarat and the Prime Minister of India for the second time with a majority of 353 seats in the parliament.

Modi has managed to acquire a pro-poor image. He has got the image of a strong leader after the Balakot success, where he hit out against Pakistan. The people of India are fed up with Pakistan, especially the people living in the border areas, and emotionally get hurt seeing a number of Indians dying/getting injured by terrorism sponsored by Pakistan. In Modi, the people see a strong leader who can take on Pakistan if the need arises.

Modi's handling of the Coronavirus spread has been appreciated by all Indians and many world leaders, and they want him to lead the world task force to fight the deadly virus.

For fighting elections, Modi's speeches are more like the speeches made by the US Presidential candidates; once he is elected, he chooses specialists to advise him on various subjects of governance, and he is not corrupt.

If the Congress does not choose a suitable candidate to fight Modi in the next general elections, he is bound to be elected as the Prime Minister [Chief Executive Head].

For good governance, a nation requires good Politicians, good Bureaucrats, and good Citizens – What sort of a person you would like to be- A or B ???

Politician-A	Politician-B
One, who would like to parachute from the top without any experience	One, who would like to start at the grass route level and gain experience?
One, who selects his subordinates for his personal gain.	One, who selects his subordinates on merit.
One, who does not deliver the promises given	One, who gives promises and delivers them.
One, who looks after himself first and then the Nation and the people	One, who looks after the Nation and the people first and then himself.
One who, in communal unrest, adds fuel to the fire with lies that create more violence and destruction to government property for his vote-bank	One, who tries to understand and controls the situation and promotes communal harmony
One, who takes advantage of the minorities for their votes and keeps them where they are socio-economically	One, who helps the minorities to lift up from a lower level to a middle- class level.
One who create a ruckus during the session of the Parliament/State Assembly and is unproductive.	One, who respects the sanctity of the Parliament/State Assembly and is productive
One, who Indulges in corruption and make a lot of money	One, who is corruption-free.
One, who is remembered as an unfit politician and is a bad example to the youngsters who want to become a politician	One, who is remembered as a good politician who did a lot for the Nation and the people and a good example to the youngsters who want to become a politician

Bureaucrat - A	Bureaucrat - B
One, who would just pass the files	One, who would go into the depth of each case and gives constructive comments, suggestions and recommendations.
One, who serves only his masters by being a 'Yes-man' for his own promotions	One, who serves for good governance
One, who is like a passenger in the bus and plays safe	One, who is an asset to the office
One, who Indulges in corruption and makes a lot of money	One, who is corruption-free.
One, who gets subordinates to serve his/her interest	One, who gets good subordinates for better governance
One, who avoids challenging appointments	One, who face challenging appointments

Citizen -A	Citizen - B
One, who always criticises the government's actions	One, who appreciates the governments action. If in disagreement, puts up a case through the correct forum
One, who does not pay his tax dues and expects all the government benefits	One, who pays his tax dues
One, who does not follow the civic responsibilities	One, who follows the civic responsibilities
One, who does not follow the traffic rules	One, who follows the traffic rules
One, who gets into riots and violence	One, who avoids getting into riots and violence.
One, who takes money for voting	One, who cannot be bought be bought

GLOSSARY

Adivasis - India Tribals

Admi - Man in Hindi

Akali - Member of a Sikh political group

Andolan - Movement

Artha - Meaning

Ayushman - Health of the people of India

Ayodhya - Place –where Lord Ram was born

Awas - Sound

Bahar - Outside

Balakot - Place in Pakistan

Bajrang - Name of a Political Party

Bahujan - Name of a Political Party

Bharat - India

Bharatiya - Indian

Bhima - Insurance

Chhodo - Quit

Chor - Thief

Crorepatis - Billionaires

Dal - Party

Dalits - Depressed class of people in India

Fasal - Crop

Desam - State of the Telegu speaking people

Godhra - Name of a place

Gram- Panchayats- Village councils

Harijan - Untouchable

Hindutva - Indian culture as identified by the Bharat Janata Party

Jallikattu - A sport where the participants catch the bull's horn and attempt to bring the bull to a stop

Janata - Public

Jawan - Soldier in Hindi

Jiva - Life

Kar Sevaks - A person who offers services for free for a dharmic cause

Kharif - Monsoon crops

Kisan - Farmer

Kranthi - Revolution

Mamla Hai - Pertaining to

Mandal - Name of the person

Mandi - Farmers market

Mantri - Minister

MODVAT - Modified Value Added Tax

Mohalla - Street

Moksha - To attain eternal liberation [spiritual word in Hinduism and Jainism

Mudra - Movement or pose in Yoga

Mukti Bahini - Name of the Bangladesh resistance group

Nala - Drain

Nawab - Muslim Ruling Prince

Ragi - Finger Millet

Rajmata - Kings Mother

Pandit - Priest

Rashtra - Country

Rashtrapati Bhavan - Presidents Residence in India

Patwari - An Official who visits and maintains records of agricultural land

Pradhan - Principal

Rath Yatra - Journey of a Chariot

Samajwadi - Socialism

Samastipur - Name of a Place

Sangh - Confederate

Sarpanch - Head of the Village

Seva - Service

Shiv Sena - Name of a Political Party

Shiromani - Name of the Political Sikh Party

Swachh - Clean

Taluka - Subdivision of a District

Tur - Name of a Lentil

Vishwa Parshad - Name of a Political Party

Yojana - Plan

Zilla Prashad - District Council

REFERENCES

Part – 1

Parliamentary System in India/Presidential System in the USA	The author has referred to the respective websites
Comparison between both the Systems	The author has referred to the discussions on the website on this aspect
Indian Political Events and the Present Political Situation	Author referred to the contents in periodicals, editorial columns and '40 years ago, 'column in the 'Indian Express' newspaper, editorial columns in the 'Times of India' newspaper and web-sites. The author has referred to books/columns written by Kuldip Nayar on political matters, Sanjay Baru's book on 'The Reluctant Prime Minister' - that brings out Former Prime Minister Manmohan Singh's 10 years tenure with Sonia Gandhi, holding the power. The book also brings out former Prime Minister P V Narasimha Rao's sound political background/experience and how he handled the political management when India was moving from 'Licence Raj' to a developed/ growth economy. Manmohan Singh was the Finance Minister under P V Narasimha Rao. The author has referred to Coomi Kapoor's book on 'The Emergency', Dominique Lapierre and Larry Collins book on 'Freedom at Midnight' and Brigadier John Dalvi's book on 'The Himalayan Blunder'.
Fault Lines	Author's views based on the political events
Why the Change?	Author's views
How to bring about the change in a democratic and peaceful manner	Author's suggestions

Part – 2

Economy	Author referred to the contents in the periodicals and editorial columns in the 'Indian Express' and the 'Times of India' newspapers and websites. The author has also referred to Arvind Subramanian's book on 'Of COUNSEL – The Challenges of the Mody- Jaitley Economy and to Raghu Rajan's articles on the Indian economy – the present situation and how to move forward, especially with the banking system.
National Security	Author referred to the contents in various periodicals, editorial columns in the Indian Express and the 'Times of India' newspaper and websites. The author also referred to the article on the 'Battle of the Bulge and the interview with General Bipin Rawat' by Sandeep Unnithin in the 'India Today' magazine of January 21, 2019.
Homeland Security	Author referred to the contents in the periodicals and editorial columns in the 'Indian Express' newspaper and in the 'Times of India' newspaper.
Communal Harmony	Author referred to the contents in the periodicals and editorial columns in the 'Indian Express' newspaper and the 'Times of India' newspaper. The author has also reproduced extracts on 'Inter-faith Platform', from the author's earlier book 'Repentance', [Page.105 to page113]
Minority Rights	Author referred to the contents in the periodicals and editorial columns in the 'Indian Express' newspaper and the 'Times of India' newspaper.
Climate Changes	Author referred to the contents in the periodicals and editorial columns in the 'Indian Express' newspaper and the 'Times of India' newspaper.
Environmental Protection	Author referred to the contents in the periodicals and editorial columns in the 'Indian Express' newspaper and the 'Times of India' newspaper.

BOOKS BY THE SAME AUTHOR

Everything Will Fall in Place	Published by Minerva Press India Pvt Ltd
Repentance	Published by IUniverse [The book was one of the finalists in the 'Foreword Magazine Book of the Year Festival-2007', at New York]
Right to Know	Published by Strategic Book Publishing & Rights Co

INDEX